Family Fortunes

Family Fortunes

Faith-full caring for today's families

JOHN DRANE

and OLIVE M. FLEMING DRANE

First published in 2004 by
Darton, Longman and Todd Ltd
1 Spencer Court
140–142 Wandsworth High Street
London sw18 4JJ

First published as *Happy Families? Building Healthy Families* in 1995 by
HarperCollinsPublishers.
This revised and updated version published in 2004.

ISBN 0 232 52542 0

A catalogue record for this book is available from the British Library.

Designed by Sandie Boccacci
Phototypeset in 10/13.25 Palatino by
Intype Libra Ltd
Printed and bound in Great Britain by
The Cromwell Press, Trowbridge, Wiltshire

Contents

Preface   vii

A family prayer   ix

1 Family history   1

2 Who are today's families?   21

3 Being a child in today's family   42

4 Adults in today's family   58

5 Parenting   80

6 Bible families   99

7 Nurturing the spirituality of the family   118

8 The family and the church   142

9 Families in times of crisis   158

10 Growing old   179

Notes   195

Booklist   207

Index   211

For Andy, Fiona, Mark, Laura and Alethea:
faith-full family builders of today and tomorrow.

Preface

This book has taken a long time to write – more than thirty years, in fact, ever since we first got together as teenagers. In the ensuing years, we must have learned something about family life, which gives us confidence in sharing it with a wider readership. During that period, we have helped countless others explore these topics, both on an individual level and in several parenting groups that we have facilitated. For more than a decade, Olive was a chairperson of Children's Hearings – part of the Scottish legal system, roughly equivalent to Family Courts elsewhere. We also bring the experience of teaching a course on 'Theological and Pastoral Perspectives on the Contemporary Family' in seminary and university contexts around the world.

The family has become a political and religious battleground in recent years, and we are conscious of negotiating some contentious territory here. We have deliberately avoided most of the debates, especially those on ethical topics. Our primary purpose is to help people to understand the reasons for the fragmentation and diversity that is the post-modern family, and explore how we might live in wholesome ways within this context. This is therefore a work of practical theology, beginning from the lived experience of today's people and reflecting on it in the light of the Christian tradition. In the process of doing so, we have learned much from the insights of social scientists and lawyers as well as theologians, though we chose not to engage in extensive discussion of other people's theories. Fearing that our primary aim might otherwise become lost, we tend to make statements rather than present arguments, and to be impressionistic rather than prescriptive – though those who want to understand some of our reasoning should find plenty of guidance through the endnotes. To those academic purists who feel uncomfortable with this approach, we simply affirm that this, in our opinion, is the primary calling of practical theologians, who – unlike more traditional theologians – fail in their ultimate purpose if they speak only to members of the scholarly community.

Our one regret is that this is a book only about the western family. We are well aware of the fact that some parts of the world still operate with what we have called here a pre-modern pattern of family life. We also know personally people from many different ethnic groups, all around the world, who struggle to connect their traditional family patterns to the incessant demands of western culture, exported in the form of movies, foods, clothing, and moral values. In this context, we hope that we can help people in other cultures to understand what motivates the agenda of globalization, while also encouraging them to have confidence in their own traditional insights, some of which might easily be more life-giving than those being promoted in the west.

Many important topics are hardly mentioned – marriage being one of the most obvious, along with the increase in singleness right across the world. These are just two of the subjects impinging on the family that would require entire books to themselves. So this will not by any means be the last word. It will not even be our final word, as we are still ourselves engaged on the journey, searching for new and relevant ways of living that will reflect the values of God's kingdom and will create the kind of family that offers a safe environment within which children can be nurtured, their parents can be sustained, and old people can be valued and respected (Isaiah 65:17–25).

JOHN DRANE *and* OLIVE M. FLEMING DRANE

A family prayer

Creator God,

You have placed each one of us in a family.

Today it seems like a stroke of genius on your part;
Tomorrow it could feel as if you made a big mistake.

In our family relationships we experience the height of
acceptance, and the depth of rejection:
- the excitement of finding you, even as we discover our
true selves through sharing with those we love;
- the spiritual claustrophobia of evil forces, as we injure
and damage those who are closest to us.

You are the one from whom all families seek blessing.

You are our caring Father, our loving Mother, our protective
Brother and our ever-watchful Sister.

We are women, men, and children created in your glorious
image. Bring us through the pain of repentance into the freedom
of your forgiveness. Make us whole, that we may bring healing
to our families.

Come, Holy Spirit, renew and restore our homes.

We pray in Jesus' name

Amen.

1 Family history

Images of the ideal family

The cheerfu' supper done, wi' serious face,
They, round the ingle, form a circle wide;
The sire turns o'er, wi' patriarchal grace,
The big ha'-Bible, ance his father's pride.

. . .

He wales a portion with judicious care,
And 'Let us worship God!' he says, with solemn air.

That was how Scottish poet Robert Burns depicted the perfect family of the eighteenth century in his poem 'The Cotter's Saturday Night'. But the time and place could be anywhere in the western world during the last two hundred years or so. In so far as there is a widely held concept of the ideal family, then this image captures its spirit pretty well. It begins with a graphic description of a man returning to his cottage after a hard week's work, to be welcomed by his eager children and greeted by the smile of his wife who has made their simple home warm and welcoming for his arrival. This family enjoys open and generous relationships, in a social context where everyone knows their place and stays within prescribed boundaries. Children and parents gather round the fire for a cosy Saturday night in the security of a home dutifully preserved by the mother as a shelter from the harsher world outside, in which not only the father but also their elder daughter has worked all week. Burns's language evokes a vivid image of the father's physical and emotional renewal in the company of those whom he loves and provides for, while the mother (who is only mentioned briefly in any detail) takes pride in the fact that her working daughter has brought home a young man with whom she is clearly in love, happy in the knowledge that this developing relationship will secure the family for the next generation. As sure as night follows day, the daughter will marry, leave paid employment and create a new home for her own husband and, in due course, their children. But the high point of this particular poem is the way the family derives its identity from the values that are reflected in the father's habit of reading the Bible and leading his family in worship. A later line in the poem describes him in transcendent language as 'The Saint, the Father, and the Husband . . .'. He might be a nobody in terms of the way prosperity is understood by the world outside, but the spiritual qualities that he and his family enjoy within the privacy of their own home are of such magnitude that 'The Cottage leaves the Palace far behind . . . '.

This is not a distinctively Scottish understanding of family life. Similar images prevail in the writings of the nineteenth-century English novelist Charles Dickens. *A Christmas Carol* is one of his best-loved novels, and a key reason for its popularity is the contrast between the miserable loneliness that characterized the home life of Scrooge and the warm relationships enjoyed by his humble employee Bob Cratchit. Like the hero of Burns's poem, this marginalized man is transformed by being with his family, and reveals a more profoundly human – and spiritual – side to his personality than the one he displays in the world of everyday work. After a hard day's labour in an office from which all vestiges of humanitarian spirit have been systematically elimi-nated, the warm fireside and the open generosity of wife and children are just what Cratchit needs to recharge his batteries before returning once more to the drudgery which is Scrooge's place of business. He may be poor, but he is a good provider within his means, and in his home he takes on an almost saintly identity. As in Burns's poem, each member of this family knows their place, and thrives on both the security and the responsibility that brings them. Bob provides an income, while his wife supplies comfort and affirmation, and the children live in happy dependence on their parents, blissfully unaware of the harsh realities which their father faces every day. Meanwhile, the innocent vulnerability of the entire family is embodied in the character of Tiny Tim, the handicapped child whose plight eventually melts even Scrooge's hard heart.

North American culture offers corresponding images of

traditional family life. Laura Ingalls Wilder was brought up in a covered wagon among the early pioneers of the American west and later recorded her story in a series of *Little House* books. Her vivid memories of family life in those days was subsequently taken to every corner of the world through the long-running TV series *Little House on the Prairie*. *The Waltons* has enjoyed similar success, and again is based on the childhood memories of its creator, Earl Hamner, and the struggles of a rural Virginia family in the early twentieth century. None of these images bears any resemblance at all to the way most families actually live today, but that in no way diminishes their continued popularity. Out of curiosity, we put 'Laura Ingalls Wilder' in an Internet search engine, and it came up with almost 60,000 websites![1] Though *The Simpsons* is a more accurate portrayal of contemporary families, the amazing resilience of these images from an earlier period can only be explained by assuming that such lifestyles still evoke a strong sense of admiration, coupled with a nostalgic feeling that, if only we could somehow manage to live that way, things would be much easier in today's world.[2]

Christians and the family

We could never turn the clock back and return to the values of these earlier generations, but this sort of romantic idealism about family life is still deeply embedded in the thinking of many people. Christians seem particularly prone to such wishful thinking, and have often exalted the virtues of this style of family to the point where it has been given an almost sacred status, as 'the Christian family'. When Christian pressure groups call for a return to 'family values', this is invariably what they have in mind. Yet the perpetuation of this image as being the 'Christian' family raises at least as many questions as it claims to solve. For one thing, it does not even begin to connect with reality for most people. With the exception of communities such as the Amish, who have taken a conscious decision to distance themselves from everything that characterizes contemporary life, no one can live this way in today's world, Christians included. But for most, the suggestion that family life could or should be like this is just incredible, and when Christians attempt to recreate the images and social structures of yesteryear they mostly succeed only in adding to the guilt that already oppresses the lives of so many within the church – not to mention the fact that, as often as not, their own children see no relevance in that kind of faith, and give it up as soon as they have the opportunity to do so. People outside the church are mystified by such attempts to turn the clock back, and the irrelevance of doing so merely reinforces their image of Christians as being hopelessly out of touch with changing social realities.

These practical questions are increasingly urgent in today's world, for they reflect the contradictions with which many Christians struggle every day of their lives. Even as we have written these few paragraphs, we have more than once asked ourselves whether we have created a caricature here. Alarmingly, a visit to our local Christian bookstore assures us that we have not, because all the books on Christian family life perpetuate this very image, and a fair number of them do so in an even more conservative form than we have described. The insistence that this understanding of family is the only authentically Christian model, and the apparent refusal of many Christians to engage with the reality of families in today's world (let alone to reflect theologically on them) raises some urgent questions that go well beyond relational pragmatism. For a start, we need to ask whether there is in fact such a thing as a 'Christian family' at all. If we take the Bible as a starting point, then it certainly provides no blueprint for any such social entity. Paradoxically, there is not one single Bible family that corresponds to this so-called 'traditional' image. The fact of the matter is that the notion of family means different things to different people at different times and places – and it always has. Though it is probably correct to claim that 'the family' provides one of the significant building blocks of society in all cultures, those blocks have never all been the same shape as one another, and throughout history Christians have followed the norms and conventions of the cultures in which they lived by accepting, supporting, and perpetuating many different models of family. That is why we believe it is misleading and unhelpful to talk of 'the Christian family', as if that was something qualitatively different from other families. It is more accurate to say that there are families, some of which are Christian. But the challenges that Christians face in the home and in wider relationships are exactly the same as those with which other people struggle. This is why – as we shall also argue – the recognition of many different forms of 'family' and the creation of safe spaces for families in all their diversity will not only reflect the values of the Christian message, but also have the potential to fulfil the missionary calling of the church by sharing the good news in relevant ways with those who are as yet not Christian.

Family in context

What then is a family? A major research industry has grown up around that question, with scholars from many disciplines addressing it from their own perspectives: sociologists, anthropologists, economists, psychoanalysts, politicians, historians, and lawyers, as well as leaders within different faith communities.[3] Our primary focus here is on pastoral and practical theology, and though we have drawn extensively on the researches of many others, we will review their findings here only as they impinge on the church's pastoral role. Indeed, so much has been written about it that a book of this size could never explore all the nuances of the question, let alone consider every possible answer to it. It is, however, important that we set our understanding of the family, and of the church's responsibilities for ministering with families, within a wider perspective. A quick backward glance at our own history, tracing the origins of some current assumptions and expectations, will provide a useful entry point into the contemporary debate. One of our favourite Chinese proverbs observes that 'Those who do not know the village they have come from will never find the village they are looking for.' To see clearly who we might yet become we need to own who we are, and be aware of some of the factors that have made us this way. Nowhere is this more strikingly true than in the family.

People are made to live in community, and interpersonal relationships are a fundamental part of being human. But from the very dawn of time, the relationships that characterize what we choose to call 'the family' have always been regarded as distinctive and special. Two unique characteristics identify a set of relationships as occurring within a family: the significance of the gender roles occupied by male and female, and the corresponding differentiation between parents and children. The practical outcomes of the power dynamic implied in these two sets of relationships might vary in different circumstances, but they constitute the fundamental defining elements of those forms of relationship that have always been identified as family. All other distinctive aspects of family life arise out of or are related to these two. In her definitive book, *The Family in Question*, Diana Gittins lists four basic features of the family: common residence, economic co-operation, reproduction, and sexuality.[4] These characteristics in turn imply further elements that all generally impinge on the concept of family, such as the nature of the power relationships between women and men, adults and children; the responsibility for domestic labour; parenting roles and sibling relationships; along with understandings of kinship, marriage, and so on that are held in the wider community – though even some of these supposedly foundational characteristics of a family are being questioned and redefined today, certainly in practice if not always in terms of social norms expressed through the legislative process.

Not all families will necessarily display all these characteristics, especially not today when the whole notion of what constitutes a family is in a state of much upheaval and redefinition, and when several of these constituent elements are themselves undergoing radical transformation. Nevertheless, this kind of list still provides a useful starting point, and while none of these elements on their own will point conclusively to a set of relationships that necessarily constitute a family, the criteria proposed by Gittins serve to give some shape to the debate, and to provide some way of distinguishing family relationships from other forms of human interaction.

Once Gittins moves beyond interpersonal relationships as such, every other characteristic of a family is connected to economic needs. As far back as it is possible to look historically, the economic purposes of a family have always been primary, and the most noteworthy changes in patterns of family life have all had their origins in the economic opportunities open to families, and the alterations in working patterns that have resulted.

Contemporary definitions tend to project a more romanticized and sentimental image, in which the emphasis is on relationships between individual members of a family group, but economic circumstances have always been more influential than any other single factor in determining the character of family life. The nature of work has always provided the frame of reference which defined the possible ways in which family members would be able to express and develop their personal relationships, and in this respect today's families are no different from the generations which preceded them. Changing work patterns are still one of the most significant influences of all on the shape of family life.

From generation to generation: the pre-modern family

Like other social institutions, the family remained virtually unchanged for centuries until relatively recent times.[5] Long after the emergence of the great civilizations of the ancient world, the underlying family pattern differed surprisingly little from the hunter-gatherer lifestyle of our earliest ancestors. Family life was dominated by non-relational matters such as economic survival and employment, while also functioning as the agent of socialization and education. Families were groups in which people could survive, through which they could find useful things to occupy their time, and within which they learned how to live with other people. Different family members naturally adopted different roles: in particular, the role of adult men and women tended to be defined by reference to their sexuality (procreation being vital to survival), and to what was practical, which almost amounted to the same thing. Both men and women died at what would nowadays be regarded as a young age, and for women that meant they were either pregnant or nursing children for most of their adult life. It would, however, be a mistake to describe women's role in ancient families as purely domestic. More accurately, there was no differentiation between 'domestic' work and work that was economically productive, because in a pre-industrial age the home was central to economic prosperity, and everyone who lived there had a part to play, if only because their survival depended on their willingness to work together. It would be anachronistic to claim that the ancient family operated on a basis of the recognized equality of all its members, but it is nevertheless true that everyone's role – though different – was of equal value. Because they did not bear children, men had greater mobility, which meant they were the ones who operated in the public sphere outside the home, whereas women were more restricted in their options through their physical connection with birthing and nurturing children. This was almost certainly a purely pragmatic arrangement: despite fanciful claims to the contrary, there is no evidence of a widespread matriarchal culture in ancient times.[6] Everyone was involved in the economic life of the family. In this primitive, or pre-modern period, the family was quite literally a building block of the community.

This was the pattern of early Bible families, where the household typically consisted of several generations living together. They included not only the head of the family and his sexual partner(s) and offspring, but also servants and their relatives, as well as widows, orphans, stateless persons and others who contributed to the economic wellbeing of the whole, in exchange for which they enjoyed the safety and security of the family unit. Over time – and this transition can be traced in the Bible itself – the nature of family relationships changed, largely as a result of economic pressures. Once family units were able to amass economic surpluses, opportunities for trade with other families also developed. Relationships outside the home gradually assumed greater importance than internal family structures, and the base of social organization became increasingly separated from the household, a trend which accelerated with the emergence of formal political structures. Because of their freedom to operate independently of children, and also their generally greater physical strength, men tended to be the ones who dealt with things in the public sphere outside the family, where matters of property, production, trade, and politics became dominant. In due course, such concerns came to be regarded as an exclusively male domain through the development of a patriarchal outlook which confined women to the private sphere of the home, and indeed classified them (and children) as part of the goods with which a man could barter in the wider world of commerce. Women's contribution to the life and economy of the family remained significant and indispensable, but when compared with more primitive family structures their role was gradually diminished and squeezed into a much narrower definition of what it meant to be a woman. Of course, none of this happened overnight, and such changes as there were took place almost imperceptibly over many generations, with a gradual evolution from ancient times through to the feudal system of the Middle Ages. The driving force behind this development, though, was fluctuating patterns of work. The same thing is still true today, and the changing nature of work is one of the major forces that continues to impact and shape the family unit in the twenty-first century.

The development of the family as we know it today has been influenced above all by that cluster of events that can be referred to as the Enlightenment, and the Industrial Revolution which emerged from it. Beginning in the fifteenth century, the first tentative voyages of European explorers coincided with an expansion of knowledge about astronomy, philosophy, medicine, science, and technology so great that, as western thinkers of the time compared their understanding of things with the previous knowledge of all the great civilizations of the ancient and medieval world, it seemed as if a new light was shining right across the world. The magnitude of the new discoveries made everything that had gone before look like mere super-stition, mythology, and intellectual darkness – hence the use of the term 'Enlightenment' to describe this period. Though the worldview of the Enlightenment ('modernity') has been seriously eroded by the rise of so-called 'post-modern' thinking and culture, its way of looking at things – especially its rationalist-materialist-reductionist philosophy – continues to have a pro-found impact on today's people, and it is impossible to understand what is going on in the contemporary family without taking some account of this. Indeed, almost all the turmoils which we can see in the family today have their origins in this period of western history.

Industrialization: the modern family

Philosophically, one of the key outcomes of the thinking of modernity was the claim that life could, and should, be divided into two spheres. From now on, things would be classified according to whether they belonged in what was increasingly regarded as the public world, concerned with things like science, economics, politics, and employment, and governed by 'laws of nature' that were supposedly true in some absolute sense – and the private world, whose preoccupation was with morality, values, opinions, and religion. Previously, no one had ever thought to separate these two aspects of human existence, because in economic terms the means of production in the home had been indispensable to the market-place where goods were bought and sold – while it had been taken for granted that religious and moral values had universal validity in relation to politics and economics as well as personal behaviour. But now all this changed. With the growth of capitalism and the concept of the market, any sense of mutuality between the home and the public world soon disappeared. Instead of the family serving as the basic unit of economic production, work was centralized and mechanized so that all significant economic activity had to take place in the organized industrial context of factories and the associated activities that became necessary to resource and fuel them. Within a very short time, access to the public world of employment and economic production was (at least in theory) the sole preserve of men, while the domestic world of the home became the place where women found their role in life.

It was inevitable that the family itself would be redefined, as its traditional functions of providing its members with economic support, employment, education, and socialization were now taken over by outside agencies. Once the family no longer had a productive economic function, it became the consumer of goods from elsewhere. With such a massive displacement of the original purposes of the family, it was necessary to work out its purpose in the new circumstances, and the simplest way to do that was to prescribe the roles that were now to be played by the various members of the family circle. In future, men were to be fathers and providers, while women were to be devoted wives and mothers, offering support and nurture, and childhood would be an age of innocence. As a consequence, patriarchy (which previously had been more pragmatic than ideological) was institutionalized, and the male public world came to dominate. Of course, the private world of the home where women held sway still had its usefulness, but even that was determined by the needs of the public world. This is the origin of the traditional image reflected in Robert Burns's poem, with which we began this chapter – of a man going out to work on behalf of his family, and then retreating into the home at the end of the day to be revived by the caring attentions of his wife. For her part, the wife would also in due course find herself redefined as a consumer of marketable goods. In addition, since values and faith had been relegated to the private world of the home which, by definition, was not the place where men did anything productive (that male role having been located exclusively in the public world, which was also now considered to be non-religious), she would also become the primary (even sole) provider of moral and spiritual guidance for her children.

All this reflected the prevailing worldview of the day, in which everything was understood in accordance with the scientific models of people like Francis Bacon (1561–1626) and Isaac Newton (1642–1727). Things had to be explained, with a clear sense of order and a neat theory of cause and effect to elucidate how it all worked. In human terms, this meant it was very important to know where everyone fitted in. Social class assumed a new significance, and the preservation of appropriate boundaries and demarcation lines became a priority. By identifying this neat rational process with so-called 'laws of nature' that were believed to be built into the very foundation of the cosmos itself, anything that fitted this paradigm was therefore by definition 'right', because that was the way the universe itself had been designed to function. By the same token, anything that seemed to question the received wisdom could be dismissed as non-rational, and therefore of little consequence. That all sounds quaint and simplistic in a world where the working models of science are taken from Einstein's theory of relativity, together with chaos and complexity theory. Yet in spite of the collapse and virtual abandonment of the previous ideological foundation of western culture, its legacy in terms of differentiated family roles is still exceedingly strong in some circles, and continues to contribute to the misery suffered in today's changing families. It has also had a significant impact in some Christian circles, particularly in relation to defining the respective roles of women and men in the spiritual nurture of children.

The actual realities of life in the eighteenth and nineteenth centuries – as distinct from the theories of the social engineers – often threatened to destroy even this minimal understanding of the family as a cohesive and mutually supportive unit. Economic necessity quite often forced all members of a family into paid employment, children as well as women, whether they wanted it or not. Yet ordinary working people generally viewed the model of the industrial nuclear family as an ideal form, even when for most of them the reality was very different. As living standards gradually increased, however, more and more families were able to live the dream, and by the middle of the nineteenth century most British families were probably organized this way. Instead of having the central role in economic production, occupied by families since the very dawn of time, the only things left for the family were the provision of emotional fulfilment for its members and the creation of new generations to ensure the continued viability of the consumer society. Governments encouraged the growth of this kind of family as an instrument of social stability, arguing that men who were providers were less likely to be criminal than those who were not. There was also a growing emphasis on the family as a place for the nurture of children, because no 'real' family would be complete without them. In the process, children came to be thought of as 'possessions', or even status symbols.

The rationalized society that emerged from this major cultural shift remained as the prevailing model of family until the last quarter of the twentieth century. Indeed, some aspects still survive, most notably the belief that to have a 'proper' family people need children – an opinion which has led to much heart-ache for those who find they are unable to have them. If the pre-modern family could genuinely be regarded as a building block of the community, this model regards the family pre-eminently as the servant of the community, an essential part of the consumer society. The 1940s and 1950s were probably the heyday of this style of 'modern' industrial nuclear family. This is clearly reflected in the kind of literature produced for children at this period, none more typical than the stories of Dick and Dora and their family which constituted the first introduction to reading for generations of British children.[7] They were the very model of children who were 'seen and not heard', amusing themselves with their friends and in the company of their dog and cat, Nip and Fluff. Though it sounds like a caricature, after a day's work their father quite literally came home to his pipe and slippers, while their mother was compliant and supportive, with her identity defined by reference to the needs of the rest of her family. Even in the mid-twentieth century, the reality for many families was quite different from this idealized picture. By today's standards, women were certainly exploited, spending hours in drudgery such as washing clothes with primitive implements – and probably suffering no less abuse and violence than they do today, without even the minimal protection that is now available. And in spite of appearance, it was no fun for men either, most of whom did not have the sort of comfortable job enjoyed by Dick and Dora's father, but spent their lives at hard physical labour in exchange for pitiful rewards, frequently dying at an early age as a direct consequence, either through industrial accidents or diseases related to the workplace. Those who survived generally found themselves locked into social class structures that offered them little chance of improving their situation, no matter how hard they worked.

We still romanticize about such families, and even today TV adverts offer plenty of images of the perfect industrial nuclear family, with the subliminal message that if you buy a particular product, your family can be like the one on the screen. Apart from those Christians who have invested this form of family life with a kind of religious aura, no one would wish to turn the clock back to these grim social realities. But a disturbing number of families still struggle with problems that, for them, have changed little over the generations, while some of the more destructive trends of today's social scene have their origins in the legacy of the Industrial Revolution and, behind it, the philosophy of the Enlightenment.

The post-industrial, post-modern family

Wherever we look, western culture is changing fast. Because of the ease with which information can now be exchanged, we could well be living through the fastest period of cultural change there has ever been. In the past, change tended to happen gradually and in subtle ways, with new generations slowly altering the way their predecessors had done things, and allowing an appropriate period of time for the changes to be integrated into people's lifestyles and understandings. Nowadays change is instantaneous and global. The confidence with which some Christians describe and analyze 'post-modernity' is scarcely justified when we try to sort out the many conflicting meanings given to that term. We have argued elsewhere for a more cautious approach to understanding this cultural change, especially in relation to the notion that it is driven by some overarching philosophical ideology.[8] This is not the place to repeat that, except to reaffirm our conviction that the need to invent labels to describe what is happening is in direct proportion to our perceived inability to make any difference: in a world where no one really knows what might happen next, applying a name to it tends to give us the false reassurance that we can somehow control it all. Yet in spite of our scepticism about some of the over-precise definitions that are offered, it can scarcely be denied that the trends identified by the label 'post-modernity' are indeed real, not least because of the obvious impact they have on our everyday lives. As a culture, we have a love-hate relationship with the industrial and technological age that emerged from the Enlightenment. No one would wish to turn the clock back, especially not in terms of scientific or medical knowledge, but neither are we all completely happy with what this knowledge seems to have brought us, as we struggle to make sense out of the discontinuities and contradictions.

Nowhere is this more obviously true than in the family. Some challenges are bound to persist from one generation to the next, for any social environment that involves relationships with other persons will always create squabbles and disagreements that can lead to friction and breakdown. The more intimate the relationship, the greater the potential for both good and ill within it, and families have always struggled with this. Even Bible families were not immune – indeed, the lasting usefulness of the Bible in relation to family matters is largely determined by the way in which it depicts the trials and tribulations faced even by people of faith, with no effort to disguise the messy details. But whereas pre-modern and modern families both operated within an agreed cultural framework about the nature of the family itself, and how meaningful and life-giving relationships might best be expressed, today's post-modern family finds itself adrift on a sea of conflicting opinions and ideas as to what actually constitutes a family. Paradoxically, and critically, the family (which until recently was assumed to be a reflection of the norms of the wider community) is now left to its own devices to create its own community, if indeed there is to be one. That is possibly one of the toughest challenges that we humans could ever face: not only are we presented with the timeless existential challenges of understanding ourselves and our relationships, but we are also now charged with the responsibility of redefining the entire frame of reference within which we might come to that self-knowledge. We can trace several major issues that are involved in meeting this challenge.

New values

One of the major driving forces in western culture has been the emergence of a technological or technocratic society, with its insistence that all human needs are technical in nature. Technical needs require specialists and experts to understand them, who then translate basic human needs into economic programmes, management procedures, and pieces of merchandise. Though we all eagerly embrace this understanding of life – indeed, we have no other option – its widespread adoption lies at the heart of much contemporary dissatisfaction and personal pain. It has been responsible for the alienation that many now feel, and it has also played a significant part in the developing environmental crisis. The technocratic outlook leads to a very narrow definition of what constitutes 'value', with anything that is 'natural' being regarded as of no value at all – and that includes the family. Edward Goldsmith has expressed it succinctly:

It is fundamental to the worldview of modernity that all benefits are man-made – products of scientific, technological and industrial progress, made available via the market system. Thus health is seen as something that is dispensed in hospitals ... with the aid of the latest technological devices and pharmaceutical preparations. Education is seen as a commodity that can only be acquired from schools and universities ... *natural benefits – those provided by the normal workings of biospheric processes*, assuring the stability of our climate, the fertility of our soil, the replenishment of our water supplies, *and the integrity and cohesion of our families and communities – are not regarded as benefits at all; indeed, our economists attribute to them no value of any kind. It follows that to be deprived of these non-benefits cannot constitute a 'cost' and the natural systems that provide them can therefore be destroyed with economic impunity.*[9]

With the dominance of this kind of outlook, no one should be surprised that the essential nurturing function of the family as a place of safety, security, and personal and spiritual growth for those who live within it has been marginalized as being no longer a worthy objective. Yet historically, the family has played a key role in the socialization of its members and the develop-ment of their ability to forge appropriate relationships with others. The commercialization of the family itself, as these values have increasingly been regarded as products that can be bought and sold, has arguably played a significant part in the breakdown of civil society that seems to be taken for granted in western democracies – and is a key reason why people in other parts of the world are concerned about the impact that globalization is having not only on world markets, but on human nature itself.

Economic realities

Historically, the major responsibility of the family has been as an economically productive unit, and the changing nature of work plays a decisive part in affecting today's family lifestyles, in two ways. One is the obvious fact that women are now a significant part of the employed workforce, alongside men. The other is the fact that the nature of work itself is changing. There is no doubt that many good things were achieved in the world of paid work during the course of the twentieth century. Though in many ways the Industrial Revolution actually made women's lives harder, this period also sowed the seeds of their ultimate empowerment, and when the need for workers in the market-place was accentuated by the absence of men during the First World War, the tendency to exclude women from productive work was reversed for all time.[10]

The invention of labour-saving devices for housework in the 1950s, together with the development of reliable contraception in the 1960s, opened up new possibilities for both men and women. But ironically, the sense of freedom has been short-lived. By the 1980s, what seemed like a new freedom was transformed by rising inflation into economic necessity, which made it imposs-ible for most families to live on only one income, and actually required that all the adults in a family be active in paid employ-ment. At the very same time, however, the nature of work has itself been undergoing radical change. In Britain in the 1970s (and the western world more generally) virtually all those who were in paid employment worked for an organization or cor-poration of some kind, and enjoyed job security and the prospect of pensions that would see them through a worry-free old age. Today, the number of people in that kind of paid employment – especially with any guaranteed future security – is diminishing fast, and this is having far-reaching repercussions for families. Those people who still work as employees are finding that there are fewer of them, and they are having to work harder. They may be getting more money, but the hours they have to work are often bad for relationships, and therefore for families. A minority of British workers now work what was once a 'stan-dard' 9–5 day, and the rest are forced to fit their lives around working hours that have been reorganized not for their benefit, but for the good of their employers. In the US, the pressure on workers is greater still, and it is not uncommon even for man-agers to take part-time work in their 'spare' time in order to maintain their family's standard of living. Working long hours with little vacation time wears people out, and can have serious demographic implications. In Japan, for instance, which has one of the most intense working weeks in the world, the birth rate is running at only half what is required to sustain a stable population, but Britain and the US are not far behind. On top of this, many more people have no work, or insecure part-time temporary employment. No work and too much work are both equally bad for families.

At the same time, the reorganization of work is not all bad news. The emergence of so-called designer lifestyles in which people create their own portfolio of work, selling a product or a service rather than their time, offers a new and potentially beneficial way of dealing with the conflicting pressures faced by today's families, as it offers greater flexibility in the way we use our time, and therefore more opportunities to be available to our families in different ways at different stages of their life. Moreover, it is not an option that need be limited to only one type of work. It is as easy for a carpenter or a plumber to have a portfolio of different kinds of employment as it is for a lawyer or an accountant, and the resultant flexibility could easily have a positive effect on families.[11] But for that to happen, we need to be intentional about it, and that includes governments and other public agencies as well as concerned individuals.

Individualism

The one thing that may hinder any positive development is yet another legacy from the Enlightenment, namely a stress on individualism. The Enlightenment elevated human reason to an almost divine status, with great emphasis on individuals being free to choose. In the event, the choices available turned out to be no more free than they had ever been, because the options were always closely defined by technological and bureaucratic structures. But the resultant mind-set that put people and their individual needs and choices first is still deeply engrained in most people who, faced with several possibilities, will generally choose the one which has most in it for them. This phenomenon lies at the heart of many of our difficulties with the family today. Self-centred individualism clearly raises some ethical questions, but they are not our concern here, nor do they constitute the key issue to be addressed if we are to tackle it effectively. For the entire structure of the consumer society not only thrives on individualism, but also requires it. Sociologist Ulrich Beck has stated it somewhat baldly, but nonetheless truthfully:

> the labor market demands mobility without regard to personal circumstances. Marriage and the family require the opposite. Thought through to its ultimate consequence, the market model . . . implies a society *without* families and children. . . . The market subject is ultimately the single individual, 'unhindered' by a relationship, marriage or family. Correspondingly, the ultimate market society is a *childless* society – unless the children grow up with mobile, single, fathers and mothers.[12]

That structural reality lies beneath just about all the circumstances that people in families struggle with today, and which feature on political agendas related to family matters. It encapsulates perfectly the predicament of post-modernity, and explains why so many family issues appear to be so intractable – for as consumers we embrace with enthusiasm the very systems that are themselves the cause of so much of our anxiety.

Fragmentation

The irony is that the thing most people seem to be searching for today is a place to belong and to be accepted. With all our concern for individual freedoms, no one seems to know who they are any longer. The post-modern angst of which we hear so much is essentially a crisis in personal identity. On the dustjacket of his best-selling book *Life After God*, Douglas Coupland asked these questions: 'How do we cope with loneliness? How do we deal with anxiety? The collapse of relationships? How do we reach the quiet, safe layer of our lives?'[13] None of these will ever be addressed on an individual basis, for they are all relational questions.

Moreover, they are not just the questions of dysfunctional families. Even in those families which appear to be making it, many men find themselves struggling to redefine their personal identity in the light of changes in family structures. Women find that, far from being set free by changing patterns of work and economic interdependence, they are struggling with a new form of enslavement, as they wrestle with two jobs instead of one. Many children are faced with the reality of their own vulnerability both within the home, as victims of violence and abuse, and beyond it as they wonder what might happen to them should the family disintegrate. In addition to that, there are growing numbers of non-traditional family homes, including increasing numbers of single people as well as couples with no children. All these groups face their own unique challenges, and there are no simple answers or quick fixes for any of them. As a culture, we will only begin to make progress when we recognize the importance of community and go on from there to find new models for living together in the light of today's new circumstances. For generations past, the family has provided people with their first experience of living in community. It is therefore inevitable that the fragmentation of the family will have wider social repercussions: it may not be too extreme to suggest that if our families are consistently malfunctioning, our entire civilization could well be in danger. The renewal of the vitality of western culture will depend to a significant extent on our ability to create new models of family that will take what is best from the past and match that with the social realities of life in the twenty-first century. We earlier characterized the postmodern family as the creator of its own community, but that could be too optimistic a statement in a world in which there are very few relevant role models to demonstrate what a life-giving and nurturing community might look like. As a result, large numbers of people – even well-intentioned ones – have no idea how to create community, because their entire lives have been starved of meaningful belonging. This crisis provides both a challenge and an opportunity for the Christian church.

2 Who are today's families?

Given the profound change currently being experienced in western culture, it is no surprise that the family is in a state of flux. The adult members of today's families wrestle with challenges that would have been unthinkable even for their parents, let alone for previous generations. It is not just that our forebears would have offered different solutions to the problems: for the most part, they would not even understand the pressing issues that are now forcing so many people to ask fundamental questions about what we really want the family to be.

It would be easy to become paranoid about this, and some Christians are. But we should keep it in perspective and recognize that family life has never been straightforward. How could it be, when it has involved interpersonal relationships in all times and cultures? Every kind of human relationship is susceptible to squabbles and disagreements that can result in the breakdown of mutual understanding on either a temporary or a permanent basis. The more intimate the relationship, the greater its potential for both good and ill. Family life offers ecstasy and agony in equal measure, and in most families both extremes are taken for granted as part of the ongoing personal growth that hopefully arises out of all such relationships. When the agony seems to exceed the ecstasy, though, something has to give – and when the parameters of society's understanding of the relationship itself are changing, it is harder still to try and make sense of things, because there is no accepted norm of what it is that we are supposed to be working towards. Yesterday's families faced the struggle with a clear notion of what constitutes a family. Today's families are also striving to redefine what it means to be a family, which is why even quite straightforward relational issues can become exceedingly complex and, in personal terms, life threatening – in a metaphorical sense for many, and quite literally for some.

By comparison with the past, today's families generally have fewer children, and all the relationships (between parents, between parents and children, and between children themselves) are a good deal less stable than they were two generations ago. One-parent families are a growing phenomenon right across the western world,[1] while there are more non-traditional family homes than ever before, including increasing numbers of single people as well as couples who either choose to have no children or are unable to do so. All these changes – and others – are manifestations of much bigger shifts that are happening in western culture, and they are leading to the emergence and acceptance of many new forms of family, as people struggle to make sense out of it all.

We can trace at least seven distinct types of family structure and domestic arrangements in western culture today.[2] In later chapters we will be considering in some detail how the church can support people in these varied lifestyles. But first it will help to have a bird's eye view of the whole family landscape. Our purpose here is not to offer a critical evaluation, but rather to explore the ways in which Christians might make a useful contribution to the life of today's families, in all their diversity. The fact that family norms are changing can be viewed as a crisis, or as an opportunity to create something new out of the death of something old. Christians, of all people, should be inspired by a vision of change and resurrection, and be ready to engage in creative reconstruction while recognizing that any new thing that involves God is more likely to surprise us than to conform to our prior expectations.

Husbands and wives[3]

This is, if you wish, the traditional family style, with two married parents living together, along with those children who are bio-logically related to them. In cultural terms its evolution has been deeply affected by the Enlightenment and Industrial Revolution, while in relational terms Christians would point to the teaching of Jesus, especially his endorsement of the monogamous lifelong commitment of one man and one woman to each other, as pro-viding some kind of normative expectation that this sort of family will try to fulfil (Mark 10:6–7). Even within this one model of family life, however, there are several possible variations, and it will come as no surprise to realize that these are related to the role of the family as an economic unit, and the changing nature of work.

Both parents in work

In most families of this type, both parents will be in full-time paid employment outside the home. The major incentive for this is likely to be economic necessity: unless one partner has extraordinarily high earning power, or either or both has inherited wealth, then most people find it simply is not possible to survive on only one income. Poverty creates its own problems, and though many people say they would rather be poor and happy, given the chance most of us would prefer to be financially secure. The creation of a viable economic unit has always been one of the prime functions of a family. But achieving this understandable aim does not come cheaply, and has its own impact on another important purpose of family life, namely the promotion of secure, stable, and nurturing relationships.

Adults cannot avoid conflicts as they try to balance the demands of two jobs alongside their family obligations. They are in turn required to be parent, sexual partner and companion, career worker, and domestic worker – or more accurately, they need to be all four at the same time. Given that today's parents of young children tend to be older than their counterparts in previous generations, they might easily find that they are also called to fulfil a fifth family role, caring for their own ageing parents. When people are squeezed at so many different points, it is much easier to talk of personal growth and fulfilment than it is to achieve it. Even those who appear to succeed in this complex balancing act frequently harbour unresolved doubts about the impact that their pressurized lifestyle is likely to have on the development of their children. They struggle to locate adequate and affordable child care (at least in their early years), but even when they find it they are probably going to feel more or less guilty about handing over so much of the nurture of their offspring to someone else, who may or may not share their own sense of standards and values. When politicians and social service agencies assume that the ideal is for all adults to be in full-time paid employment, but at the same time insist that the major responsibility for raising children lies with parents, it is predictable that many people will go through this stage of life convinced of their own inadequacies, and with enormous burdens of guilt building up that can easily afflict them for years to come.

Men at work

Not all husband and wife families find that both partners either wish, or are able, to work full time outside the home. There are still a fair number in which the husband is the only wage-earner. Those who are struggling with the pressures of juggling home and outside work, often imagine that these people have it a lot easier. But the truth is that they face their own particular challenges. Though this arrangement undoubtedly relieves some of the pressures connected with domestic work and child care, women who opt for this lifestyle can find themselves put down and misunderstood even by their friends. While the term 'housewife' might once have been an honourable one, it generally has a negative connotation nowadays, as if being a 'housewife' is an inferior form of being. Even in its original usage it could be demeaning and depersonalizing, implying that such women's lives were concerned with serving inanimate objects (houses) rather than working in partnership with other persons (husbands and fathers). In the US, the term 'homemaker' is the preferred description of such people, and it is certainly a more accurate (and affirming) way of referring to the lifestyle of women (or men) who choose to be full-time partners and parents instead of taking up outside paid employment. But in Britain there is still some way to go on this issue, and when we have used this term in seminars we have sometimes been accused by Christians of being 'trendy' (another epithet that is not intended as a compliment). But it is not about trendiness for its own sake, nor is it anything to do with political correctness. The language we use expresses our attitudes, and we should always choose our words carefully so they communicate the values of God's kingdom, which (among other things) are about lifting people up and affirming their worth, not putting them down.

Being called a 'housewife' can be bad enough. But to be asked the question, 'Do you work?' (often expressed that way in all innocence by those who take it for granted that 'work' only happens in paid employment) can be an even more provocative and demeaning experience. Unless they take specific steps to develop their assertion skills, such women are likely to go along with the prevailing tide and admit that they do not 'work' – even though they probably put in at least a twelve-hour day in the family home. It is but one of many ironies in society's attitudes to the family that the only people who as a matter of course place a value on work within the home are life insurance companies paying out on their policies. The American insurance company New York Life advises its clients that to cover the financial loss incurred with the death of a homemaker who would otherwise have been in that position for another fifteen years, 'the appropriate amount of insurance protection for the stay-at-home spouse could be as much as $750,000'.[4] On that basis, a full-time homemaker is worth about $50,000 a year to the family budget. British insurance companies are more reticent about making such estimates, but a simple calculation using the minimum wage and assuming an average working day in the home of seventeen hours produces a comparable figure of just under £40,000. Most women who choose to stay at home and raise children would be surprised by these figures. The majority feel undervalued by society, and as a result suffer from a low self-esteem, which later in life may inhibit them from exploring other avenues of self-fulfilment, because of their lack of confidence in their own abilities.

It is often imagined that men whose wives choose to be full-time homemakers must be zealously patriarchal, and while that may be true for some, being the sole provider in a family is not a role that most men would seek for themselves, as it creates its own burdens for them as well. The economic stress of having both wife and children totally dependent can be quite devastating, and sometimes life-threatening. Men in this position can – and do – literally work themselves to death. Those men who choose to be the sole provider because of their patriarchal outlook are likely to face additional pressures, maybe finding themselves under threat from workplace practices which put them in direct competition for jobs and promotion with women who are working in the market-place, whom they regard as ideologically unacceptable and personally threatening. Managing to solve the day-care problem by having one parent give up work outside the home can have far-reaching knock-on effects in other areas of life, which then impact the dynamic of family life every bit as much as having two partners in paid employment. Many traditional Christians find themselves caught up in this particular dilemma.

Women as providers

This does not exhaust the possibilities for husband and wife families. In other circumstances, families find either that the wife is the only one with paid employment outside the home, or that neither adult is working. Some people choose the former as an option, and agree by mutual consent that the woman will take outside employment while the man cares for the home and children. We know all about this, because at one stage of our life together we ourselves lived this way. It undoubtedly demands a strength of character and self-confidence on the part of both partners, for others frequently misunderstand them. When a man is referred to as a 'house husband' it carries the same pejorative overtones as a woman being labelled a 'housewife', while women in this situation can find themselves being asked, 'What kind of man have you got?' – implying that they are married to wimps. In addition, the prevailing system will tend to militate against both of them in terms of job security and promotions if they should want to swap roles for a time. In practice, this course of action tends to be open only to those with a good deal of underlying economic stability, and even the provision of paternity leave from full-time paid employment has not really made much difference in that respect. Moreover, when a father is the main carer for his children, he is likely to come across problems that would not be faced by their mother. Men in this position can find themselves disadvantaged in dealing with public agencies which – despite many policy statements to the contrary – still tend to be operated at local level by individuals who assume that it is women who will be responsible for the care of young children in particular. Things like the provision of baby-changing facilities in the men's washrooms of shopping malls, or of parent and toddler groups, rather than the traditional 'mother and toddler' groups, give the impression that society has changed – but if as a man you've ever tried changing a baby in a male washroom in the UK (as distinct from the USA), the comments you will be likely to hear from other men will tell you otherwise. While every little helps, these are all merely cosmetic changes that need to be matched by a much more radical shift in public perceptions than many people seem to be ready for.

It is more common for the situation where the wife is the sole earner to be brought about unintentionally through economic deprivation (triggered by the husband losing full-time employment) or ill health on the part of the male partner. In families where both parents have been earning, the wife naturally continues to do so (though with renewed intensity), while in those where the wife was not previously employed in paid work, the increasing availability of part-time jobs, many of which are geared to the recruitment of women (and poorly paid), may have to provide the family's only financial lifeline. When caused by underlying poverty, families in which the woman is the only one in paid employment face the same pressures as those where neither adult has paid work. Partners who find themselves forced into spending more time together without adequate financial resources suffer increasing levels of stress, which all too often can lead to personal frustration, and spill over into violence and eventual breakdown within the family.

One-parent families

We have deliberately chosen to use the terms 'one-parent family' and 'lone parents' here in preference to the widely used, but ambiguous, notion of the 'single parent', except where we refer to government statistics which explicitly categorize people as 'single parents'. There is a great deal of unclarity about exactly what it means to be designated as 'single'. In the past, a single person would have been either someone who had never been married, or someone whose partner had died. Today, those who are classified as 'single' are more likely to be divorced than never-married or widowed, and many of them will be living in long-term relationships with a sexual partner, and quite possibly with children. If we used the designation 'single parents' we could with some justification, therefore, include a number of different family types under this heading. For the sake of clarity, we will consider here only those that can be described as 'one-parent families', that is where one adult is living in a home with their children, and that one parent is responsible for their care without the help of another adult.

There is some debate as to how long one-parent families have been around. It can be made to seem that the number of families headed by lone parents has increased markedly during recent years, but that has to be balanced against the fact that, in the UK at least, the government never collected any statistics under this heading prior to 1967. In fact, the phenomenon as such is not a recent development, and many women in previous generations found themselves single-handedly bringing up children: husbands were killed in wars, they migrated leaving their families behind, or they deserted their wives and just disappeared. There was always unmarried pregnancy as well, and the persistent fact that men have a shorter life expectancy than women has also played a part.

Despite the fact that there is a discernible and highly publicized trend for women (especially celebrities and middle-class professionals) to have babies without any desire for a long-term relationship with their fathers, very few people set out with the intention of creating a one-parent family. Though lone parents can, and do, make a good job of raising their kids, most of them regret that they are in that position. Quite apart from any psychological, social or economic benefits, common sense tells you that two parents are better than one. To mention just a few of the obvious benefits: there are two sets of eyes to keep track of the kids; when two adults agree, that offers stronger guidance for them; and two people provide a more diverse set of role models than just one.[5] One-parent families generally come about as a result of unexpected – or certainly unplanned – circumstances: the death of a spouse, divorce, or a man abandoning his unmarried female partner as soon as she becomes pregnant. It is less likely that a woman will abandon both her children and their father, though that does sometimes happen. In the past, partners who hit on hard times in their relationships tended to stay together: they either resolved their difficulties, or reached an understanding to live separate lives while sharing the same home, or accepted a deteriorating domestic situation simply because in economic terms there was no alternative, at least not for women. Changes in the nature of available work have now altered all that – at least in theory – and the possibility of living independently, coupled with more relaxed divorce laws, have been major factors in the growing number of one-parent families throughout the western world. For all these reasons, the lone parent plays an increasingly significant part in family life today. In the UK, the average single parent has 1.7 children, which is only marginally lower than the average 1.9 for a married couple, while 32 per cent of all births are to single mothers – only marginally lower than the USA, where the figure is just over 33 per cent. Just as husband and wife families come in several different forms, so one-parent families can be divided into two very obvious categories, namely those headed by women and those headed by men.

Women as lone parents

The majority of one-parent families are headed by women (91 per cent in the UK), and in spite of the image projected by a few high-profile celebrity single mothers, the vast majority of them are poor. It is not an easy life, and most women bringing up children by themselves are living below the generally accepted poverty level and need to rely on some form of state assistance in order to survive at all. This fact is so obviously indisputable that in many situations being a woman and a lone parent is synonymous with poverty – the 'feminization of poverty' as it has been called. The reasons are not hard to comprehend. If it is difficult for families with two parents to juggle successfully with all the demands of daily life, then for many lone parents it is virtually impossible. When it comes to finding employment, all the odds are stacked against them, and it is exceedingly difficult to get jobs that are financially worthwhile in the short term, or that have any long-term prospects. Most employers demand 100 per cent commitment to the job – something that, by definition, lone parents find even harder to give than those who are living with a partner. In any case, many lone parents are relatively unskilled, often because they have committed themselves whole-heartedly to marriage at an early age, and as a result it is only poorly paid or casual work that is available to them.

They also face other problems. On a personal level they fre-quently suffer from intense loneliness, lacking any resources for emotional and sexual fulfilment, and unable to create space to forge new and meaningful adult relationships because of the time commitment demanded by their (often young) children – not to mention the attitudes of other people who can be hope-lessly patronizing and unsupportive. Even when a lone female parent does manage to obtain work she can expect to find herself subjected to unfair discrimination, and to verbal and sexual harassment – on the one hand by men who see her as easy game, and on the other by married women who feel threatened by her lifestyle. Many women also live with the ever-present possibility of physical violence from a former spouse or lover, not to mention other men who will always be looking for short-term relationships with no strings attached. Even when new relation-ships are formed, without adequate commitment to the children they can be unhelpful at best, and stressful – even destructive – at worst.

Men as lone parents

One-parent families headed by men come into being in more or less the same ways as those headed by women. Generalizations can be misleading, but on the whole fathers seem to have an easier life than mothers as lone parents. For one thing, men are usually economically better off than women. In addition, because of the way the legal system looks at matters affecting the custody of children, they are more likely to be parenting older children. This presents its own challenges, of course, but caring for older children is a different and, on the whole, less intensive commitment (certainly in time) than caring for toddlers. As children grow up they do not need attention for twenty-four hours a day, they can feed and wash themselves, they are usefully occupied in school – and they are also capable of accepting responsibility for some of the everyday tasks that need to be done about the home.

Statistically, men also tend to stay single for shorter periods than women. But they have many problems in common with lone female parents: finding adequate day care for children, personal loneliness, social isolation, a lack of emotional and sexual fulfilment, plus all the conflicting demands of career, housework, and parenting with which families of all types must wrestle.

The attitudes of society at large toward families headed by lone male parents can vary enormously. Sometimes friends and neighbours will be extraordinarily protective, sharing meals and services with fathers in a way they would never dream of doing for a lone mother. On the other hand, men can find themselves unfairly subjected to suspicion about their motives. In spite of policy statements to the contrary, by social work agencies and others, a man living alone with children is more likely to be accused of abusing them, either physically or sexually, than a woman would be in the same circumstance. 'Why else would a man want to bring up children alone?' is often an unspoken question, and one that is rarely addressed to lone female parents. When men are faced with such hostility (on top of all the other pressures of heading a one-parent family) they are inclined to distance themselves as far as possible from social service agencies, which in turn effectively cuts them off from some of the assistance that might, in theory, be available to help them and their children cope.

Blended families

These come about as parents whose relationships have broken up forge new relationships and bring their children with them, so as to blend them all into a new cohesive family unit. Like the one-parent family, step-parenting is not a new phenomenon. Parents faced with the loss of their spouse, for whatever reason, have always been inclined to remarry, and have then faced the prospect of trying to help children who are not directly related to one another to live harmoniously in the same family. With increasing levels of divorce and remarriage, more and more parents find themselves in this situation, and in the UK 10 per cent of all children now live in a blended family. But the form this takes today is much more complex than it was in the past, and many people not only work hard to blend families together in their own immediate home situation, but at the same time are also trying to be absentee parents to other children who are blending in a different home. The fact that this is happening at all says something important about the way the family is still regarded as being fundamental to human welfare and happiness. The breakdown of one set of relationships is not leading to the death of the family, but to its reorganization. Being a step-parent is itself a major challenge, but the more children that are involved the more difficult it becomes. It can take years for husband and wife to blend their own pre-existing families into a new social unit, and if in the meantime other children are born out of their own relationship with each other, that merely adds further complexity to the situation.[6]

Churches seem to find it especially hard to relate to blended families. Some will not countenance remarriage after divorce under any circumstances. Others want to have it both ways, and refuse to remarry people, while still recognizing such marriages as valid. Yet others say one thing and do another. As a result, families in this situation can get the impression that there is no place for them in the church. We have been involved in the formation of several church parenting groups, and we inevitably start the first meeting by inviting people to share their stories. It is always interesting to hear other people talk about their own families, especially the kind of language they choose as being appropriate for the church context. In one such group, a couple described themselves as a near-perfect example of the industrial nuclear family, but then after hearing the stories some of the rest of us told, the man of this particular partnership indicated that he wanted to say more. He went on to reveal that the family he had first mentioned was not his only family. He also had other children from a previous marriage, and they had subsequently been blended into a new family with their mother and her new husband. He spoke with warmth and appreciation of them, and though we were encouraged to know that we had created an environment that was safe enough for him to break out of his preconceived ideas about Christians, it was depressing to realize that his initial assumption had been that, however important all this was to him, he needed to keep quiet about such things if he was to find acceptance in the church. This kind of scenario is increasingly common, and churches that do not know how to accept blended families will be isolating themselves from effective ministry among a growing sector of the population.

These families, like all others, face their own particular pressures and challenges. Internal competition within the parents' own relationship can be a major stress in blended families, with unaddressed emotional baggage to sort out, as well as new styles of relationship to be developed with former spouses. But there will also be different levels of relationships within the new home, and in that context the predictable challenges for all parents are likely to be magnified, with increased problems of sibling rivalry, competition for the parents' attention, and emotional manipulation of one group by the other, not to mention conflicts over who receives discipline from whom. Some children in such circumstances might even try to wreck the new family, seeing it as the cause of all their problems, rather than a possible way out of them – especially when other children are born who are biologically related to both parents, instead of just one of them.[7]

In principle, the extended family circle should be able to help out here. But in reality, in-laws are often a big problem anyway, and the more sets of them there are to deal with (as grandparents, if not strictly in-laws), the more complex and problematic the situation can become. Nevertheless, when this kind of intergenerational care is exercised with sensitivity for the needs of both parents and children, it can provide stability and continuity that will support the personal development of both. On the other hand, for many couples trying to blend families together, the hassle is just not worth the effort and they are cast back on their own resources as they try to cope.

Cohabiting couples[8]

An increasing number of people choose to cohabit – live together unmarried – in committed relationships, and to have children. This kind of family appears in different versions, and comes about for many different reasons, though in terms of pastoral care their issues are very similar to those challenges facing the husband and wife family or the blended family. Many of the general observations made under those headings will also apply here. Cohabitees face exactly the same difficulties of balancing full-time paid employment, parenting, and work around the home as their married counterparts. The only really distinctive feature is that this family has a differently structured relationship between the parents, who instead of getting married have chosen to live together unmarried. Even here, though, there is more than one reason why people choose to do so. For many, it is a short-term measure forced upon them by the fact that they are still married to other people, and it is not possible to remarry until divorce proceedings have been finalized. Others, though technically free to marry, choose to cohabit for a period in order to ascertain whether the relationship is likely to work out in the longer term. Yet others find themselves forging cohabiting relationships on a temporary basis, while their main ongoing family style is that of single person (and maybe also a lone parent).

It is easy for Christians to take a negative attitude toward all this. But the fact is that neither families, nor faithfulness in relationships, are dying out. There is some statistical evidence to suggest that couples who cohabit are less likely to form stable relationships than those who marry as a first step, though it is also undeniable that many cohabiting relationships display an extraordinary degree of fidelity, and last longer than a lot of marriages. In addition, a large number of cohabiting relationships do in any case eventually lead to marriage. Whether that will continue in the future will depend on a variety of social and economic factors. With western governments increasingly offering those who live together unmarried the opportunity to register their partnerships in order to secure the same rights as married couples, the precise legal status of both cohabitation and marriage – and the relation between the two – is clearly going into the melting pot. It may be that we are returning to a more primitive understanding, even perhaps along the lines of the culture of biblical times, where marriage was the final stage of a more or less extended period of betrothal marked by several stages of increasing commitment.[9]

Couples without children

Since many of the tensions identified in family life relate to the problem of balancing the needs of adult relationships with those of children, you might think that an obvious resolution would be for adults to choose to have no children. Presumably being childless would then remove a major obstacle to the achievement of human happiness. But life is not that simple, and for some couples the absence of children creates at least as many problems as their presence does for others.

Some couples voluntarily choose to be childless. No western country has yet followed the example of China which for economic reasons tries to limit every couple to just one child. But they don't need to, as the economic pressures of affluence can have a similar effect. For couples where both partners are engaged in fulfilling work, progressing steadily along clearly defined career tracks with rising expectations of both personal fulfilment and financial prosperity, the whole system is geared up to persuading them either to delay having children for as long as is physically possible or (what often amounts to the same thing, by default) never having them at all. Considerations motivating such choices include the likelihood that the woman will never be able to regain her position in career terms after the birth of a child, no matter how short a leave she takes from paid employment, as well as the fact that both of them are probably having to work so hard that they literally would have no time to fulfil a parenting role in any adequate fashion.

When those who have work are being forced into longer and longer hours, the pressure on couples to decide to remain childless is increasing all the time. When John first started teaching in a British university, it was a very family-friendly employment situation. Though the system was far too conservative to ever think of using a word like 'flexi-time', that is effectively how it operated: there was a specified amount of work that needed to be done, and within that framework there was considerable flexibility. Today, that has disappeared. Not only are teachers in universities being expected to work longer hours – including in some cases evening and weekend work (in addition to daytime Monday–Friday hours), as well as work during what would otherwise be vacation periods – but they are also being pressurized to produce quality research publications, for the execution of which most institutions are either unwilling or unable to provide time or facilities within the boundaries of what might be regarded as an ordinary working week of forty hours or so. As a result, many academics find that the only way to fulfil all their employer's expectations is to work long hours, and the easiest way to do that is to cut down on time spent with families. Either they spend all their evenings and weekends doing the research work for which there is no time provision in the working week, and thereby lose out on quality time spent with their family; or they choose different priorities in the home, and thereby lose out on promotion in the workplace. This scenario is by no means unique to academic life. It is rapidly becoming the norm for many people, and not just those in so-called professional occupations. With ever longer opening hours in shops, factories, and offices – all of them organized for the benefit of the employers rather than for the personal wellbeing of the staff – is it any wonder that more and more people are choosing to remain childless? They simply have enough to do already, without adding to their busy lives the demands of parenthood. Indeed, many of them are too tired to have sex at all, whether for procreation or pleasure.

In social terms, no one yet knows where this trend will lead, but in almost all western nations the present birth rate is insufficient to renew the population, even in the medium term. When so many people who would be otherwise well equipped to raise mature people for the future choose not to do so, that is bound to have far-reaching repercussions for the whole shape and balance of the culture of future generations. Precisely because they are aware of such considerations, many couples who choose to be childless often suffer from guilt for the rest of their lives, always wondering whether or not they have done the right thing.

In addition, though, many couples are involuntarily childless, for a variety of physiological reasons. Far from finding this a blissful state, they too are under stress. In terms of their own self-image, they can be made to feel inadequate. Not only will they never be one of those 'perfect families' so beloved of TV advertisers, but they have to live with the nagging thought that 'I can't even perform the most basic of human functions' – so how can they be whole persons? That in turn can lead to the apportioning of 'blame' for their childless state, which can easily prove to be the death blow to a relationship. And if they survive all that, they are probably still faced with angry relatives who feel they have been deprived of their rights because they have no grandchildren, nieces or nephews.

Other homes

Finally, there are a number of other possible forms of social structure that are redefining the family, but of which we can make only brief mention.

Living alone

Single-person homes are increasing in number today. People become single for a variety of reasons. Some just grow from adolescence into adulthood without forging a lasting relationship with someone they might marry. Others cohabit, but are still classified as 'single', while many more move from one short-term relationship to another. Then there is divorce and death, both of which increase the number of single people. When we conflate the figures from these various categories of singleness, the UK 2001 census shows single people accounting for almost exactly half the adult population (49.1 per cent).[10] In common with some other emerging lifestyle patterns mentioned in this chapter, the increase of singleness in today's world is a topic to which the church should be giving urgent attention. The fact that we are unable to do more than note its importance here is not an indication that we treat it lightly, but quite the opposite: to do justice to it would require an entire book to itself.[11]

Living in community

There is an increasing trend towards living in community, especially in the USA. Young singles, or couples, find themselves unable to afford a home of their own, and live with other people who are in the same situation, either in a single house divided into separate apartments, or by taking a share in a larger housing complex, even part of a street, which can become a community in which meals might be shared as well as living accommodation. In the US, growing numbers of churches and seminaries are establishing intentional communities along these lines. People who become single as a result of homelessness, divorce, and so on can find this kind of arrangement particularly appealing, but couples with young children are also discovering it to be a safe nurturing environment in which they and their families can make friends with others who share similar values.

Same-sex families

There is also an emerging family model based on gay relation-ships, both between homosexual men and lesbian women.[12] Gay couples not only foster and adopt children, but also conceive their own, whether through short-term liaisons with members of the opposite sex who act as surrogates, or through artificial insemination or IVF techniques. This is a topic which excites many Christians, and if some churches have problems with blended families, then it is merely stating the obvious to say that they have a mountain to climb if they are to have any effective ministry with families headed by gay people. Given the sort of pronouncements made in the media not only by individuals but by mainline denominations, in both the UK and the USA, Christians will have to work hard to shed the homophobic image they have so effectively created for themselves in recent years. Indeed, it may be that in some places the door has already been closed on any meaningful Christian pastoral care within the gay community. The various theological and moral arguments that have dominated church debates about homosexuality will no doubt continue. Whatever the outcome, gay families are a social reality in western culture, and if Christians are concerned to care for the family in all its diversity, then this particular form of family and its pastoral needs cannot be ignored. Much of what we say in this book will be relevant to the experience of gay parents, though it would have been too complex a task to adopt language throughout that could apply equally well to these families as to others.[13]

Extended families

In addition, variations on the extended family home are becoming more common in some contexts. There is an increasing trend for grandparents to be short-term carers for their grand-children in order to enable their parents to go to work, or to have custody of them on a longer-term basis while the parents sort out their own relationship difficulties. Such arrangements can offer a way of dealing with family breakdown internally, within the wider family circle, something which is likely to be encouraged by social workers as it avoids children being taken into care or into foster homes. Custodial grandparenting can be very successful, but evidence shows it can also be stressful, for grandparents as well as children.[14]

Families in transition

The family is clearly in the midst of enormous upheaval and change. Though most of us will identify with some of the models mentioned here, none of us is likely to match any of them on a permanent basis. As time passes, families change, and a majority of people anticipate that and plan for it. Change is a constant factor even within the life span of each of these different family patterns. No one can be a full-time parent for ever, because children grow up and their parenting needs change, which in-evitably affects the lifestyle of the whole family. Most parents would probably hope that one of them could be a full-time parent while their children are small, but would not regard that as a permanent situation, and would expect to resume paid employment outside the home on a progressive basis as circumstances change. In the short-term, harsh economic realities often make it difficult or impossible for people to fulfil this aspiration. They simply cannot survive following the expiry of a statutory period of paid parental leave from work immediately after the birth of a child, and as a result they are forced to return to full-time employment sooner rather than later, regardless of what their personal preferences might otherwise be. In any case, it is not always easy for a parent to plan to return to work some years in the future. The nature of particular jobs might undergo radical change in the meantime, necessitating retraining, and there are very few careers where it is possible to take several years out and then return to the same rung on the promotion ladder. There is a major social challenge here for governments. If we want to have enough babies to renew the population, while providing families with lasting economic security and supporting people's expectations of having meaningful paid employment, then there will need to be appropriate provision to enable that to happen.

Beyond these internal changes within the categories we have identified here, there are also more significant shifts in family styles and allegiances, which make it difficult to forecast what the future may bring. It might well be that new versions of what in the past would have been called the extended family could provide a way forward, this time not based on kinship in the strict sense, but on networks of unrelated friends and associates as well as those bound together by genetic links. Whatever happens next, we can be sure that the redesigned family will feature in the emerging social landscape. But the shape of the new design is not yet clear, nor is it likely to be for some time to come. As a culture we are still at the drawing-board stage. The question for Christians is whether we can think creatively enough to make a positive contribution to this process. It is easy to say that the family today is in crisis, but that is merely to state the obvious – and a crisis is not always a bad thing. The Chinese, as is well known, have two characters which define the concept of 'crisis'. One speaks of 'danger', and the other means 'opportunity'. For Christians to focus on the danger, and to be constantly bemoaning the disappearance of the industrial nuclear family, is the way of death. To see the situation as an opportunity will require careful discernment to enable us to identify those new emerging values that reflect God's will (and in spite of much confusion, there are plenty of signs of hope), and to work alongside other people of goodwill to ensure that these values make a positive contribution to the new image of the family that will take our descendants safely through the next generations.

3 Being a child in today's family

Children learn what they live

A child who lives with criticism learns to condemn.
A child who lives with hostility learns to fight.
A child who lives with ridicule learns to be shy.
A child who lives with shame learns to feel guilty.

A child who lives with tolerance learns to be patient.
A child who lives with encouragement learns confidence.
A child who lives with praise learns to appreciate.
A child who lives with fairness learns justice.
A child who lives with security learns to have faith.
A child who lives with approval learns to like themselves.

If children live with acceptance and friendship,
they learn to find Love in the World.[1]

Since her poem was originally penned in 1954, Dorothy Law Nolte's sentiments have been widely acclaimed, and can be found in many different versions around the world. The poem's title expresses succinctly some fundamental truths about human development. Who we become as adults is to a very large extent shaped by our experience as children. It is by no means impossible for people to change direction in later life, but doing so almost always involves a lot of painful heart-searching in sorting out the baggage of our childhood past. Childhood has a profound and lasting effect on us all, for good or ill. The way children develop a sense of their own identity and image depends on their interaction with adults, their parents and others who are significant in their lives. It follows that any disruption in the quality of a child's early relationships is bound to have far-reaching repercussions. In turn, anything that affects today's children will have consequences for tomorrow's adults and ultimately, therefore, for the whole shape of our communities. No one yet knows what future effects there will be for society as a whole as a result of the difficulties faced by so many of today's children. The only certain thing is that, with increasing numbers of children having negative experiences of the family, the impact is likely to be considerable.

Adults and children

Prior to about the seventeenth century, no one thought of 'childhood' as a separate stage of human development.[2] It was not that previous generations did not care about their children, but they valued them for their future potential rather than seeing any intrinsic worth in the state of being a child. Childhood was just a necessary prelude to becoming a full adult member of society, and children were therefore valued not so much for themselves but as a contribution toward society's investment in the future. The family itself was regarded as an institution that was bigger than its individual members, and for which it was worth making sacrifices and commitments that would lay solid foundations for generations yet to come. Few people today have that sense of hope for the future, either because they believe things are irredeemably heading for disaster or, more often, because they live only for the present and for themselves – attitudes that are encouraged by consumerism and the technological mindset that assumes everything can and should be delivered instantaneously. This uncertainty about the future and our ambivalent understanding of the nature of happiness affects the way we think of and relate to our children.

Though enormous numbers of people long to find meaningful relationships with others, very few have a concept of happiness which centres on living in community, or understands human fulfilment in terms of personal commitment and self-sacrifice. The corrosive effects of selfish individualism are widespread, and Christians are not exempt from its pervasive influence. Indeed, historically the Church has played a major role in promoting it:

we do well to remember that the Enlightenment emphasis on the autonomy of the individual is not entirely separable from the values of the Protestant Reformation, with its insistence that so far as God is concerned each person stands individually and personally accountable only for him or herself.

All this is reflected in the contradictory attitudes to children that can be found among parents as well as in society more generally. Unlike our forebears, we do not have children for future security, still less for economic gain: on the contrary, they actually cost us a lot of money! Instead, we say we have children for emotional satisfaction. Paradoxically, though, we are tempted to treat them as mere possessions, to be disposed of as we see fit. When we read Bible stories in which parents sacrificed their children, we rightly have many questions, but though we may not sacrifice them to the gods nowadays we can still assume that we have property rights over our kids, and 'sacrifice' them in other ways. At different ends of the relational spectrum, we are as likely to deprive them of our time and attention as we are to fight for custody rights over them in court – both attitudes assuming that children are the property of their biological parents, and therefore we can do what we like with them.

As a society, we also regularly exhibit the same double standards. We say we want to provide opportunities for parents to be fulfilled through paid employment, while at the same time we make half-hearted provision for their children, whether in terms of the structuring of employment, or in the offer of appropriate day care. The problems faced by many children can be traced directly to the conflicting demands that society places upon their parents. Everyone knows the phenomenon of latchkey kids, forced to fend for themselves at an early age before and after school each day and for long hours during holiday periods. The plight of children left 'home alone' while their parents take vacations is not just a Hollywood fiction, but is reality for some – almost certainly for more of them than hit the headlines. This sounds scandalous and irresponsible when it expresses itself in that form. But the fact is that some young children are left unattended on a regular basis while their parents work, because no other choices are open to them. The inaccessibility of proper day care affects parents as well as children, and that can have knock-on effects in all areas of their life. Stress easily spills over into conflict in both home and workplace. It affects health, lowers productivity, and undermines the stability of all kinds of relationships. None of this is good for children. In addition to such identifiable issues, many children find themselves treated with indifference, even by those who think they are good parents. For successful, ambitious parents children are both a necessary social accessory, and also an enormous inconvenience, and there is always the temptation to keep them occupied with watching TV, videos, or playing computer games instead of investing ourselves in them. These things might not look like neglect, but at the end of the day they all amount to a failure to take seriously the full humanity and worth of our children – which, in a Christian context, is to question their essential nature as persons made 'in the image of God' (Genesis 1:27).

Children can also find themselves in a no-win situation because of the laissez-faire attitudes among adults over the issue of discipline. This too amounts to a devaluing of the child as human person. The emergence of the industrial nuclear family, combined with the Victorian obsession for structure and religious opinions that emphasized the intrinsic corruption of human nature, led to the view that children needed regular discipline in order to 'beat the sin out of them' – a notion that could be justified from Scripture passages such as Ben Sirach 30:1–13, where the following advice is given:

> He who loves his son will whip him often . . . He who spoils his son will bind up his wounds, and his feelings will be troubled at every cry. Pamper a child, and he will frighten you; play with him, and he will give you grief. Do not laugh with him . . . Give him no authority in his youth, and do not ignore his errors. Bow down his neck in his youth, and beat his sides while he is young . . . (RSV)

We have rightly rejected all that, but as a reaction to such excesses some parents offer their children no disciplinary framework whatever. They say they are giving their children the freedom to develop their own lifestyles. What they are really doing is refusing to take responsibility for their own offspring, and abandoning them to a life with no structure, limits, or values – often assuming that it is not their job anyway, but a service that should be provided by the wider community. At the same time as parents neglect to offer a framework for the socialization of their children in terms of values, they are quite likely to be making very specific demands of them, by expecting them to dress, wash and feed themselves, and be responsible for their own welfare while the parents are at work. Children who are regularly left by themselves before and after school each day are bound to be more vulnerable than those who have proper adult care and supervision. The chance of getting involved in delinquency is only one manifestation of this. Many more of them are, in effect, expected to be the managers of their own homes, doing the shopping, the cleaning, perhaps even being the regular cook for the entire family's evening meals. Of course, children need to be empowered to play their part in the running of the home, and it is not necessarily a bad thing for young teenagers to be expected to help in these ways. But when such responsibilities are placed on children as young as seven or eight years old without support from adult family members, then children can find themselves literally enslaved in their own homes.

There is no doubt that at the present time the emerging models of family are creating more problems than they can resolve, and they affect children in every social class. That is not to say there can be no resolution of them. But if our children are to grow up as whole and balanced people, it will require more realism about their predicament on the part of adults. The one indisputable fact is that children never create the circumstances in which they find themselves. It is easy to say that parents have the primary responsibility for giving their children the love and commitment they deserve and need. Governments love to say it, because they think that absolves them of any responsibility. But if we expect all adults to be productively employed and also caring for their children, adequate support will be required for parents who are trying to juggle so many balls at once. One way or another, these challenges impinge on the lives of most of today's children. But they are not the only factors with which as a group they are having to contend.

Poverty

Poverty is hard to define, because it is not just about economics. Whenever it is discussed, it invariably becomes a political issue. Governments are embarrassed by it and tend to minimize it, while their political opponents are inclined to exaggerate it. However you quantify it, the last twenty years have seen a massive increase in poverty on a worldwide scale. It is not uncommon to see even children begging in the streets of all our major cities, and homelessness and poverty are obvious facts of life throughout the western world. Moreover, many of the poor are very poor – and there are a fair number of others who, though not quite poor enough to be officially classed as 'below the poverty line', are still suffering significant economic deprivation. The serious dislocation of populations all around the globe, and the increasing numbers of refugees and asylum seekers, is only highlighting an issue that has existed for some time.

Politicians always tackle this matter by asking who is to blame, and whether people are responsible for creating their own poverty. That is a valid question, but whatever the answer might be, it is never children who create their own poverty. Yet increasing numbers of them are finding their lives affected by it. A couple of generations ago, old people were the ones most at risk from poverty. Some still are, and with the growing pensions crisis more of them might yet be, but in general it is children and young families who are more likely to be among the poor, especially one-parent families and two-parent families with only one adult earner.

Children can be very resilient to hardship, and even those who know they are deprived will hope for something better. But unless things do actually change, they internalize their situation and lose hope. To deprive a child of hope for the future is a form of abuse whose consequences for the rest of their life are incalculable. Is that not one of the things Jesus had in mind when he condemned so stridently those who might cause a child to lose faith (Mark 9:42)? To be a child and to have no hope is a contradiction in terms, but it is the reality for very many children today. Imagine, if you can, what life is like for a child in poor circumstances in a temperate climate: living in a damp home, missing school because of frequent illness caused by the damp and the cold, having to share a bed with your brothers and sisters, or even with adults, unable to participate in all the activities at school because your parents are unable to afford some of them, not always having clean clothes to wear when you go to school, and never having a place at home to do homework. Hope might be kindled for a while by the promise that one day you will have better housing. But the reality is that the poor often have to move from one temporary home to another, and they can stay on waiting lists for public housing for years without anything happening. Is it any wonder that when children realize that for them there is no escape, they handle the problem either by withdrawing into their own private world, or venting their anger in delinquent activities – or, increasingly, in self-harm or suicide? There seems to be a link between poverty and ill health, lower educational achievement, delinquency, and many of the other maladies afflicting children.

What is more, poverty affects the models of community living that parents can pass on to their children. It can lead to violence between parents, and interminable arguments over how whatever money they have is to be spent, and who spends it. Adults caught in this situation often look to alcohol or drugs as a way of escape – and children get caught in the middle. At best, many children raised in poverty grow up to repeat the same cycle themselves. At worst, they are forced into homelessness as teenagers and spend the rest of their lives as a liability to themselves and to the wider community.

The relationship between poverty and family breakdown is undoubtedly a complex matter, but changes in family structures certainly constitute one factor in the increase in family poverty. For example, divorce almost invariably means a lower income for the woman, and relative poverty for her (and her children, if they end up living with their mother as a one-parent family). Men go their own way, and in spite of the best intentions of government agencies they often manage to evade substantial financial responsibility for their children. In the 1990s the UK government attempted to redress the balance by setting up the Child Support Agency to collect cash from fathers and redistribute it to their children and former wives. This move met with some resistance from men who had remarried and had second or third families. They claimed that meeting their government-determined financial targets would jeopardize their new families, and there would be no sense in robbing one family to pay another. Who could blame them? Within less than two years, the Agency was radically restructured to take account of such matters. But the nature of these arguments, focusing on the perceived happiness of the adults involved, merely serves to highlight the extent to which children are almost always the victims in such circumstances. Nor is this a matter of social class, for even children who are born into relative affluence can suddenly find themselves plunged into poverty as the result of the breakdown of their parents' relationship.

Emotions

Separation and divorce also have a significant emotional impact on children. It is very difficult to identify a specific cause of this, as children tend to see breakdown as one single episode, whereas adults are inclined to think of it as a process and they therefore compartmentalize the different elements contributing to it. It may not be the divorce itself that causes emotional disturbances for children, but the tensions and pressures that precede it and the economic deprivation that often follows. But the whole process creates major trauma. For a child, it is not just the immediate effects of separation that make a difference, but what breakdown represents in terms of their lost expectations, their broken relationships, and shattered dreams.

The negative effects of losing a parent through divorce last well beyond childhood. Role models provided by parents are a vital factor in influencing a child's own later family formation, and the rise in emotional and psychological problems faced by children, not to mention the increasing incidence of teenage suicides, is all related in some way to changing support systems within the family.[3] In fact, in the medium- to long-term, divorce can be much harder to handle than the death of a parent. Children go through the same kind of grieving process in both instances, though in the case of divorce there is never a final separation, which means that the agony is constantly prolonged and may never be resolved. Adults rarely see divorce the way a child does, because their whole agenda is different. Adults divorce for many different reasons, but the majority do so only reluctantly and after giving the matter much serious thought. So within their own terms of reference, their reasons are mostly good ones. Children, however, find it hard to imagine that anything could possibly be important enough to be worth splitting up for. In many respects, adults' needs in a contemporary marriage are different from those of their children. They look for love, fulfilment, and personal satisfaction. A child also needs love, not so much in terms of personal fulfilment but in the form of protection and security. For a child, to exchange those essentials for an adult's version of personal fulfilment will always seem a bad deal, or just selfishness on the part of one or both of their parents. Adults also need to remember that breakdown for a child means the loss of a person with whom they have a unique and irreplaceable relationship: you can only have one father or mother. Divorce is not without its emotional trauma for adults, but they are losing a lover, who can eventually be replaced: parents cannot.[4]

In the short-term, divorce has many different and unpredictable effects on children, partly related to their age when it occurs. Some experience an overwhelming sense of loneliness and insecurity, afraid that both parents will eventually leave them. They may take sides, blaming one parent for what has happened and regarding the other as a victim. Adolescents probably suffer the most, and their loss of security at this crucial time in their own development can create worries about whether they will be able to make relationships, or what levels of personal intimacy they can handle. Children's immediate symptoms can range from physical side-effects such as nightmares, sleeplessness, or unexplained aches and pains, to unexpected delinquency or running away from home, or openly expressed anger and disapproval of their parents – especially if remarriage is in view, because that means there is no chance at all of going back to the past (something that most children in divorce secretly hope for). Young adults can find their parents' divorce especially stressful, and forego any possibility of an adult relationship with them as a result. In the longer term, the trauma of divorce can affect children's own choices about relationships. They might become cynical and suspicious of marriage and less likely to want children of their own.

In helping children in such circumstances, we need to remember that we all resolve our own stresses in different ways, depending on our varying temperaments and personalities. And of course children do survive the disintegration of their family. Nor should we generalize and say that in the long run divorce per se will always be a bad thing for a child. For a child who is trapped in a close relationship with an abusive and violent parent, divorce can very obviously turn out to be a good thing. But even in that situation, family breakdown is still costly in terms of a child's emotions. Church workers called upon to advise in these situations need to be very sensitive to what is actually going on. It is too easy to advise parents to stick together at all costs – 'for the sake of the children' – while ignoring the sum total of unhappiness that such a situation perpetuates. On balance, it is probably children trapped in unhappy homes who suffer the most, but we also need to realize that children of divorce do have to handle a lot of emotional distress. We might regret that these are the only alternatives available to some children, but this is how it is and we need to find ways of living with it.

Violence

Physical violence can take different forms, but for many of the world's children it has become a way of life, whether experienced through starvation, disease, the ravages of war, slavery, or organized sexual exploitation. One of the most obvious facts impinging on the experience of western children is that the family itself – the place where they have a right to expect to be given care and security – has all too often become a place of cruelty and violent oppression. Public awareness of this has grown significantly in recent years, and it is a topic that will keep cropping up in subsequent chapters. Here we will concentrate on its impact on children. It is difficult to know whether current levels of domestic abuse and violence are one of the by-products of changing family structures, or whether things have always been like this, the only difference being that people are now more open than they were in the past, and so it just seems as if violence is increasing. But it is difficult not to imagine that in many instances there must be some causal connection with other factors that are impinging on family life, because it is not just adults who perpetrate violent acts against children: there is a growing incidence of children being violent to adults (their parents included) and to other children. In very many of these cases their own experience of family dysfunction and breakdown plays a major part in determining the behavioural patterns of such children.

Violent domestic abuse is an extremely emotive subject, and we must not fall into the trap of overstating the size of the problem. It is still only a minority of children who suffer physical abuse – but it is a bigger minority than most adults imagine, or are prepared to face up to.[5] There are different estimates of how common physical and sexual abuse is, but there is a general consensus that it tends to be under-reported. Part of the problem is a matter of definition as to what constitutes 'abuse'. For example, if children are left unattended and uncared for by parents who are addicted to alcohol or drugs, then that clearly constitutes neglect – but does it also constitute abuse? Not all abuse is physical. There are many non-physical ways to abuse a child that do not involve what most people would think of as violence, but which are every bit as damaging.

Many children are consistently put down by parents and teachers, by being repeatedly told how useless they are at doing things, and how far short they fall of their parents' ideals and expectations. Religious parents are particularly prone to this kind of behaviour, reinforcing their own preferences by identifying them as 'the will of God', and then invoking eternal sanctions against children who fail to conform. Both of us were brought up in religious families, and suffered from this to a greater or lesser extent at different points in our childhood. At the age of eight, Olive was abandoned by her parents to the care of a foster family whom she had never met before, and who lived hundreds of miles away from all her relatives (of whom she had very many) – to free her parents to go and evangelize other people's children. It took her years to work through the traumatic emotional and spiritual consequences.[6] John has distinct memories of being told as a child of about nine years old that he was so bad he must be the 'man of sin' referred to in 2 Thessalonians 2:1–4. Such accusations are easily recognized as expressions of the frustration of adults who had a particular religious language available to them. All parents will understand the frustration, and most will have said things they subsequently regretted. But many adult Christians suffer from a lack of self-esteem as a result of such childhood encounters – and then go on to inflict similar injustices on their own offspring.[7] The fact that Christian parents can do and say such things probably reveals more about the lack of support they receive from the church than it does about their personal commitment to the welfare of their own children. Whatever the reason, many children still suffer repeatedly from verbal and psychological abuse, especially in middle-class families, because the more educated a parent is the more words they have at their disposal. Then there is smacking. Does that constitute violent abuse? Even with heightened public awareness of the issue it is still not uncommon – in the UK at any rate – to see an angry parent physically harassing a child in a public place such as a supermarket or shopping mall. In spite of efforts by politicians to ban it, this behaviour is also generally legal, though it is often difficult to know where to draw the line between what might constitute a legally acceptable level of physical punishment and what becomes in effect violent assault. Among Christians, some of the most heated debates on parenting centre around this issue.

A number of things contribute to violence in the home, and while it is tempting to blame traditional patriarchal men,[8] that is not the only factor, and probably not the most important. We are all increasingly under stress, and this is a major cause of relational dysfunction that can easily open the door to violence in the home.[9] Some families know of no other way to relate to one another, and find themselves trapped in a cycle of violence. Occasionally, other psychological factors may be involved. In particular, we know that many abusers have themselves been the victims of abuse, or otherwise subjected to emotional deprivation, parental rejection, and family conflict (though not everyone who suffers these things necessarily becomes an abuser). Violent parents may also be psychopaths or sociopaths, or suffer from other conditions associated with low self-esteem and high levels of insecurity. Whatever the explanation, many children are suffering from unprovoked violence at the hands of their carers. Some end up dying either through deliberate physical assaults, or as a result of neglect. One of the most disturbing trends, however, is the growing number of children who no longer regard the family as a place of safety and security. Many of them spend increasing amounts of time on the streets and in shopping malls, because they feel safer there than at home. One result, however, is that they are vulnerable to being recruited into gangs, prostitution, and other forms of delinquency and racketeering. For others, the suffering they encounter in the home is so great that they come to believe that death could be a real release. Suicide is the ultimate act of hopelessness and despair, and over the last twenty years the rates among children have been rising. Some researchers suspect the true figures for child suicide are higher than the statistics suggest, because suicide as a real cause of the death of a child is hard to prove conclusively, and can be so painful for relatives that police and social workers often accept incomplete explanations. Whatever the truth, a dysfunctional family is undoubtedly one of the key reasons for childhood and adolescent suicide, particularly when a child feels somehow responsible for the mess at home, and can see no way of improving it or resolving the conflict.

The crisis in the family is most keenly felt by children. They are not responsible for what is happening to them. They have not created the situations within which they have to live, and even in the most stable home situations it is easy for them to be overcome with a sense of injustice and unfairness. Of course, parents usually try their best, and at stressful times in their own relationships many people will find support from informal networks of relatives and friends to look after their children. But for many more, there is no way to cope and they find their children taken into care. For some children that can be the answer to their prayers. For others being in care can be as traumatic an experience as the original home situation was. If such children grow up without adequate support from their families, then as teenagers they can easily slip out of the care system, taking with them unrealistic ambitions to set up their own homes in the community, only to find themselves trapped in a cycle of loneliness, unemployment, and poverty. For children to be in care can only ever be a temporary solution to particular crises. The majority of them have two possible places in which to find their identity: the street, or the family. In that situation, it makes sense to work to support the family, rather than making long-term care arrangements elsewhere, or paying the social costs of having large numbers of homeless youngsters living rough.

If we have painted a bleak picture in this chapter, then that fairly reflects how life is for huge numbers of children around the world today. We do not wish to exaggerate the challenges facing children, and it is important to acknowledge that most families are neither seriously dysfunctional, nor are they perfect. They work with what Michel de Certeau calls 'making do', that is they follow their ideals, achieving what they can and succeeding to a great enough degree to be able to nurture the children within them.[10] But we should not use that fact to close our eyes to the dysfunctional elements that are to be found in all families, even those that on the surface seem to be coping well. Families that are dangerous and debilitating for children tend to be damaging for everyone else in them as well, which is why we will return to this theme more than once in the chapters that follow.[11]

Bearing all that in mind, church leaders need to adopt approaches that will encourage families to live up to their best ideals in relation to their children, and be prepared to support them when things go wrong. Theologically, this invites us to reconnect with some fundamental Christian beliefs, most especially the doctrines of creation and incarnation. The very first page of the Bible makes the breathtaking claim that people are 'made in the image of God' (Genesis 1:27), while at the heart of the New Testament is the equally challenging claim that the character of God is to be uniquely seen in the person of Jesus Christ (John 1:14). That would be exceptional enough if it were a claim made only for the adult rabbi, Jesus of Nazareth, but (in the face of claims to the contrary by Docetists and others) the Gospels are unanimous in their conviction that Jesus the child was both fully divine as well as being fully human. While it might be argued that the Genesis statement was only meant to apply to adults (it is certainly only adult women and men who are specifically mentioned there), the New Testament leaves no room for any such notion. There, the state of being a child is itself a vehicle for transcendence, and Jesus was as fully divine as a newborn baby as he was at the time of his death. This message is further emphasized in those stories which highlight the importance placed on actual children by Jesus himself. The disciples no doubt had Jesus' best interests at heart when they prevented children from coming to him, for their culture generally viewed them not only as incapable of rational behaviour, but also as a distraction from the more serious business of spiritual life: they might become disciples only once they had grown up. Jesus would have none of this, and insisted not only that a child could be a disciple, but could also be a model for other disciples to follow (Mark 9:33–7, 10:14).

This biblical teaching has clear and obvious consequences for the opportunities that the church should afford for children to play a full part in the life of the Christian community. But it also highlights one of the key contributions that a Christian worldview can make in respect of the place of children in the family, and focuses our attention on the fact that a distinctively Christian understanding ought to be more bothered about what families do than what they are supposed to look like. In architectural jargon, form follows function. And in relation to children, a key function of the family is to honour and nurture their humanity, recognizing that in their humanness they – like adults – are made in the image of God. This also challenges parents to a different way of being adult. One of the reasons we are so easily tempted to hurry our kids along to becoming adult as quickly as possible is because that can be a way of avoiding our own vulnerability. For, as Jesus himself suggested, children invite us to recognize and live within our own childlike nature, and they assure us that the creation of meaningful community requires us not just to acknowledge, but even to celebrate our vulnerability, weakness, openness, and dependency. These are not the characteristics that are most valued in a consumer society, and as a result, 'It is an irony of our time that infants in less-developed countries, where neediness and dependency are the norms of living and modern conveniences are less available, often have a better chance of growing up healthy'.[12] A key reason for this is that their parents, generally for reasons beyond their control, have no option but to demonstrate that dependence on God that even Christian parents are inclined to discount in today's western societies. We cannot countenance the exploitation of non-western peoples that is part of that situation, but there are important human – and Christian – values reflected there that those of us in more 'developed' cultures need to rediscover before it is too late.

4 Adults in today's family

While the nature of the relationships between women and men may be changing, and the acceptable diversity of family-creating adult relationships is now wider than ever before, the way in which women and men get on with each other is still fundamental to the ethos of the home and the growth and development of those within it. Though a child's perspective is vital for any holistic understanding of the family, in the final analysis adult relationships will always determine the lifestyle of families. The pressures faced by women and men, and how they deal with them, have a direct bearing on the experiences of children. By identifying some of these pressures, we will hopefully develop lifestyles in which we can support one another, and help create family structures that will be to the benefit of both adults and children. Some Christians believe that relationships between women and men (and, indeed, children) constitute a theological question rather than a sociological one, and we have something to say about that in a later chapter. But it makes sense to consider the question initially in terms of the everyday circumstances within which people have to live. This is important to us, for two reasons. First, our understanding of theology requires us to do so. We do not see 'theology' in terms of abstract notions that are disconnected from the realities of daily life. If theological reflection is not rooted in human experience, then we are unlikely to find the right questions to address to God, and about God – let alone to uncover any answers that might help us to actually live in ways that reflect the distinctive values of the gospel. The emphasis on doctrines of creation and incarnation, already highlighted in the previous chapter, reminds us that a biblically based Christianity can never be a disembodied collection of propositional statements, but starts from the recognition that it is precisely in the experience of being human that we encounter the fullness of God through Jesus Christ. In addition, any Christian reflection on the family needs to be rooted in the realities of family life for the simple reason that significant numbers of church people struggle to connect what they perceive to be the idealistic patterns of Scripture with their own experience. As a result, they either end up in denial about what is happening with their own homes and families, or leave their Christian belief on one side as being irrelevant to everyday life.

Influences changing families

This is a convenient point at which to summarize some of the factors that are involved in the massive change that the family is currently undergoing. Some of them have already been hinted at: they are all an inescapable consequence of the cultural shift from modernity to post-modernity. Christians can be especially resistant to change, telling themselves that they are preserving trusted and tried values that will last forever – a notion that is often reinforced by hymns declaring that God never changes (so why should we?), or that portray change as a bad thing ('Change and decay in all around I see . . .'). This is a curious attitude for those whose sacred Scriptures contain many invitations to see things in new ways (e.g. Isaiah 42:9; John 3:5–8), and whose Founder was constantly surprising people by doing things differently (e.g. Matthew 5:38–42, 19:30; Mark 2:12; 1 Corinthians 1:25), while his first followers were charged with turning the world upside down (Acts 17:6). Change is not only a natural and inevitable aspect of life, but something to be welcomed. Even conservative Christians do that in the rest of their lives: like everyone else, they buy new products, go to new vacation destinations, update their cars and TV sets. Yet people who would never dream of wanting to turn the clock back in those respects are frequently dismayed by the fact that the family is changing. But change can be the agent for both good and ill, and the important thing is how we respond to new challenges. For those who would give pastoral support to families in today's tough environment, this is the central question: how will we respond, and what will be the guiding principles that lead to practical outcomes in specific situations?

There are several obvious factors that have impacted family

patterns and lifestyles, all of which can create significant challenges that, if not dealt with carefully, can lead to dysfunctional relationships.

Mobility

Fifty years ago, most people spent their entire lives within a twenty-mile radius of their place of birth. Today, more than 60 per cent of us can expect to move away from our birthplace, and among some sections of the population the figure is higher still. The majority of children in the western world no longer have everyday access to their grandparents or other members of their wider family. In the past, relatives provided natural networks of support for parents of young children, but today child-minding is a commercial enterprise. This change can be beneficial: once paid, you don't owe a babysitter anything else, unlike grandparents who can imagine you should be indebted to them forever. It can also have drawbacks, though: you don't know who these people are, whether they share your values, or indeed whether they can be trusted with your children (though not all relatives can be, either: most abuse of children is at the hands of their own family members). The previous pattern also provided a shared pool of wisdom to young parents struggling to know if their child's behaviour was 'normal', and what to do about things they found difficult. The same with teenagers, for whom grandparents often operated as therapists. Today, many teenagers don't personally know any adult beyond their own parents, and some don't even know both of them.

Economic pressures

Today's families find it harder to resist expectations about how people are 'supposed' to live – pressure which is now more than the traditional 'keeping up with the Joneses', if only because there is much more to keep up with. It is taken for granted that eating out will be a regular part of life, something that was less available in the past. And whereas even twenty years ago it was possible to feed a family for a week on soup made from a bone, regulatory controls have made it increasingly difficult to buy the ingredients, quite apart from the amount of time required to cook every meal from scratch. As little as a single generation ago, it was perfectly possible for parents to choose for one of them to be a full-time homemaker (typically the mother), at least for a time. Today only the most well-off parents, or those prepared to make considerable sacrifices, can do that. The resulting pressure on home life is, in many cases, destructive. Economic pressures related to employment (or the lack of it) are a major source of misery and breakdown.

Sexual revolution

Unlike their grandparents, today's women choose whether or not to have babies. In reality, however, this is not as free a choice as it seems, for the overwhelming expectation in society is that it is a good thing to be a parent. This message is more insistent as politicians realize that, with few exceptions, western populations are ageing rapidly, and the workforce of younger people will therefore shrink dramatically within a few years. It is also widely believed that parenthood is good for social stability: men who are fathers are less prone to criminality, and men with a prior criminal record are more likely to reform once they become parents. But we receive mixed messages from the media, and general social expectations – and so we find one section of the population desperate to have babies, and willing to pay large sums of money in order to conceive them by any means possible, and others who are so anxious not to have children that the abortion rate in Britain is currently one of the highest anywhere in the developed world. Without entering into the moral arguments behind all this, it has to be obvious that people today are faced with questions that no previous generation had to deal with. These questions become even more complex when multiple sexual partners are introduced into the equation, along with the fact that sexually transmitted diseases are widespread in some sections of the population. Add to that our insatiable appetite for continual sexual experimentation, and it is not hard to see why sex is now both a major preoccupation, and a major problem, for so many people.

None of these influences affecting today's families can be labelled right or wrong in themselves. They are all, in one sense, good things. Mobility has brought greater integration and understanding of different cultures and family groupings. The changing economic scene has improved the standard of living of the average family exponentially when compared with families of fifty years ago. And the sexual revolution has offered women enormous opportunities for personal fulfilment that have been beneficial to society at large. At the same time, however, each of them has also created new pressures and problems.

Challenges for women

Theoretically, women should have a much easier time today than their mothers and grandmothers could ever have imagined. Reliable contraception has delivered them from the rigours of repeated pregnancies, and great advances have been made in empowering women to be good parents, loving partners, and successful career people all at the same time. Some countries are more intentional about it than others, but throughout the western world there is no shortage of legislation aimed at making life easier and more fulfilled for women. The reality, though, is often different – sometimes very different indeed – so that in practice women can still find themselves oppressed. No amount of legislation can change the attitudes of men, or indeed of the cultural norms. Though the law may no longer officially subscribe to a patriarchal way of thinking about the relations between women and men, in practice many people still operate with that mindset, and ironically (especially within the church) women as well as men can think and behave that way.

Even among those who are self-consciously trying to redefine roles in the family, there can be an enormous gap between theory and reality. It is easier to pay lip service to the ideals of sharing and partnership than it is to do anything concrete about it. In terms of what actually happens in the home, women still generally find themselves assuming the major responsibility for what goes on there at the same time as they are trying to hold down demanding jobs in the workplace. Not only has the 'new man' failed to materialize in any serious way, but in addition women are expected to be available to help men deal with their own identity problems. They are usually the ones who need to handle the tensions that arise in blended families, and there is an almost universal expectation that it is women who should pick up the pieces from separation and divorce, especially in relation to children and their needs. In most countries this assumption is formally enshrined in both legislation and child-care practice.

Because of the individualistic way we define 'freedom', some things that look like greater freedom for women can actually have the opposite effect because of a lack of supportive resources in the wider community. For example, single teenage parents are actively encouraged to raise their children in a way that would not have happened a couple of generations ago. There are many good reasons why, as a general principle, most reasonable people would support that course of action – in theory. But in reality it does not automatically lead to freedom, nor necessarily to a greater level of happiness and fulfilment for either parent or child. All too often it results in poverty and deprivation for all concerned, and the loss of opportunities for education and self-improvement on the part of those who arguably need them most. Society at large should pay more careful attention to the practical outworking of such double standards. The church, for its part, ought to be more realistic about what is going on and recognize that many of those with whom it finds it hard to minister are actually being sinned against by the very structures that, in other ways, are claiming to set them free.

All work and no play . . .

Most women still do most of the everyday tasks of housework, and whenever men assume any responsibility they generally avoid routine and boring things like washing, ironing, and cleaning. This fundamental imbalance in home responsibilities is magnified when children are involved, because in addition it is almost always women who are expected to be responsible for child care, either by doing it or arranging for it. In such circumstances, women unavoidably come under stress, which itself can lead to absenteeism from work and the breakdown of physical or mental health. Mothers under stress always have a negative impact on family relationships. The 'superwoman' myth dies hard, and most women probably try and fill this role at some time. Some succeed, but the majority find themselves forced either to limit or abandon their career ambitions or to cut back on the amount of energy they invest in the home, thereby sacrificing some of their aspirations for the family.

This double – or even triple – burden borne by so many women is almost endemic in the average western home today, and is the point where women need most support and affirmation in their roles. Choices are not easy. To have a decent lifestyle, families need two earners, and in the process women are forced in effect to have two jobs – housework and employment – which can easily lead to stress and resentment. Most men are either unwilling to change or incapable of doing so, and as a result women have either to accept the pressures, or choose divorce and lone parenthood as the lesser of two evils. That analysis might sound simplistic, but give or take the odd detail, this is reality for very many women. To break out of this vicious cycle, the problem needs to be tackled at two levels.

First is the role of women and men as partners within the family. To create and maintain a successful relationship in circumstances like this, men must be realistic about women's needs. To put it bluntly, the way to a woman's heart, and a mutually affirming relationship, is more likely to be through washing clothes, cleaning bathrooms, ironing the washing, and scrubbing the floors, than through any number of romantic candle-lit dinners and the like. The church can do a good deal to encourage this kind of responsible partnership. It is not enough merely to accept that men may do these things if they wish. We should be saying loudly and clearly that it is part and parcel of a contemporary – and Christian – relationship. One way of doing that is for churches to make fewer demands on the time of their members, so they can actually commit themselves to their families without feeling guilty because they are not at church meetings. Another is to model partnership between women and men in church structures, whether the leading of worship and the making of strategic decisions – or the serving of food in church kitchens. Even in churches that say they believe in opportunities for all, it is not uncommon to find that women still carry out only traditional roles such as child care, cooking, and so on. People learn how to live in partnership when others model it for and with them, and churches should work hard at doing this.

Christians should also be taking a lead in raising fundamental questions about the role of parents in bringing up children. We have already mentioned the problems of self-image faced by women who want to be full-time homemakers. This is not a minority concern, for a very large number of women find themselves in this role at some stage of their lives, if only on a temporary basis. They work hard, are generally unpaid, and because they produce no 'marketable' product, find themselves undervalued by a consumer society. They might easily also be devalued even by their friends, who see them as a free child-care service because they have 'nothing to do all day'.

The assumption that parents can find 'real fulfilment' only through paid employment outside the family actually raises some far-reaching questions about mutual accountability, which impinge on fathers as well as mothers. Whom do we want to provide the primary role models for our children? Parents? The state? The companies we work for? Independent child-minders? Different parents will give different answers. The same parents might easily give different answers in relation to each of their children. But, however we resolve it, there is no doubt that children who spend insufficient time with a parent at an early age are likely to have relational and identity problems in later life. The experience of those countries which provide either or both parents with paid leave from work for several months, or even longer, at the time of a child's birth seems to suggest that it is not crucial whether this care comes from fathers or mothers, or a mixture of the two. Maybe even that is scarcely radical enough. Back in the mid 1990s, management guru Charles Handy proposed the idea of 'time-banking', allowing parents to take almost indefinite amounts of paid leave when their children are young and need them, which they will make up in later life when their circumstances have changed.[1] Such a scheme would require more visionary social structures than most politicians seem capable of devising. But in the medium term it might also be less costly to society as a whole. However we quantify it, there seems to be an obvious and clear connection between early negative experiences in the family and criminality and personal breakdown in later life. How can we put a value on security and loving relationships? With difficulty – which is why social policy all too often ignores and devalues such things. But Charles Handy (writing as a business consultant, and therefore by no means disinterested in making money) offers a better vision with his reminder that 'there are satisfactions and achievements which cannot be measured by money'.[2] Growing numbers of workers are agreeing with him, and for many – especially women – the work-life balance is assuming greater importance than the size of their pay cheque.

Working hard for little reward

The economic pressures for women do not stop once they have secured paid employment outside the home. When they are in work, women are generally paid less than men, sometimes for doing the same jobs. A majority of women have only low-paid jobs readily available to them, for several reasons. The constant pressure from the world economy has resulted in a greater proportion of jobs being part time and low paid anyway. But when there is internal family pressure to maximize total income by having two earners, women will tend to take any job they can get, which usually means a low-paid job with few prospects and little to offer by way of personal fulfilment. Even well-qualified women working in professions where, in theory, there is equality of opportunity, still regularly find themselves paid less than men because the structures of those professions do not facilitate promotion for anyone who is unable to give 100 per cent of their time and energy to the job. That tends to exclude women with children, because the reality for them is that family stability can depend on a woman being prepared to give up or in some way modify her personal ambitions in terms of career prospects. Even employers who claim to be enlightened and sympathetic by offering 'flexible' working hours usually do so at the expense of promotions and career advancement. The fact that women take this in their stride by making 'invisible' modifications to their ambitions (not going for extra training or refusing promotions and transfers) does not make the economic injustice any less real.

In practice most women make compromises of this sort without any direct coercion. But they rarely have any option to do otherwise, which is one reason why some (especially in well-paid jobs with prospects) defer having children. This avoids an interrupted career, and in one sense is the obvious thing to do, because ultimately it is the presence of children which disrupts adult ambitions and lifestyles. But that just highlights the nature of the difficulty, because almost any choice available to a woman is going to involve personal costs of a kind that men do not have to reckon with – whether by postponing the emotional satisfaction of having children for as long as ten or twenty years, facing the increased physical risks of having children at an older age, or indeed choosing not to have them at all.

This interconnected web of economic and emotional conflicts is a major reason why family breakdown is becoming increasingly messy and painful. In traditional families, women's role was clearly related to work in the home, as a result of which they became dependent and vulnerable. We are right to regret that, but we are deluding ourselves if we think anything substantial has changed. In the new situation women are doubly vulnerable: men are now less disposed to accept mutual accountability because they think women are, or should be, financially independent. As a result of convincing ourselves that reality matches theory, and that women can in fact easily be self-sufficient, most female one-parent families find themselves poor and with little sympathy from men who tell them when relationships fail, 'You wanted to be independent in marriage, and you can't change the rules now just because things didn't work out.'

Emotional support

Women have always been expected to carry the emotional responsibility for family life, providing a warm, secure, loving home environment for husband and children. In recent years it has become fashionable to talk of men needing to develop their 'feminine' side, usually defined in terms of intuition, sensitivity, personal openness, and generally having a gentle image as distinct from the macho attitudes traditionally associated with men. Whether these differences are real, in the sense of having some

physiological basis, or relative, in the sense of being the products
of socialization, need not concern us here. Either way, they highlight yet another example of double standards at work. For while
'feminine' characteristics are, in this context, seen as a good
thing, traditional psychology still generally regards the 'female'
characteristics as inadequate, and the 'male' ones as normal or
healthy.

There is no shortage of examples to demonstrate the impact
of these attitudes. A mother's personal needs are often sacrificed
for the good of the entire family. Not only that, but she is regularly blamed for the dysfunctional behaviour of others, such as
violence on the part of a husband or the delinquent and anti-
social behaviour of her children. It is a well-documented fact
that the incidence of depression and phobias of all kinds is much
greater among married women than single women or men, and
their consumption of tranquillizers is correspondingly greater. In
the light of our previous analysis of the changes in family life,
this is hardly surprising, for most women have a low level of
control over a situation whose demands and pressures are
increasing all the time. Moreover, men can have an unhelpful
functional approach to the emotions, most obviously highlighted
in their different attitudes to sex, which they regularly regard as
the starting point for emotional intimacy, whereas women see
it the other way round.

All these things apply in relationships that are outwardly
stable. Breakdown and divorce introduce yet other emotional
struggles, though on balance they seem to be greater for men
than for women, at least in the long term. That does not mean
it is easy for women. Being a lone parent usually means economic
disadvantage for women, which in turn affects their relationships
with children, and possible future partners. But a woman is also
realistic about the alternatives, and knows that remarriage is
unlikely to be the end of emotional pressures, because the same
burdens are still there, only a second time round they will be
expanded to include two different sets of children as well as a
new adult relationship (not to mention elderly relatives and
responsibilities to the wider family circle). In addition, all this
will have to be worked out in the shadow of memories of past
failures, and the likelihood that any future failure will also be

blamed on her. Men typically adopt a more utilitarian approach to relationships, content to see how things work out, whereas women always invest much more emotional capital even into relationships that might have no long-term future.[3]

To imagine that women have been set free from emotional bondage is to take a very unrealistic view. The fact is that at the emotional level women today struggle with infinitely more complex demands than previous generations, facing contradictions and tensions all along the way. Today's woman is to be her own person, independent and free – yet also at the beck and call of others. She is to work at a job to make her contribution to the family budget, but she is also to be responsible for maintaining the home. She is to be free to choose whatever will bring her personal fulfilment, but her choices are constantly circumscribed by the responsibilities of being wife and mother. She is to be independent, but always there when others need her. There is just one thing that distinguishes her from her grandmother: she has a choice to leave relationships that are destroying her – though in exercising this choice, she might well find herself subjected to physical and sexual violence which will damage her even more.

Violence

Recent years have seen a general rise in awareness of violence against women. Even now, we cannot be sure that we know the full extent of it, because what happens in the home is still the most secret of all areas of life, especially when it concerns intimate partnerships. By definition there are rarely witnesses to testify to what goes on, and even when violence against women clearly occurs it is not always taken seriously. Despite much public debate, the authorities and society at large still generally assume that for a woman to be raped or beaten by a man she knows – particularly one she loves – is less serious than to be assaulted by a stranger, and in just about all cases there is a tendency, one way or another, to blame the woman for what happens. As well as domestic violence, there has also been an increase in all forms of harassment of women in the workplace, through physical, verbal, visual, and other means.

Violence is rooted in the need to control other people.[4] It is a way of punishing those who break accepted norms of power and privilege, and society finds it easy to accept this in relation to racial or political violence. At a time when political leaders justify acts of war by reference to the need to 'punish' or 'teach a lesson' to those who step out of line, it can seem logical to set violence against women within the same frame of reference. Yet many people are resistant to this, and instead of enquiring about the social structures and attitudes which provoke domestic violence they prefer to understand violent men as individuals who are deranged or need help in some way. All the available evidence, however, shows that rape and violence are not about sex or personal gratification, but about control and domination. One consequence of violence against women is to make them more afraid, and therefore more controlled and restricted in what they can do and where they can go. A woman who is alone in a city street is statistically less likely to be violently assaulted than a man in the same circumstances. But the perception of most women is the exact opposite and they, not men, are the ones who stay indoors out of fear. Similarly, women who are beaten by their husbands often remain silent because they are afraid of them and the public shame that could result from being open about what is really happening.

We will return to violence in a later chapter, because it is a major factor in family dysfunction – and women are not the only victims. Violence always has a cause, but the same immediate cause may not necessarily lead to violence in every case. People who try to resolve conflict this way frequently learn it from their own formative experiences in violent families. Men beating their wives is not a new thing, though quite possibly the extent of it, and the reasons for it, may be different now than they once were. In old movies violent men were regularly the heroes, beating their women when they defied patriarchal authority, or when they were drunk or angry about something else, even because their meals were not to their liking. Abusive words qualify as 'violence' just as much as physical assault. Indeed, violent individuals often use psychological and physical violence alternately, to keep their victims in suspense not knowing what might happen next, and thereby undermining whatever vestiges of security and self-esteem they have left.

Middle-class professional people tend to report domestic violence less than other groups. That probably means they are better at concealing it. There is certainly no reason to suppose that the families of Christians are immune. There is no one simple cause of violence against women. Patriarchy can be one element in male violence against women, and certainly when other factors are present it offers a conceptual framework within which violence can appear to be 'justified'. Some theologies have a tendency to encourage this thinking, even if they do not overtly approve of personal violence as a means of enforcement. Obviously this is not the only contributing factor to domestic violence, but it is often present. Anything that challenges a man's dominance can easily become a catalyst for violence. There is some evidence of a link between economic stress in men and violence against women, suggesting that loss of control in one area of life may lead to a need for greater control to be expressed somewhere else, and the home is the easiest place for insecure men to assert this.

So far as women victims are concerned, the long-term effects of violence can be totally destructive, including a severe loss of self-esteem, self-hatred, withdrawal from contacts outside the home, drug and alcohol abuse and, eventually, disintegration of the personality (the ultimate submission). Short-term effects are physical injuries, or even death. Women can be murdered when they try to exercise their right to leave a relationship (though in such cases moving to end the relationship is more often an effect of previous violence, rather than its first cause).

Challenges for men

For a long time, it was widely believed that marriage is bad for women, but good for men. This view was first proposed in the 1970s by Jessie Bernard, who argued that married women were more depressed than married men, while married men were less depressed than single men.[5] More recent work by sociologists at La Trobe University, Melbourne, carried out in 2002 on a very large sample of more than ten thousand adults (all of whom were interviewed personally), has questioned this finding and claims that when every type of mental illness is taken into account (rather than just those to which women are particularly susceptible), there is no difference between the struggles that men and women encounter in family relationships. In fact, their findings offer a balancing perspective in our reflections on the challenges of family life for adults, because they demonstrate that, in spite of all the hardships people face today, married people are emotionally better off than either divorced or single people. There could be several reasons for this (for instance, people with few mental health problems may be more likely than others to get married), but the La Trobe researchers are in no doubt that 'Marriage seems to have the same mental health effect on both men and women and that is in the direction of protecting them against mental disorders.'[6]

It is not difficult to identify some of the challenges that today's men face. John Gray's book *Men Are from Mars, Women Are from Venus*[7] became an instant best-seller because he put his finger on something that large numbers of people recognized: many men have difficulties with relationships, and can be clueless in dealing with women. They love them, yet they are afraid of making wholehearted and open-ended commitments to emotional intimacy. They are dependent on women, but they fiercely oppose any notion of mutual accountability. They desperately want women to approve of them, but find it well-nigh impossible to ask for acceptance. They want – sometimes, expect – women to be there when they need them, but only to deal with immediate (and sometimes trivial) needs, rather than entering into open relationships. If they are honest, most men will recognize something of themselves in here. Most researchers trace men's uneasiness with themselves to an excessively mother-dependent childhood, and the lack of a helpful male role model during their formative years. As boys grow up, this often leads to a love-hate relationship with their mother. On the one hand, she has great power over them, but on the other she is unable to do everything, and in a patriarchal context may be prevented from doing the most important things. For many males, their first step toward personal autonomy occurs when they challenge the authority of their mother. It is only a small step from that for men to define their own identity by reference to being 'set free' from women. Unless men have specific opportunities to work through these attitudes, the scene is set for a lifelong love-hate attitude to women in general. For boys raised in families where the father is rarely involved in matters relating to home life, this image can be very powerful: to be a man is to be 'free' from women, and being a real man must involve psychological superiority over women in all male-female relationships.

For these and other wider cultural reasons, the role models commonly available to men mostly define them by reference to such values as independence, power, and aggression. Maleness becomes identified with the need to have power and control in all areas of life. Notwithstanding some cosmetic changes, the world of work still generally operates on these principles. They are damaging in any context, but when they are applied to the family they can only serve to destroy any possibility of intimacy and openness in relationships. Needless to say, these under-standings of what it means to be a man are also profoundly unChristian.[8]

Men and money

Even those men who might subscribe to some of the values just described are not always happy with the practical outworking of such views. While many women in the past felt oppressed *within* the traditional patriarchal family, many men felt oppressed *by* it, and particularly by the burden of having to be the sole economic provider. A man was traditionally judged by his ability to feed, clothe, and house his family. His main ambition was to rise as high as possible in the employment market to ensure that his family's standard of living would be as secure as he could make it. He threw himself wholeheartedly into the rat race of paid employment, and no matter what the discouragements, he stuck with it, courageously doing the best he could for the sake of his family. When, inevitably, he was less successful than others, then he knew he could go back to the family for psychological respite. In the home, he would always have a special position and privilege. To his family, he was the best man in the world, and even when he lost out to competitors in the world of work, he could still wield great power in the home.

It is fashionable to imagine that the patriarchal family made life easy for men, at the expense of women. The truth is that it dehumanized them both. Men were defined purely in economic terms, their worth determined by their work. This is an insidiously destructive understanding of human nature, and many men still find that the loss of a work-defined identity leads to personal disintegration, whether through unemployment or retirement (significant numbers of men die within five years of retirement). Even today, men rarely define themselves by reference to their relational roles as husbands or fathers, preferring instead to talk about their jobs. This is all far removed from the Christian understanding of women and men together being 'made in the image of God' (Genesis 1:27). It will be a long, hard slog, but we need to take seriously the challenge of enabling men to feel happy with defining themselves as persons in relation, rather than in functional terms.

Despite all that, one might argue that the industrial nuclear family at least offered men some sense of 'security', in that everyone knew where the boundaries were, and who was responsible for what. Today, some men feel that the changing shape of the family has removed from them even that limited sense of their own value. Generally speaking, it is no longer possible for a man to be the sole economic provider for a family, certainly not without taking on spare-time work in order to do so (though some men will choose this option to their own detriment rather than accept the inevitability of economic partnership with a spouse). In any case, even if a man manages to provide for his family single-handedly to his own satisfaction, he is likely to find himself disapproved of by society at large as a person who has stuck with old ways of doing things. If he manages to handle that, he is still likely to find himself disadvantaged by tax regulations in many western countries. With the exception of people with inherited wealth or other forms of private income, the sort of family in which it is financially possible for men to be the sole economic providers has all but disappeared and is unlikely to be revived in the foreseeable future. As this has happened, even those men who think of themselves as progressive are being forced to make some more or less painful adjustments in their self-image.

The economic realities of life for men in situations of family breakdown are also challenging, and largely parallel those faced by mothers as lone parents, though, as has already been indicated, men hardly ever find themselves in such desperate poverty as women.

Men and their feelings

There is a major crisis today about how to define what it means to be a man, and much of this concerns emotional issues. As men come to terms with the changing face of family values and structures, they are having to handle levels of emotional stress which were unthinkable for their fathers and grandfathers. The collapse of traditional male roles is threatening enough, but that pales into insignificance when compared with the challenge of discovering new ways of being a man. For if the 'new man' is to function as an effective partner in the modern family, he will need to be a good deal more emotionally open than any of his ancestors have managed to be. Nor is he likely to get too much assistance from women, who from a man's point of view can seem unhelpfully ambivalent: they still want men to be tough and strong, while they are also demanding that they be intimate and open about their feelings.

So what does it mean to be a man? This is not a silly question. After forty years of the women's movement, we have some sort of consensus about the possibilities for women, even if all women are not yet able to exploit them. But men are just at the start of this search for a new identity, and there is very little to guide them. The popular media promotes images of a new breed of celebrity fathers and husbands – sport and movie stars – who are eager to take responsibility for the life of their family. Such individuals undoubtedly offer better role models than men who abandon responsibility for everything, and there is no question that their example is inspiring many younger men to take more seriously their family responsibilities. But juggling career, house-work, children and marriage – the so-called 'Atlas syndrome' – creates the same pressures for men as trying to be superwoman does for their partners. It is a good deal easier for celebrities to appear to juggle all these things with apparent success than it is for ordinary people who do not have the same resources. The same could be said of many of the programmes claiming to offer spiritual understandings of the nature of manhood: much of what is on offer is again esoteric and distanced from the interests and possibilities available to the average man.[9] There is a major opportunity for the church here.

For centuries, men's psychological wellbeing has been inextricably bound up with their expectations of marriage and the family. It is well known that men do not have the same open relationships with other men as women do among themselves. This is encouraged by the way the workplace has been structured. When competition is the basis of career advancement, it stands to reason that you would never want to expose your weaknesses to those whose main ambition in life is to take advantage of you. Consequently, the only place where most men could ever open up – to however limited an extent – was in the safety and security of the home, especially in the days when women took it for granted that their job was to give their men whatever they wanted, with no questions asked. We have already noticed how women were oppressed and exploited by this situation. But the other side of the coin is that men actually needed the family for their essential security, and without it they can be exceedingly vulnerable. Statistics over a long period show for example that, on average, married men live longer than single ones, and are less likely to be criminal or to commit suicide. This is why divorce and breakdown come as a great shock to many men. A man can truly love his wife, but be so insensitive that he has no idea how she really feels, and that she is about to leave him. That kind of man can experience a profound loss of purpose and personal value from which he may never recover. Not all men suffer that way, of course, and there are others for whom breakdown is more about the disruption of lifestyle and their loss of public image than about the loss of a particular family. They can move on to new relationships more easily.

This is the context in which we should set the issue of domestic violence by men against women. It goes without saying that there is never any excuse or ultimate justification for violence.

But those who are involved in ministering to men in this situation will do so more effectively if they try to understand some of its likely underlying causes. Though it is hard to quantify, most researchers have a strong feeling that the increase in domestic violence is – at least in part – somehow related to men's feelings of frustration, failure, and insecurity in the new situation. Inflicting pain on women and children can offer men who struggle to cope an easy outlet for their anger, hence the rising incidence of abuse in the home, and harassment in the workplace. Women become scapegoats for men's own insecurities. If a man fails to win promotion in work, he can blame the female competition, or female managers. If his marriage breaks up, he assumes it must be his wife's fault. By gradual increments, men can cast themselves in the role of helpless victims, and thereby justify (at least to their own satisfaction) victimizing others. Some western countries have experienced this on an organized level, with the rise of groups attempting to reclaim 'father's rights', flexing their muscles by, for example, going to court to get injunctions preventing their partners from having abortions, or from moving away with their children to start a new life in another city, or by campaigning for what they call 'equal' treatment of women and men in divorce settlements (which almost always means worse treatment for women).

Men deal with these pressures in different ways, depending on their personality, temperament, and the nature of their family relationships. The conflicts will be magnified for traditional men, because they face the economic pressure of being solely responsible for adequate financial provision for their families, combined with what they are likely to regard as unfair and disagreeable competition from women in the workplace. If their wives share their traditional views, they may be able to mitigate some of this, but if not the pressures can become overwhelming – and one of the features of changing divorce patterns is the increasing number of people who separate later in life after marriages that have lasted for twenty years or more.

Danger – men at work

Men face the same conflicts between work and home as women, though they experience them slightly differently. Men who try to be good parents and partners do not always find it easy to balance the quality of their home life against the insistent work pressure to go for promotions and to improve their position in the workplace. Promotion often involves moving home to some distant area, which can be unsettling for children. Or it might require a journey taking several hours a day, with a consequent reduction in the time available to him to be with his family. This has always been a problem for some men, leaving home before their children are out of bed in the morning, and not returning in the evening until long after they have gone to bed again. This obviously increases stress for any man who takes his parenting responsibilities seriously. It also makes weekends and vacation times particularly valuable – something that churches should take far more account of in relation to the way they organize their activities. Despite many changes, men still find the world of work is at odds with their responsibilities in the home. Their jobs are organized and defined as if their family did not exist, and whenever they allow family responsibilities to impinge on work, by leaving early or missing meetings, they are likely to get more negative reactions than women would in the same circumstances. Men can easily find themselves in a no-win situation: they know their families need them, but the opinion of their work colleagues (at least on an official level) is that the job should always come first. Any man who refuses to comply is regarded as a wimp and is likely to lose out on promotions. It can be hard to live with conflicts like that, and wrestling with them in the midst of all the other challenges presented by family life is never going to be straightforward.

When men are also coping with the aftermath of separation and divorce, the same problems are magnified many times over. One-parent families headed by fathers can have acute problems simply because it is impossible to be in two places at once, though lone fathers have medium-term advantages over against lone mothers, because they tend to have higher incomes and generally stay single for a shorter time. But for periods during which they are lone parents, men probably face more social isolation than women. The fact that the role of the lone male parent is not always well understood or socially acceptable means they typically have fewer networks for emotional support than women in the same situation.

Two things clearly emerge from this survey of the problems of adults in today's family. First is that there are no easy solutions, and we will not find the answers by looking to the experiences of the past. We are constructing families today with no role models, and no agreed blueprints, and that is naturally scary. When it works out well it can also, of course, be exciting and rewarding. The second thing is that neither women nor men will be able to redefine the family single-handedly. We will need to learn to work in partnership, which in turn requires openness and a willingness to be in constant negotiation over family roles and responsibilities. Maybe our respective responsibilities will change at different stages of the family's life cycle. But co-operation and genuine sharing will be the only things that will enable us to create the new community for which we are all looking. As an ideal, that accords well with some distinctive Christian values, and modelling this may well be the most useful thing that the church can do for today's parents.[10]

5 Parenting

How do families work?

Family therapy begins with understanding the dynamics of family life, on the assumption that if you can appreciate what is going on, then it should be possible to find ways of dealing with it.[1] A classic way of doing this draws on the insights of developmental psychologists like Erik Erikson, and regards family life as a series of stages through which every couple will pass.[2] By understanding the challenges and opportunities presented at different stages of the cycle, it is possible to identify typical crisis points and work for their resolution.[3]

The notion that life is a series of fixed linear stages has some significant weaknesses. But thinking of a family as a social environment that develops through more or less predictable stages still has much to offer not only to those who are involved in the pastoral care of families, but also to those individuals who want to understand their own intimate relationships. A traditional cycle began with a 'premarital' stage, marked by the engagement of a couple to be married, followed by the 'marital couple' stage in which a couple worked out how their relationship would operate. The birth or adoption of a first child marked stage three, and here the couple would adjust to their role as parents. Stage four, the 'completed family', begins with the birth of the final child, then three more stages follow: adolescence (as children begin to differentiate their own identity, and parents come to terms with the teenage years); 'launching' (children become independent, forming their own families, parents work to accept their departure); and 'post-launching' (the last child leaves home, parents reinvent their own relationship). On this understanding, the earlier stages provide a necessary foundation for progression through the later ones, and anyone who offers support to a family will begin by placing them within this cycle.

Some therapists insist that if previous stages have not been worked through adequately, they should be revisited, especially the foundational relationship between husband and wife.

This way of thinking about families is better suited to some topics than others, but parenting is unquestionably one aspect of family life that can helpfully be understood by such developmental analysis. Once you are a parent, you are always a parent. It is not a role that can be given up or abandoned, but neither does it remain static: being parent to a thirty-something is not the same as caring for a five-year-old. All parents relate to their kids in some way from the moment they are conceived to the moment when death (of either child or parent) separates them. Though older people may think of themselves as grandparents, they only occupy that position because they are already parents, and the way they connect with their own adult children will actually determine how they relate to their grandchildren. Reviewing the various stages of parenting can therefore be of considerable value not only to parents themselves (who can place their own concerns in a wider perspective) but also to those who offer pastoral support to both parents and children, whether in the church or some other caring context. Before exploring that, however, we need to appreciate the limitations of stage-development thinking, as well as recognizing its strengths. At least five factors make things more complicated than it sounds.

Family structures

When this notion of family stages was first articulated, the industrial nuclear family was the norm. Today such families are very much in the minority, even in the church. A simple stage-development model by itself cannot take account of the changed work patterns of husbands and wives, nor does it automatically connect with all the various non-traditional families mentioned in a previous chapter. Families formed by a cohabiting couple, for example, may or may not experience a neat sequential movement from one stage to another. Families that experience breakdown, remarriage, and blending certainly will not. Moreover, none of these will automatically have the sense of shared memory which is at the heart of this way of understanding family life.

Children

This approach defines a family by reference to the presence of children, and takes it for granted that children will live with their birth parents until adolescence or beyond. In times past, the term 'family' always implied children – otherwise, you might be talking of human relationships of one sort or another, but they would not be families. Nowadays, the definition of a family tends to be expressed in much wider terms, to match the actual realities of the social partnerships that we form. Though children are still central, they are no longer regarded as the non-negotiable foundational core of what constitutes a family. Nor do marriage and parenting necessarily go together: cohabiting couples have children, divorce and remarriage mean that some people become parents without ever having conceived their own children, and married couples may choose to remain childless or delay parenting until later in life. People who become parents later in life may well experience some of the same stages as those who have children while they are younger, but there will be differences for couples whose first child is born to a father in his sixties and a mother in her forties, when compared for example with our own family life cycle (we first became parents in our early twenties).

Life expectancy

In western societies, life expectancy has increased quite dramatically, and the phase of life after children have left the family home ('post-launching') can now account for as much as half of the time span of the typical family system. When Erik Erikson formulated his classic taxonomy of 'the eight ages of man', he described just one stage after the age of sixty, which he called 'facing death'. Some men today are still becoming fathers at this age, and this 'final' stage itself is getting longer all the time: the number of people living well into their eighties and nineties is increasing, and will continue to do so. Old age itself now requires to be understood as more than one stage, especially in relation to the 'oldest old' (over-eighties), increasing numbers of whom live independently in their own homes for longer – which in turn creates new demands for their children. In addition, increasing numbers of adult children are now quite likely to remain in the parental home, and the 'launching' stage can last for up to a decade for each child, which in turn means that parents might still have their children living with them well into what in the past would have been their old age.

Individuals and groups

Classic developmental models of the family tended to focus on individuals, and regarded families as just the sum total of their members. Relationships are invariably more complex than that, and the family, along with other social organisms, is more than just the totality of the disconnected actions of its constituent parts. The typical family consists of several relational systems interacting with each other (parents to each other, children among themselves, children to parents, parents to their own parents, children to grandparents, to name just the most obvious).[4] The more layers of relationships there are, the more complicated things become: in the case of blended families, for example, any one family will typically be linked with the relational systems of at least two others. Understanding how an individual relates to other individuals can be helpful in working with families, but processes of *family* development also interact with and affect the developmental processes of individuals.

Life in straight lines

A simple developmental model of the family sees it progressing in a straight line from one stage to another. But it has always been more complicated than that. Even in the heyday of the industrial nuclear family, couples who were 'launching' teenagers might find themselves with a pregnancy (their own, or that of their adolescent son or daughter). Today, 'launched' young adults can – and do – return to the parental home, perhaps bringing their own children with them; and their parents increasingly find themselves raising their grandchildren. Life is infinitely more complicated than it once was, and we need to think of stages of family life in correspondingly flexible ways.

Despite all these limitations, however, the general idea of developmental stages can still be helpful, as long as we regard it as a descriptive way of thinking, rather than a prescriptive formula. We need to treat it more like a compass – giving a general sense of direction – than as a detailed road map describing every twist and turn in the journey.

Stages of parenting

One of the most useful accounts of this topic has been provided by Ellen Galinsky, President of the Families and Work Institute, based in New York. Her book, *The Six Stages of Parenthood*, offers a particularly accessible analysis, because though she takes account of the wider insights of developmental psychologists, her argument is not based on theoretical constructs but on interviews with more than two hundred parents at various stages of life, and from different socio-economic backgrounds.[5] This connects her categories with the lived experience of real people, and is a major reason why we will follow them here, to clarify the challenges facing parents at different stages, and also to identify starting points for the pastoral care of families in their ongoing development. Not all details will be an exact fit for every parent. Anyone with more than one child will by definition be living in more than one stage at any given time, and for those whose children belong to blended families and other forms of multiple family relationships, things will be even more complex again.

Image makers

Becoming pregnant for the first time is a unique occasion. Subsequent pregnancies may evoke excitement and anticipation, but this one changes life forever. Even those who desperately want to become parents find themselves asking significant questions of meaning, purpose, and identity. Parents-to-be naturally speculate about what things will be like. Do they really want to have a child? Will they ever be the same again? How different will home life be with a baby? Will there be a baby at all? Most pregnant women fear at some time that their baby might be dead, or deformed – so even supposing the child is born alive, what will the rest of life look like for them? Pregnancy can raise significant spiritual questions. Thinking about the meaning of birth brings the reality of death into sharper focus – not only literally, but also in the metaphorical sense that becoming a parent spells the death of a former way of life, and offers the possibility of new birth as mother and father become different people. In his account of the reasons why people become Christians, John Finney discovered that pregnancy and childbirth were, for many, crucial catalysts in the process of either finding faith for the first time, or rekindling a dormant faith.[6] Churches that are serious about mission will recognize this, and take account of it in their approach to pastoral care and evangelism.

This can be a challenging time for men: though the child could not have been conceived without them, their partner now seems to hold all the power. Sexual relationships may become less intense, and arguments can blow up out of nowhere, inducing guilt in the prospective parents who worry that they might have harmed their unborn child. Some people revert to adolescent behaviour, as their insecurities take over while they struggle to work out how each of them will deal with the child. If addressed openly, this question can make discipline issues easier to handle later on, while neglecting it can sow the seeds of future conflict. Some men find all this too much to handle, and leave their partners, so that women who thought they were in secure relationships end up as lone parents even before they have actually given birth. Pregnancy brings relationships into sharp focus, and can as easily become an opportunity for rekindling old arguments as for laying past disagreements to rest. If the pregnant couple's own parents are dead, or no longer in touch, old wounds can be reopened and past grief experienced again.

Early pregnancy seems unreal, but once the baby starts to move parents begin to relate to it. They wonder who the child will be, what he or she will look like, what kind of person he or she will become, and so on. They might worry about giving their child the best possible start in life. Beneath all this is a big question that is more about the parents than the child: what kind of parents do we want to be? Will we live out the dream of western culture that depicts parenthood as a state of fulfilment,

happiness, fun, and moral worthiness? Will we manage to repli-
cate the things that our own parents did well, and avoid what
we think they got wrong? These questions will be revisited with
every subsequent pregnancy, because the birth of a new child
always offers the chance to make a new start.

Nurturers

Once a child is born, we know the answers to some of these
questions. We know who the real child is, which probably does
not correlate precisely with how we imagined he or she might
be. We also get some idea of who we are going to be as parents,
both individually and in this new three-way relationship. An
obvious way to start exploring that is to reflect on the birth itself.
Did we do as well as we wanted? If something happened that
we did not cope with – in a situation which, after all, is 'natural'
and instinctive – then what chance do we have of handling more
challenging things? New parents can be incredibly vulnerable at
this time, especially if perceived shortcomings in their performance at the birth are then followed by difficulties with feeding,
crying, or whatever. Those who befriend them might wonder
why new parents can be so obsessive about repeatedly rehearsing
every little detail of the birth, but there is a simple answer to
that, for this is one of the ways we work through reconciling
what we thought the child might be like with what he or she
actually is like. In pastoral terms it is an invitation for expressions
of warmth and approval: the one thing all new parents need to
hear is that they did well, for that brings with it the reassurance
that they will probably make a good job of the remainder of the
parenting task.

Accepting the baby in all his or her uniqueness is often the
easiest part of being a new parent. Accepting yourself can be
more demanding. Being a parent to a newborn is harder work
than most people imagine it will be. This is especially true for
the mother: regardless of how supportive the father is, being the
mother of a small child is an all-consuming commitment,
requiring not only time but considerable physical and emotional
energy. The round-the-clock care needed at this stage means that
both parents will lose sleep, and that in turn affects how they

can operate in other areas of life. New parents easily end up feeling helpless and stressed out – and, as likely as not, guilty about being that way. Our image of who we thought we were (the perfect parents who can do everything) has to be reconciled with who we actually are. Dealing with these issues can form the launch pad for significant growth within a relationship, or can mark the beginning of a destructive cycle. Lone parents are likely to have an especially tough time, as by definition they have no intimate relationship within which they can be honest about themselves, and where they can receive the kind of support that they most need.

Others can help, of course – and do. A traditional African proverb reminds us that 'It takes a whole village to raise one child' – and there is a good deal of truth in it. In a culture where our support networks are no longer geographically based, but are communities of interest, the church has an increased opportunity to be that village, a place that will 'create an environment in which pregnancy and birth are filled with promise, in which nurture and discipline are possible, in which children are valued and families protected for the sake of every individual and for the sake of the community.'[7] All new parents need help – but there is a thin line between help and interference. Grandparents frequently overstep that line, eager to help (even seeing it as their duty), but acting as if they own the baby. Churches can be the same. Too much interference and well-meaning advice can become paternalistic and patronizing, creating dependency and instilling in new parents a low sense of their own self-worth and a consequent limitation in their potential for developing new skills themselves. But too little involvement suggests that no one cares and easily results in young parents concluding that the church has nothing to offer, and all its claims about being community are so much hot air. It is worth working at this to get the balance right, because whatever the community does, it will still have an impact.

Beyond the actual business of caring for the new baby, the developing of relationships, both old and new, is also important for parents at this time. If there are older children in the home, they need to be included or they will become jealous of the attention given to their new sibling. Parents can unconsciously expect their other children suddenly to grow up and act older than their age by being responsible for themselves in ways that would never have been required had it not been for the new arrival. As the new baby grows, both parents and child begin a relationship of mutual learning from one another. Erik Erikson famously remarked that 'a family can bring up a baby only by being brought up by him [or her] . . .'[8] and while this is the case at all stages of a child's life, it is especially true in earliest childhood. In order to facilitate their child's development, parents need to be aware of the child's response in different circumstances, as they each work out how much to give and how much to receive. All three are learning things about themselves and about one another, and this requires space and time. A willingness to trust a child is also vital at this time, for it is in this relational matrix that our first images of God are formed.

Parents also redefine their own relationship. A three-way relationship is certainly different than one involving only two people, but babies rarely create problems. They tend to highlight existing unresolved issues – though having a baby can also improve things (parents might, for example, be less likely to have stormy arguments). One of the most paradoxical relationships concerns the new grandparents. Most of us wish to some extent to be different from our own parents, yet at the same time – if we are close to them at all – we need them to encourage us and affirm that we are doing alright. Parents of young children also get to know other parents with kids the same age. These relationships can also play a vital role in defining us as parents. By comparing notes with others in similar circumstances we get a sense of what is 'normal' for both parents and children, and also a critical perspective that enables us to see how our own kids are doing by comparison with others.

Mothers usually have more extended leave from work than fathers, but sooner or later in the majority of cases both parents find themselves back in full-time employment outside the home. Apart from practical arrangements for child-care facilities, there are other well-documented pressures associated with returning to work: guilt about doing it at all, difficulties in coping with the change of style between workplace and home, jealousy of those who look after our kids because they see more of them than we do – and on and on ... the list is seemingly endless. This nurturing stage of parenting offers endless possibilities for churches that will listen to the needs of new parents. We will return to some specific things in a later chapter, but for now we will simply ask a question: when did you ever hear any of this being addressed – or even acknowledged – in a church?

Legislators

Ellen Galinsky calls this 'the authority stage'. Though it is not age determined, it generally starts with the so-called 'terrible twos'. A child of this age is learning new physical skills – walking, talking, feeding, toilet training – and may also be facing psychological challenges ranging from the birth of a younger sibling to moving into a 'big bed'. Over and above that, behavioural boundaries also come into the picture. Parents face questions about what the rules should be, who will set them, and how they will be enforced.

There is no single 'right' way of doing this, but several factors affect the way we go about it. Our own prior experience of rule-makers inevitably plays a part. People who vowed they would never behave like their own parents end up doing just that. We get angry without intending to, sometimes reverting to childish behaviour ourselves. Our children can also turn out to be unex-pectedly aggressive, and when they scream, 'You are horrible, Daddy' – worse still, 'I wish you were dead' – parents naturally wonder what has gone wrong. Sometimes there is an answer. Sudden changes in a child's behaviour can be provoked by new circumstances: divorce, moving house, death, or unemployment. When that happens – especially when these changes were specifically chosen – parents feel guilty, and can easily project that onto their child, which only makes matters worse. More often, though, there is no obvious cause for aggressive behaviour, apart from the fact that the child is growing and developing. Growth always involves change, but even parents who know that can still be taken by surprise when it happens.

Since our children are changing all the time, parents need to do the same. That does not mean we should just muddle through issues of boundaries and rule-setting, but it does imply that the resolution of particular issues will always be provisional, and further growth will lead to new perspectives. As children grow older, this becomes ever more complex, but at this stage there are some specific matters that can be used as a framework. Clothes, for example, can become a springboard for working at the fundamental question of 'who is in charge of what?' Who decides what a child will wear? This classic question highlights the importance of balancing what parents regard as appropriate limits against the need for children to experiment for themselves. Getting the balance right gives children the ability to take initiatives and work things out for themselves. Getting it wrong can have the opposite effect, leading kids into a lifelong dependency.[9]

Most questions at this stage are like this: they are unlikely to be life-threatening, and offer relatively safe spaces where parents can work out their overall approach to discipline. How will the rules be communicated? Will it be 'because I say so', or will your thinking be explained? When your child is obviously heading for conflict, will you take pre-emptive action to avoid it or leave them to make their own mistakes so they can learn from them? If that happens, what about punishment? And what will 'fairness' be when you have to sort out conflicts between different children? Is there one absolute standard, or will you differentiate between them in relation to their age and maturity? The 'you' here is always plural, which introduces its own complexity. Even lone parents have to reconcile their answers with those of others, whether family members, baby-sitters, or workers in the day nursery. When these people have different expectations, whose values will prevail? The same questions arise in two-parent families, and can become a major issue in blended families in relation to who has the right to give direction to whose children.

The challenges can seem overwhelming – and any parent will testify to the fact that those listed here are not the whole story. But most parents manage to live up to their aspirations for most of the time. An underlying issue arises from the fact that our kids' behaviour often reflects our own, and thereby forces us to reflect on our own identity. Throughout life we all balance the ideal image of who we want to be and the reality of who we actually are, and children just bring that into a clearer focus. Is this part of what Isaiah was getting at, when he envisaged the ideal world as a time when 'a little child will lead them' (Isaiah 11:6 NIV) – or Jesus, with his insistence that 'anyone who will not receive the kingdom of God like a little child will never enter it' (Mark 10:15 NIV)? Instead of retreating, we need to work at turning such moments into transformational experiences.

It is no wonder that parents constantly ask themselves, 'How are we doing?' This is an important question, because as toddlers engage independently with the wider world, they represent their parents. When they bite another child in the nursery, or make a mess in a restaurant, or break something in a shop or another person's house, it is as traumatic for the parents as for the child (who may not fully appreciate the consequences of these actions). As well as challenging the parent/child relationship, it damages the parents' self-confidence, because they share the rejection of their child. Nursery owners and school teachers should understand this. Because politicians are always measuring *their* achievements, teachers can assume that parents are doing the same. But parents regularly see it the other way around: they are the ones whose performance is being graded, by reference to the way these others regard their children.

Parents of toddlers soon discover that not all public places will welcome their children, and tend to avoid them. Few churches specifically say they do not welcome children to their services, but many use more subtle means to ensure that parents know which spaces are for children, and which ones they should stay away from. Churches that are serious about ministry with families need to remember that parents pick up this kind of thing very quickly. They should also bear in mind that most parents want their children to grow up in a natural way, not to remain as toddlers all their lives. Churches that define their children's ministries by reference to what they imagine a three-year-old would like are missing the point – especially when, in the process of doing so, they insult the intelligence even of a growing three-year-old, by singing vacuous songs or reducing everything to a lowest common denominator which suits no one. Not only is that bad theology (even, sometimes, no theology), it is also counterproductive in terms of effective mission and spiritual nurture. Moreover, parents look to those who work with children in churches or other voluntary organizations to tell them how they are doing, just as they do with teachers and other authority figures. We cannot exaggerate the importance of church being a context where parents (and others) are affirmed, and where serious attention is paid to the challenge of 'speaking the truth in love' so that 'we will in all things grow up into him who is the Head, that is, Christ' as part of 'the whole body, joined and held together by every supporting ligament' (Ephesians 4:15–16 NIV).

Educators

From about age five to the beginning of teenage years, children become increasingly independent: they watch TV by themselves, choose their own reading material, and have friends whom their parents know nothing about, perhaps individuals they have talked with in an online chat room. Parents have to work out how to allow their children to grow up and develop their own separate identity, while protecting them from potential dangers. School is now the major focus of a child's life, and takes over many of the socialization functions that were previously the concern of the family. This can be a relief for some parents, but for teachers – especially in the first years of schooling – it can be a problem. Though the family is still the primary location for the socialization of children, parents increasingly either seem not to understand that, or are too busy to take it seriously, and teachers end up spending time on basic hygiene or relational skills rather than the educational tasks for which they are employed. Some issues at this time can create conflicts between the values of home and school, particularly at the older end of this developmental stage when things like sex education begin to feature on the curriculum.

When a child moves self-consciously into this wider world, he or she inevitably encounters many different value systems, and a child starting school for the first time offers parents an opportunity to think again about their own core values, and perhaps to redefine them. Even apparently trivial matters require such reflection, beginning with the kind of school to which we will send our kids, how much pocket money they get, how many clubs and extra-curricular activities they enrol in, and so on. This is the time in a child's life when they develop a sense of what Erikson called either industry or inferiority,[10] and parents can be tempted to create unrealistic expectations by projecting their own childhood ambitions (especially their unachieved ones) onto their children. Sometimes they expect different things from boys than girls, or from their first child over against later ones, or they compare their child unfavourably with others, constantly asking them, 'Why can't you be like [someone else]?' There is nothing wrong with parents making such comparisons for themselves: that is one way we gain a sense of how our kids are doing. But children need to be encouraged in who they are, not criticized for who they are not. The way that parents' hopes for them are expressed can have a major impact not only on how they think of themselves for the rest of their lives, but also on who they think their parents are.

Life's big questions tend to surface at this time. The more children know, the more they want to know: what is the world about, why are all families not like their family, what is death about – and why people get divorced. For couples whose first child is in this stage, this is indeed the time when, statistically speaking, many split up and perhaps remarry. When that happens, all the issues about values, discipline, and guidance already mentioned are magnified. In a blended family, the number of available options increases, not only within the family itself, but a child living with one parent also has to work out how to relate to the other one who lives elsewhere. Even for parents who stay together, there are still challenges related to time and work. It now becomes important to work out how to move on from a relationship in which, at the beginning of this stage, parents are the rule-givers, to a relationship based on friendship that will be more appropriate for the next stage of the journey. Other questions also arise, as parents wonder what their children think about them, and work out how openly they should share their own frustrations and disappointments. This latter question is especially important for Christian parents, who often find their children rebelling against church during these years. With our own kids, we always spoke honestly about the church, and that policy served us well. Children know that churches are not perfect, and if that is acknowledged are more likely to be able to accept it: nothing else in life is without problems, so why should the church be any different?

Teenagers

Most parents dread this more than any other stage, and despite all the publicity can still be surprised how soon their children become adolescents. It seems to be occurring at a younger age all the time, and consumerism has created yet another intermediate stage called 'tweenage' that is between childhood and teenage (typically ages 9–12).[11] For our purposes here, the actual age at which this stage occurs is not all that important: the phenomenon is a reality, whether it occurs at age ten or fourteen.

Adolescence is not just another stage, but is a qualitatively different state from childhood, because the child is actually in the process of becoming a different person. Kids are grown up but not grown up, dependent but independent, wise and silly all at once. In effect, a teen is half-child and half-adult, and the tensions this creates are both physiologically determined and socially conditioned. There has always been a generation gap between older people and younger ones, but nowadays it is much wider than many parents and grandparents realize, because culture itself has undergone rapid change in recent years, and the pace of that change continues to accelerate. Teenage children are not wrestling with the same issues as their parents were at the same age. In the past, teenage rebellion was defined by things like under-age drinking and casual kissing, but today it can involve joy-riding, experimenting with drugs, making acquaintances via websites, and absolutely taking it for granted that young people will have sex as soon as they are physically capable of it. And not just having sex, but experimenting with it in every variation possible. Some kids know more than their parents about the stock of sex shops, and talk openly with their friends about matters such as oral sex, cyber sex, sexually transmitted diseases, 'rampant rabbits', and more besides (if you don't know what some of these things are, that merely proves our point). Parents (especially Christians) can be shocked to discover all this about their own children, as they realize that they no longer have the control or influence they once did. They probably don't know the half: though most teenagers still want to live with their parents, many regularly stay overnight with boy or girlfriends, and have what is in effect an alternative life with a peer group that parents can only imagine – because their kids won't talk to them. They bemoan the fact that their kids are now getting to do things they were never allowed until they were much older – not just sex, but things like travelling on long journeys to and from school, buying their own clothes, going unaccompanied overseas, or cooking their own meals (some of them, of course, necessitated by the parents' own lifestyles because they spend so many hours working). There is no doubt that all this can be threatening stuff for parents, who feel that their authority is questioned and disregarded, especially at those times when their teens have a problem.

The communication problem is partly related to the shift from modernity to post-modernity. Today's teenagers actually communicate and process information in quite different ways than previous generations. Parents often wonder why their kids need to listen to music all the time, and why when asked a question they will simply grunt or give a dismissive reply – and continue listening to music. Music is a language, and at a time in life when it is hard to articulate your own thoughts, listening to music can be an important way of working things through. By taking time to listen to their music, parents can learn a lot of things that teenagers would like to say to them. It is important not to dismiss something just because you can't understand it. Far better to begin to dialogue. The problem for parents is that even the rules of dialogue are changing all the time. Our own children were born in three separate decades, and the oldest was already a teenager when our youngest was born. The world in which our older son grew up was quite similar to how it was in our own teenage years. Books were still a major learning tool, talking with someone else generally occupied a person's undivided attention, and the electronics industry was in its infancy. But our youngest child could do homework, listen to music, play with a computer game, eat a meal, watch the TV, and carry on a conversation – all at the same time, and without detriment to any of them. The actual ways in which teenagers communicate have changed, and parents need to appreciate this, and be part of the new style. Instead of insisting that everything else be abandoned to hold a conversation, we need to allow our teenagers to do more than one thing at once, and to be aware that they are likely to be much better at doing it than we are. Trying to make them as we once were will be a recipe for unnecessary confrontation, and can provoke crisis not avert it. Money can be a major flashpoint between teens and their parents. Teenagers often fail to understand their parents' concerns, because they are never adequately explained to them. For a teen, arguments over money are about control, not cash. But who can blame them, when they only ever see their parents acting as consumers (spending money) and never earning it (because that happens away from the home)?

We should remember that our children learn their behaviour from us. The older they get, the more like us they become, and the more adult they seem the more threatening it can be to have your own behavioural patterns reflected in someone else. Some parents dislike their teenagers because they dislike themselves. If during their children's formative years, parents have established a pattern of physical or verbal abuse as the way to make things happen in the home, then they can be sure their teenagers will imitate them with a vengeance – and it will not be a pleasurable experience to be on the receiving end. On the other hand, if open and loving communication networks have been in place from the start – particularly in relation to parents being prepared to listen to children as well as speak to them – then parents will invariably have an easier time during the teenage years.

Parents of teenagers can be under pressure for other reasons, which also affect the way they relate to their children. Obviously, the age of teenagers' parents depends on how old they were when their children were born, and that will be different for each child in a family. But parents of teenagers are generally in mid-life, and with more people delaying parenthood until their thirties or forties, this will be a growing trend. Some find this a difficult time of life anyway. Mid-life crisis may be difficult to describe in any hard-and-fast way, but at some time between the ages of about forty and fifty-five, our perceptions of life do tend to change, and some people have a real struggle to cope. By this time, adults often feel they have achieved whatever significant things they are going to do. If they missed that important promotion at work, then they are probably never going to get it now. If they passed by the opportunity to move to a different town or country, it will not come their way again. If they never got around to conceiving that other child they had vaguely dreamed about, then they have lost the chance. Some also experience a general lack of vitality, and a greater awareness of their own mortality. If you combine the emotional turmoil of an adolescent with the mood swings of a menopausal mother, then by any definition you have an explosive mixture. In all this, the diminishing possibilities for parents are in stark contrast with the increasing potential of their own teenagers. Teenagers, with the whole of life before them, remind us of who we once were – and the lost opportunities that we may still hanker for. At such a time, the natural instinct can be to preserve the status quo in as many areas of life as possible. This no doubt explains why in church life it is usually the middle-aged (men in particular) who are afraid of change, and not the elderly.

Adults handle mid-life in many different ways, no doubt related to their own temperament and previous experience. But for those who are insecure at this time, the maturing of their children can be exceedingly threatening to their own personal sense of identity and self-worth. The natural instinct might be to try and control and restrict our offspring in an authoritarian way – in effect, to attempt to keep things the same by preventing them from growing up. That is never a good idea at any stage, but whereas parents with a patriarchal attitude can at least make it look as if it works in early childhood, having a domineering parent as a teenager can lead to a total disruption of relationships. A breakdown at this stage frequently lasts well into adult life, and it can take many years to repair the damage.

Those who are prepared to work through these and similar issues will almost always find themselves emerging as better people, for their own partners as well as for their children – while those who refuse to come to grips with their own personal baggage at this time are likely to find a progressive deterioration in all aspects of relationships in the home. Increasing numbers of marriages break up when parents are struggling with teenage offspring. But even the most open families can use all the support they can get. The whole ethos of church life can make a major contribution, and those which have support groups in place already have a major asset to help parents handle the teenage years. As well as enabling parents who may be struggling with mid-life to share something of their accumulated wisdom with younger parents (something that will enhance their self-image anyway), many of the younger parents in such a group will not be far away from their own teenage years, and will be able to reflect on how they managed to cope, and what things made a difference. For parents who have no established lines of com-munication with their teens, doing things with other families whose teenage kids are friends with yours – and whose parents might be better communicators – can create a context for bridges to be built.

Like younger children, teenagers need clear boundaries: having rules ultimately says that we care what happens to them. But family rules should be flexible, transparent, and fair, and apply to parents as well as children. At the end of the day, though, Christian parents need to remember that no one is ever saved by rules. Generosity and grace go hand in hand, a theme underlined in one of the most memorable of the stories that Jesus told (Luke 15:11–32). For inspiration on good parenting, we scarcely need to look further.

6   Bible families

Christians naturally turn to the Bible for guidance on family life, as on other significant matters of faith. But many find that, far from providing an answer to their questions, the Bible is itself a part of the problem, not least because of the enormous social and cultural differences between its times and our own. How can we sort out what is still relevant, and what we may need to discard? And what are the abiding values of the gospel in relation to family life? These are major questions and we cannot engage here in a detailed consideration of the underlying hermeneutical issues that are involved in reading and applying an ancient text to the very different circumstances of post-modern culture. We do of course have an opinion on that, and those who are familiar with the debate about such matters will have no difficulty in locating our theoretical positions. This is not the place to propose a method, but rather to explore ways in which we might use the Bible in practice. For those who struggle with understanding what it means to be Christian in today's family, this is not a detached, intellectual question. On the contrary, the answers that people offer can – and do – make or break family relationships. We begin with a story to illustrate some of the pressure points. This is not an imaginary scenario, but a real-life story that did actually happen to a couple we know, and the only thing we have changed is their names. The actual circumstances are very specific, but they demonstrate well enough the issues with which Christian couples struggle as they try to be true to themselves and faithful to the biblical heritage.

The search for relevance

Clare and Martin were a young couple in their twenties. When they fell in love and decided to marry, the only thing that motivated them was their shared desire to be truly happy together, and for their new home to be a place where Christ would be honoured and served. Neither of them had previously given a great deal of thought to what marriage might involve. Most of their peers lived together unmarried, with a view to getting married later if things worked out for them – so it was not a natural topic of conversation among their friends. But as they thought about relationships in the context of Christian faith, Clare and Martin concluded that they wanted to make some kind of formal commitment that would provide them with a more secure framework than cohabiting seemed to offer. In addition – though neither of them could ever recall hearing much about the subject in regular Sunday worship – they had the impression that the church people would probably prefer them to get married rather than live together unmarried. As they shared their concerns with one or two of the older members of the church whom they felt they could trust, they soon realized that virtually none of them had any comprehension of the issues they felt they were dealing with. They expressed surprise that a Christian couple would even have considered cohabiting – something that made Clare and Martin wonder how detached from culture the church could be, because all their friends would have taken that for granted. They survived that discovery, but then as they sought further advice about what, exactly, makes a marriage 'Christian', they really did begin to think that some people in their church were totally detached from the real world. They had imagined that working out how their faith could be reflected in their relationship would be an essentially pragmatic exercise. Instead, they found themselves sucked into a theological whirlpool in which they were soon out of their depth.

As she spoke with other women in the church (including some only marginally older than herself), Clare discovered that being a Christian wife should involve her in being 'submissive' to her husband. She was taken aback by such talk – and certainly had no idea what it might mean in practice – but the more people she spoke to, the clearer it became that this was widely considered to be the Bible's pattern for marriage, and therefore one that she should adopt. Since she wanted to be faithful to Christ, as well as being a good partner for her husband, she eventually conceded that, while it may be culturally unpopular for her to allow

Martin to take the lead in all the major decisions affecting their
life together, it would nonetheless be the 'Christian' way. After
all, they were being counter-cultural by getting married in the
first place, so perhaps this was just another way of expressing
their distinctiveness. It took her some time to work through it
all, but eventually she felt happy enough with a 'submissive'
role to raise the matter with Martin. Far from welcoming her
compliance to the 'Christian ideal', he was absolutely horrified
at what she was proposing. Unlike Clare, he had been brought
up in the church, and had heard some of these ideas in the past.
If he had given any thought to them, it was only to assume that
they were quaint hangovers from the past that related merely to
older generations. It had never crossed his mind that it would
ever impinge on his own life in any practical sense. To him, the
notion of submission undermined everything that he was hoping
for in his relationship to Clare. He had no idea at all what it might
mean for Clare to be 'submissive' to him, and no inclination to
find out. He could see no reason why they should not be good
friends and equal partners in this new stage of their relationship.
They had fallen in love as two independent and equal persons,
so why should marriage change anything? Surely it would give
them a new context in which to build on what they already had?
It made no sense that he either could or should somehow be in
control of his wife. 'If this is what Christian marriage is about,'
he reflected to himself, 'then you can keep it' – and, though he
never said it to Clare, he began to think that maybe they would
be better off just living together anyway, even if it did involve
alienating their church community. In fact, he did wonder – only
momentarily – what they were doing in the church anyway, if it
was so disconnected from reality.

Clare and Martin determined to get to the bottom of these
conflicting opinions, and found a minister from outside their
own church who was a great source of strength to them both.
They took a long, hard look at various Bible passages where
'submission' was mentioned, and decided it was not for them.
By the time of their wedding day, they had resolved it all to their
own satisfaction. What happened next is hard to credit, but
believe us – we were there. At their wedding, the sermon
preached by the minister of their own church began with this

passage of Scripture: 'Wives, submit to your husbands as to the Lord. For a husband has authority over his wife . . . And so wives must submit completely to their husbands' (Ephesians 5:22, 24 GNB). They didn't know whether to laugh or cry, but having been through it all in advance, they laughed – and got on with the business of working out their own understanding of what a Christian family should be.

Others would not be able to smile so easily. It is no laughing matter for the battered wife or the abused child to be given such advice. If the submission of women to men is of the essence of the Christian family, then for many people it is going to make better sense not to be Christian. To be under the control of another person can never be good news for anyone. Yet very many Christians struggle with precisely this issue as they try to work out how they are supposed to follow Christ within today's family. Moreover, much of the advice given by Christian leaders to the victims of violence and abuse reflects the opinion that the acceptance of male domination in marriage is the 'Christian' way to live.[1]

Many Christians prefer to ignore these questions rather than deal with them. But it is central to our concern to bring gospel values to bear on the matter of what it means to be Christian and a responsible member of a family in today's world. The Bible will not simply go away, and unless we are prepared to deal openly with passages that seem to promote the exploitation of women and children by men, we will have nothing to contribute to the renewal and healing of suffering families, whether our own or other people's. Christian women who find themselves trapped in violent and abusive relationships suffer even more than their secular counterparts when they try to rationalize what is happening to them by reference to the kind of theology which regards female submission as the essential foundation stone of a happy marriage. An unexpectedly high proportion of those who call for help from shelters for battered women begin to explain themselves by saying, 'I'm a Bible-believing Christian, but . . .'[2]

A realistic view

At a time of rapid and unpredictable cultural change, it is natural to look for guidance that might provide that sense of security which we imagine our forebears enjoyed, and it is understandable that Christians should hope to find that in the Bible. But using the Bible effectively is neither simple nor straightforward.

We have already pointed out that the industrial nuclear family is a practical lifestyle for only a tiny minority of people today. We have also argued that it is not in any sense an intrinsically Christian pattern, but is culturally conditioned – like all other family styles through the ages. This kind of family cannot be found in the Bible, and the assumption that it can not only has disastrous consequences for many Christian homes, but also distorts the way the Bible actually presents the family. Instead of trying to turn the clock back to an age that has gone forever, we should be asking how we can live in the new circumstances in ways that will reflect the love of God and the values of Christ's kingdom. Our starting point for that will be the recognition that there is no single pattern for family life enshrined in Scripture, nor does the Bible contain detailed instructions which are as valid for families today and in the future as they were for ancient Israel or the first Christian communities. We have been reflecting together on this for the whole time we have ourselves been married (almost forty years), and one of the few certain conclusions we have reached is that there really is no such thing as a biblical blueprint for something called the 'Christian family'. Some will inevitably accuse us of promoting a watered-down faith that merely accommodates itself to the latest social trends. It is our contention, however, that we are doing exactly the opposite, for by going back to the teaching of Jesus in particular we are reverting to the very roots of the gospel. We are also, as we will seek to demonstrate shortly, placing ourselves squarely in the centre of the ongoing tradition of Christian history, and indeed of the Bible itself.

Christian families

Historically, Christians have always accepted that families come in different shapes and sizes. They have also recognized dysfunction as an intrinsic feature of intimate human relationships, and the idea that Christian families should expect to be free from the problems that afflict others is a recent invention. Many great heroes of the past wrestled with the consequences of their own unhappy home lives. John Wesley found it easy to leave home and embark on arduous mission work precisely because of his own unhappy relationship with his wife. David Livingstone took so little interest in the needs of his wife that she ended up effectively being a lone parent to their children, and eventually gave up on faith altogether as a result. Wesley made a virtue out of necessity, claiming that if he had been a good husband and father he would have been a much less effective evangelist.[3] But long before that, the apostle Paul may well have found himself in a similar situation, and even a cautious commentator like F.F. Bruce suggested that Paul's single state at the time he wrote his letters was best explained not by thinking he had never married, or was widowed, but by assuming he was divorced.[4] In our own time, the simple fact is that the families of Christians break up in much the same way as other families, and the rate at which Christians divorce and remarry is indistinguishable from the trend in the general population. A survey by Barna Research (a Christian organization) showed that in the US so-called 'born-again' Christians have one of the highest divorce rates in the country (27 per cent as against a national average of 25 per cent), with members of Baptist and independent churches higher again (29 per cent and 34 per cent respectively). The same poll showed the divorce rate among atheists as 21 per cent, leading to headlines like 'For a happy marriage, avoid a Christian'.[5] There is obviously no point trying to pretend that 'Christian' families are any different from others.

Yet many churches are in denial, and Christian people whose families encounter difficulties often leave the church in order to deal with them, rather than finding in the community of faith the kind of support that they need in times of difficulty. Parents whose grown-up children's relationships collapse can find themselves in a similar position, thinking that they have somehow failed to impart 'Christian' values to their kids. And because their churches resist reality, they find themselves marginalized and disempowered. Just as children regularly create imaginary identities for themselves in Internet chat rooms, so too churches sometimes cushion themselves from reality by creating imaginary identities in relation to family breakdown, assuming that if only they can convince themselves that Christian families stay together and live happily ever after, then it must be like that. Not telling the truth in chat rooms can land children in dangerous and compromising situations, and the same is true of the church, not just in relation to family breakdown but with all sorts of matters related to sexuality. Back in the 1990s when we first started reflecting theologically about these issues, we had a research assistant who carried out some qualitative ethno-graphic research for us among clergy, and one of the most consistent features to emerge was the repeated identification of Christian leaders (some quite prominent) whose behaviour appeared to contradict their beliefs. Paradoxically, on further reflection we realized that some of the horror stories we were hearing demonstrated that their behaviour *did* match their beliefs, which began with the assumption that the family is a hierarchy headed by men (responsible to God), under whom are women, children, pets, and so on in descending order. Though it is not anything like universally the case, the reality of life within some 'Christian families' (including clergy families) is that parents (invariably fathers) declare their allegiance to 'traditional family values' while their own families are seriously dysfunc-tional, often as a result of the violence and abuse that they themselves impose on their spouses and children. Clearly, we must be careful not to exaggerate this, because a majority of Christian leaders do not fall into that category. But there is no question that, within the Christian context (as elsewhere), the family has potential for great blessing, as well as for enormous harm and destruction. If, as some imply, the Bible's message is only about those families which match up to recent western images of the industrial nuclear family, then we Christians actu-ally have no distinctive insights of faith to contribute either to our own families or to those of others.

The attitudes just mentioned are easily dismissed as the convictions of a fundamentalist minority, and there is no doubt that they derive partly from an approach which ransacks the Bible looking for proof texts rather than engaging with the whole picture. But in our experience, that is by no means limited to the lunatic fringe, and there is no shortage of well-informed and reflective Christians – including some theology professors – who in theory would claim to adopt a more differentiated hermeneutical approach to Scripture, but who when faced with the practical realities of pastoral encounters still look for a single text that can be used to resolve complex issues.

So what does the Bible say about families? For those steeped in the Christian tradition, it is never easy to take a step back and read the Bible as if for the first time. Marcus Borg attempted to do so, and found himself both praised and vilified in roughly equal measure.[6] However, with increasing numbers of people having no previous knowledge at all of the Bible, it is not too difficult to find out what the unbiased reader of Scripture thinks about it. We have raised this question with many such people in workshops and seminars over recent years, and they all say the same thing: that, potentially, the Bible has a great deal to offer, precisely because its stories about families are so similar to our own experiences today. Notwithstanding their different cultural settings (and we should remember that the Bible itself bears witness to changing norms over many generations), Bible families were remarkably similar to our own, and shared many of the same struggles. Wherever we look in its pages, we find exactly the same diversity of family styles as we encounter in everyday life. Even those who are praised as people of great faith could be hard to live with: domestic violence, abuse of children, and exploitation of other family members are nothing new, even within the families of God's people. Simply by reporting these unpalatable facts, the Bible emphasizes God's concern for what goes on in family life. It also conveys some important insights into the way that faith can help make sense out of the chaos into which families so readily degenerate. It might seem unnecessary – even voyeuristic – to catalogue some of the problems encountered by Bible families, but it is worth doing, because when today's Christians turn to the Bible for guidance they easily miss what is obvious. If we reduce the Bible to a collection of abstract ideals, it has little ability to challenge and empower us to be the people whom God intends us to be. But when we read its stories in the light of our own experience, we discover that its world is not strange and alien: it is the same world of family conflict in which we still struggle to forge relationships that will bring growth and blessing into our own lives and those of others.

Bible families[7]

It would not be too misleading to describe the entire Bible story as a sequence of narratives about different families. The description of relationships in the very first family sets the scene for all that is to follow, as Eve learns that 'your husband . . . shall rule over you' (Genesis 3:16 NRSV). This is one of the earliest statements in the Bible about human relationships, and it acknowledges a universal reality: that women often find themselves put down and personally devalued even (or especially) by those men whom they love.[8] But this is not the only thing the book of Genesis says about relationships between women and men, nor is it the primary starting point. As a matter of fact, the oppression of Eve by Adam is listed as one of the consequences of the Fall. God's will as expounded on the very first page of the Bible is quite different: there, women and men are created as equals, both of them made 'in the image of God' (Genesis 1:27–8) and intended to live together in an open and harmonious relationship with one another (Genesis 2:25). In biblical terms, the structured hierarchies of the industrial nuclear family are not a reflection of the will of God. On the contrary, this is what happens when people reject the values of their creator.

Far from upholding it as the ideal, the Bible actually challenges our inherited patriarchal family model. Taking these Genesis narratives at their face value, it would not be an exaggeration to describe the patriarchal family as idolatrous, because by creating a descending social hierarchy of God-Men-Women-Children, it implies a spiritual hierarchy in which women and children have no direct access to God – something that also infringes the first of the Ten Commandments (Exodus 20:3). When men put themselves in the place of God they are denying not only the basic rights of others in the family, they are also challenging fundamental aspects of the teaching of Scripture. The Bible reflects the structures of patriarchal culture, because it describes life as it is. But in doing so it also challenges the status quo by suggesting that, far from being the will of God, this is actually a sign that something has gone wrong: the first consequence of sin is a breakdown in relationships and the oppression of one person by another. It is important to keep in mind this over-arching theological frame of reference as we consider the actual stories of Bible families.

By the time we reach Genesis 4:1–16 fratricide is on the agenda, as Cain murders his brother Abel. Neither of these children experienced their family as a place of security. Cain had suffered rejection long before he lifted his hand against Abel – a scenario that repeatedly characterizes today's families. There is no hatred so intense as that which can develop between family members. A few pages further on, we come to the central family of the entire Old Testament. Abraham occupies a key role in the story of salvation history, and when people later confessed their faith they did so in terms of their commitment to 'the God of Abraham, Isaac, and Jacob'. Moreover, Abraham was held up as a great hero of faith among the earliest Christians (Galatians 3:6–4:31; Hebrews 11:8–19). What kind of family did he have? Even a superficial reading of the narratives cannot disguise the fact that it was no 'ideal' family, and his own behaviour con-tributed significantly to its dysfunction. One way and another, everyone associated with Abraham suffered as a consequence of his greed, lust, abuse, violence, and selfishness. The Bible hides none of the unpalatable facts as it describes how he treated his wife Sarah as if she was a prostitute, encouraging the king of Egypt to have sex with her (Genesis 12:10–20); how her sub-sequent internalizing of her oppression led her to approve his sexual relationship with another partner, Hagar (Genesis 16:1–4); and how he was later prepared to sacrifice – literally as well as metaphorically – the favoured son Isaac (Genesis 22:1–14), as well as Hagar's son Ishmael (Genesis 21:9–21) – though in both cases God stepped in to save the children from the fate planned for them (Genesis 21:17–18, 22:12–14). The entire sequence of stories about Abraham gives an honest picture of a man who misused his family for personal gratification – even religious gratification – and then went on to despise those whom he had abused. Nor is this a unique case: examples of the same thing can easily be found in later Bible history.

The Bible also documents the way family dysfunction is handed on from one generation to another. Given their own childhood experiences, Ishmael and Isaac were almost certain to find themselves entangled in unsatisfactory adult relationships. Since we all learn parenting skills from our own parents, it was entirely predictable that Isaac's family would disintegrate – and it did. Jacob cheated his brother Esau out of his inheritance (Genesis 27:1–45), and then in turn his sons sold their brother Joseph into slavery (Genesis 37:1–36). At a later period, the same pattern of dysfunction over several generations brought ruination to the royal houses of both Israel and Judah, with the cycle broken only when Joash was brought up by a foster parent in the ancient equivalent of being taken into care (2 Kings 8–12). The perpetuation of destructive cycles of family behaviour through many generations is not a new phenomenon.

The family stories of other Bible characters reflect the same realities. Moses is another key player. By comparison with some others there is very little personal information about him, so it is perhaps even more significant that one of the few things we are told is that he enjoyed a good fight with his brother Aaron and sister Miriam, even as an adult (Exodus 32:1–35; Numbers 12:1–16). Samuel is another leading player in the Old Testament story, and one of the few personal things we know about him is that he suffered the disruption of his family life from an early age – this time, an enforced fostering in the name of religious devotion, as his parents abandoned him to be brought up by Eli the priest, of whom again the only thing we know is that he had already made a mess of parenting his own sons (1 Samuel 2:27–36, 3:11–14). The prophet Hosea experienced great anguish at the disintegration of his marriage relationship (Hosea 1:2–3:5). Ruth began with a happy and positive experience of home life until her husband died and she was left virtually penniless, only finding new meaning and purpose when she remarried and joined a blended family. In the New Testament, Jesus told a story about a father with two sons. In spite of all the love showered on them, one almost destroyed himself with greed, while the other shattered the family through pride, and the father was frustrated (Luke 15:11–32). Jesus frequently met and affirmed women who had been abused and exploited by men (John 4:4–26, 8:1–11, 12:1–8). Even his relationship to his own family was not exactly idyllic (Mark 3:31–5).

This is a random survey of life in Bible families, and it is certainly not exhaustive. But the sample is entirely representative and by making other choices we would not significantly change the general impression. Stories like this are highly problematic for anyone who tries to understand them as models that Christians should follow. A responsible person living next door to families behaving in this 'biblical' way today would call the police or social service agencies. They could hardly be admired as families living out the values of the gospel, because their lifestyle is self-evidently at odds with the central themes of Christian teaching. But then, the Bible never does recommend these families as examples to be followed. The problem is not with the Bible, but with the way some Christians want to read and apply it. The Bible's great strength (and a major reason why it is still worth reading at all) is its realistic honesty about human life – and that includes its accounts of family life. The discovery that Bible families were like ours is not bad news, but just the opposite – not because of the unsatisfactory nature of many of their relation-ships, but because in the midst of so much brutality the Bible also offers a story of hope. Running through all its pages is the affirmation that, even in the worst kind of family, it is still worth trusting in God. Moreover, God can be trusted to take sides with those who are oppressed, abused, and exploited. Faith is not a magic potion that dissolves the problems. Those, like Abraham, David, and the rest who make wrong choices, are not let off, but have to live with the painful consequences of their wrongdoing. That is really good news for people who suffer: God is with them in the midst of their pain – and on their side. Even when they suffer gross injustice at the hands of their nearest and dearest, God offers only unconditional love and acceptance. Bible stories are not meant to be models for morality, but mirrors through which we can explore our own identity. In the process of contemplating what we see, we can hear the good news and be challenged about our own shortcomings, as well as discovering the possibility of new beginnings even for those who have been most deeply hurt.

Jesus and the tradition

Bible stories naturally reflect the cultural assumptions of their time, and in that world three ideas were widely taken for granted:

Family rights were property rights: that is, families were patriarchal in the absolute sense that all the members of a household belonged to the dominant male. Even the Ten Commandments, which in some ways were ethically advanced and enlightened for their time, deal with adultery not as a moral or personal issue, but as a property issue: having sex with another man's wife is no different from desiring 'his cattle, his donkeys, or anything else that he owns' (Exodus 20:17 GNB).

This meant, secondly, that *women were always under the control and in the possession of men*.[9] The basic assumption underlying Abraham's behaviour was that women and children essentially exist for a man's benefit, to use as he likes. The reason that his attitude is not explicitly condemned in the Old Testament is because the whole story was handed on within the context of a patriarchal society in which that was the natural starting point. The way a man related to his family was not a moral issue. We see this especially clearly in relation to divorce, which was allowed for almost anything. The Old Testament placed virtually no restrictions on a man's rights to divorce his wife: 'Suppose a man enters into a marriage with a woman, but she does not please him because he finds something objectionable about her, and so he writes a certificate of divorce, puts it in her hand, and sends her out of his house; she then leaves his house and goes off to become another man's wife' (Deuteronomy 24:1–2 NRSV). Put that way, divorcing your wife sounds like selling a car when you get bored with its colour, or its performance begins to fall off – and, of course, a woman had no rights at all to choose to divorce her husband, or whether to allow him to divorce her.[10]

Thirdly, *the positive function of a woman in this context was economic*: she existed primarily for the purpose of producing children, who would support the family unit in the father's old age. A woman who did not reproduce was like a car with no engine, and some rabbis even doubted whether such a person would get into heaven.[11] Undertones of that thinking can still be identified in some conservative church circles today, to the discomfort of childless couples and singles.

It serves no useful purpose to criticize the biblical narratives or the way they were traditionally understood, for they simply report the patriarchal values of their own times. In any case, we have already noted the way in which the Bible's own understanding of creation puts a question mark against all this. By the time of Jesus some of these issues were being discussed within a wider context, and his own teaching on divorce and remarriage reflected debates between the leading rabbis of the day about the terms under which divorce and remarriage might be sanctioned, with Jesus challenging the prevailing opinion that a woman might be divorced for almost any reason at all (Matthew 19:1–12; Mark 10:1–12).[12]

Jesus questioned the accepted norms of his culture in other significant ways, not least by accepting women as equal partners with men in the spiritual quest. When Mary was criticized for talking about faith instead of staying in the kitchen, Jesus specifically affirmed that she was doing 'the right thing' (Luke 10:42 GNB). He had a regular group of women who accompanied him and shared his ministry (Luke 8:3), in striking contrast to other religious teachers who generally regarded women as spiritually handicapped. Moreover, Jesus regularly identified himself with those who were victimized by the prevailing attitudes. Nowhere is this more clearly spelled out than in the story of a woman who was allegedly caught in the act of committing adultery (John 7:53–8:11). The story does not reveal whether she had been formally tried and condemned, nor does it indicate the precise nature of her wrongdoing (in a patriarchal culture, merely speaking to a man unaccompanied could be classed as 'adultery'). In any event, Jesus was invited to take part in her execution, which was not only condoned, but required by the Law. Jesus set it aside – and that was good news indeed for the woman, who discovered that 'whatever human law or custom may legitimate violence against women, it cannot stand face to face with the revelation of God's affirmation of all humanity.'[13]

Paul

Jesus' concern for outcasts of all kinds is so central to the Gospels that no one could plausibly question his commitment to belief in the essential equality of women and men, and of children and adults. But things are more complex with Paul. This is partly due to the fact that his writings were all letters written in response to other letters or verbal communications, none of which now survive. With Paul we only hear one side of a conversation, and that limitation in itself should alert us to the difficulties of formulating hard and fast guidelines on the basis of what he writes. Nevertheless, some things are clear – and surprising, in view of the way he has been understood through much of Christian history. In Galatians 3:28, Paul unequivocally affirms the equality of women and men, just as he asserts that there is no difference between slaves and free people, or between different races. Moreover, throughout his letters Paul mentions women whom he accepted as full partners in his own ministry, to at least one of whom he applies the title 'apostle' (Junia, in Romans 16:7). And, in contrast to other teachers of the time, he argues that women have as much right as men to pray and prophesy in the public gatherings of the church (1 Corinthians 11).

But other statements attributed to Paul appear to say different things. What about the advice to families in Ephesians 5:21–33, including the bit about wives being submissive to their husbands? Several comments are relevant here. For a start, we can note that in its cultural context this code of conduct was widely accepted not only in early Christian circles but also in Judaism, and some Greek circles as well. Paul was not the one who actually formulated these rules, and within the New Testament they are also quoted in Colossians 3:18–4:1, 1 Peter 2:18–3:7, 1 Timothy 2:8–15, 6:1–2, and Titus 2:1–10. That might suggest that the early Christians did no original thinking on family life, and just accepted the cultural norms they knew. Yet they are distinctive in one key respect, and that is in the way that they address women, slaves, and children alongside masters and fathers.[14] This is highlighted by the way the advice begins, 'Be subject [some translations have "submissive"] to one another out of reverence for Christ' (5:21 NRSV). This is also consistent with other passages – for example, when writing about sex, marriage and divorce in 1 Corinthians 7 Paul addresses husband and wife equally, suggesting that they both have responsibilities as well as privileges. In Philippians 2:4, a similar principle appears with the recommendation, 'Let each of you look not to your own interests, but to the interests of others' (NRSV).

Historically, therefore, it is reasonable to conclude that, far from upholding hierarchical values of patriarchal households, Paul was actually challenging them, though doing so within the existing cultural framework.[15] There is certainly plenty of evidence to suggest that the starting point for all Christian relationships, in the family as well as elsewhere, is to be mutuality and partnership rather than domination and oppression. In the case of these lists of household duties, the actual Greek word used by Paul has the same implication. Though it has been conventionally translated as 'be subject' or 'submissive' the term *hupotasso* carries that meaning more in the sense of 'making an accommodation' or 'giving way to' the concerns of another, rather than dominating another. In other words, Paul is encouraging his readers to be flexible, ready to give way to each other. There will be times in a relationship when a man should acknowledge the priority of his wife's concerns, while on other occasions the woman may need to do the same. Understood this way, the statement is about the mutual responsibility of husbands and wives. To be fair to Paul, therefore, we should recognize that he is a good deal more sensitive about relationships than even his friends have often claimed: he is unquestionably more progressive than 1 Peter, where a similar list of household duties leaves readers in no doubt that a wife was expected to offer unquestioning obedience to her husband, and Sarah's tolerance of Abraham's domineering behaviour is even held up as a model to be followed (1 Peter 3:6).

Reading the text through the family

For today's families, the important thing about these biblical texts is not what they meant in their original historical context, but what they seem to be saying to us. Scholars have traditionally argued that it is illegitimate to read Bible stories through contemporary perspectives. In reality, though, we all bring our own personal baggage to anything, and to pretend otherwise is just to bury our heads in the sand. In any case, if it is not permissible to bring our own concerns to the Bible, that raises the more fundamental question: why bother reading it in the first place? Statements like that horrify the exegetical purists, of course, especially those who are still wedded to the historical-critical method of biblical interpretation, which prioritizes historical meaning over contemporary understanding (indeed, in its most pristine form dismisses that as an illegitimate concern of the interpreter). Traditionalists who are aware of the questions we have raised tend to dismiss them as 'a more or less artificial problem'.[16] A recent study of the Abraham stories claims that 'There is *no* recorded example of Jews or Christians using the text to justify their own abusing or killing of a child.'[17] That may well be true as it is stated, but all it means is that nobody has ever gone on public record to say that – as if they would! Similarly in the case of the Samuel story, from a historical angle we might reasonably ask whether his parents really did 'abandon' him to the care of Eli, as we suggested, or whether they made a great sacrifice (he was, after all, visited annually so they maintained some sort of contact). But the point is that, when stories like that are read through the experiences of today's children, it resonates with them, for whenever religious parents make sacrifices it often involves their families, and in light of the wider challenges of the gospel there is every justification for asking if that can ever be right. Ivory-tower theologians writing books in the remoteness of academic institutions will think of plenty of reasons to dismiss such contemporary readings of the text. But anyone who is engaged in the pastoral care of families knows that, far from being unusual or extreme, these are absolutely typical examples of the way some Christians use the Bible to justify their own behaviour. And for every one who excuses violence and oppression by reference to Abraham or other similar characters, a dozen or more will refer to New Testament injunctions about 'being submissive' in order to give expression to what they perversely imagine to be some God-given order of the hierarchical priority of male over female in the family. For evidence of that, just look in any Christian bookstore: in a random survey of the stock in one of our local stores, every book on family affairs – without exception – argued that submission by women to men is the key to a happy marriage, because it is 'God's way'. Many of them also claimed that for fathers to inflict regular violence on their children (disguised as 'discipline') is the pathway to their personal maturity and ultimate happiness. Again, these notions are not the products of a misguided fundamentalist imagination but are actually deeply ingrained in the western theological psyche. Even Karl Barth – widely acclaimed as perhaps the greatest twentieth-century theologian – argued that, because men are to rule over women as Christ does over the Church, this is not an equality issue. His reasoning was that, just as Christ allowed himself to be subject to God (even though he was equal to God), so for women to elevate men (even though they are their equals) is an act of humility – and therefore men owe their position to women's humility, not to their own male sense of superiority.[18]

Others try to apply the New Testament by emphasizing the nature of 'submission' as a two-way thing, and therefore implying an acceptance of the equality of women and men in relationships. There is no question that one of the major problems in the family today is the unwillingness of many men to accept any form of accountability, and in that sense 'mutuality' can only be a good thing. But at a time when the rising level of violence is causing concern in the wider society, and by all accounts is just as prevalent in the church, even talk of 'mutual submission' is unhelpful and can just become a smokescreen for aggressive behaviour. A term like 'submission' is simply inappropriate, no matter how much it is reinterpreted or explained in relation to a cultural context that has long since disappeared. Our use of language has moved on, and we ought to take account of that.

In reality, even the most conservative Christians have already done that with other positions adopted in the New Testament.

Take, for example, what is said about slavery in Ephesians 6:5–9. While the mutual accountability of slaves and masters that is recommended there was undoubtedly an enormous advance over the prevailing first-century conditions, Christians today regard that as purely pragmatic advice for a particular circumstance. We all understand that the application of wider scriptural principles makes any sort of master-slave relationship quite unacceptable. Though the seeds of slavery's destruction were always in the New Testament, it took the Church 1800 years to come to terms with it. Different social circumstances give us different opportunities to reflect on the gospel's challenge to our own cultural norms, and the time has now come for us to formulate new understandings of what it means for women and men to be made in the image of God, of equal importance to God and with equal potential not only as disciples but as human beings – and to recognize that, no matter how carefully it may be defined or reinterpreted, the language of submission does not give expression to those fundamental biblical principles.

7 Nurturing the spirituality of the family

This is one of the most important topics of all, not only for Christian parents but also for the Church as an institution. The question posed by John H. Westerhoff – *Will our Children have Faith?*[1] – is now paralleled by Walter Brueggemann's question, 'Will our Faith have Children?'[2] Churches of all traditions struggle to hand on to their children a living faith that will survive into their own adult life, and most children raised in a Christian environment give up on the Church. Some return years later when they become parents themselves, but they are just a tiny minority compared with the huge numbers of children who leave church never to come back. Not only is this a major missional challenge for the Church, it also represents a personal tragedy for many Christians that leaves them feeling a failure as parents, and disempowered as believers – for if their faith is apparently meaningless for their own children, how can they with integrity commend it to others?

Disagreement about children and church has led to endless splits and divisions among Christians, even on occasion the emergence of new denominations, and continues to be the catalyst for ongoing debates on the nature of the sacraments, of church membership, and more besides. Some – with a strong emphasis on 'original sin' – insist that children be dealt with sacramentally, regarding baptism as a cleansing ritual that can accomplish this. Others prefer to emphasize the nurture of children within the Christian community, and see baptism more as a badge of belonging than a sacramental cleansing from sin. Yet others have no time for the incorporation of children per se into the church, insisting instead that discipleship is essentially an adult thing to be experienced through personal choice and radical conversion. Much ink has been spilled in the course of these debates – and they are, of course, infinitely more complicated than this summary might suggest. Theologically and pastorally, they all have different strengths and weaknesses. But in relation to children's spirituality they all have two things in common. They start with the church and its ways of seeing things – rules, regulations and institutional requirements – and then ask, 'How can a child be fitted in here?' In addition, there seems nothing to choose between any of them when it comes to nurturing the faith of children in a way that enables them to make it through to adult Christian discipleship: no one ecclesiastical tradition is better than any other at holding onto its children.

How does faith grow?

If all our churches are failing our children, it seems obvious that a radical shift of emphasis must be required. This will likely be more problematic, because our underlying theological starting points (rather than denominational allegiances) will to a large extent determine how we feel children can or should articulate Christian faith. Those who prioritize the axis of Fall and Redemption, seeing people as irredeemably sinful until touched by the Church, are likely to view spiritual development in terms of jumping through hoops in order to conform to church order and discipline. Though their devotees imagine they are very different from one another, each of the three approaches summarized above has traditionally operated in this way. While they might mention the freely given grace of God, their real subtext is 'you can be part of the community of faith, but we'll let you in on our terms'. If we were to prioritize the doctrines of Creation and Incarnation, however, our starting point will be rather different: 'You are a person made in God's image, how can we help to develop that?' The understanding here would be that, as individuals 'made in God's image', children will belong to the family of God before they are likely to start believing the propositions of theological or creedal statements. More than that, there will be an appropriate expression of faith for every stage of life.

We have already mentioned John H. Westerhoff's book, *Will our Children have Faith?* It, and others like it, connect faith development with what we know of human nature from other fields of enquiry such as developmental psychology.[3] The following diagram illustrates this idea:

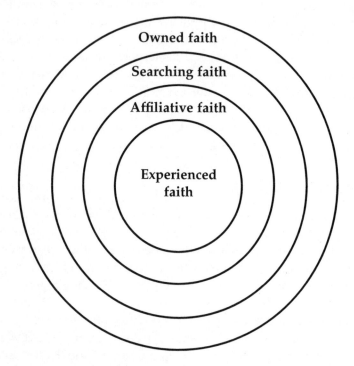

Here, faith begins in the central circle and moves out through the others, in such a way that spiritual growth corresponds to natural growth and the child's emerging sense of personal identity. *Experienced faith* is absorbed (like everything else) through relationships in the first stages of life. Though a young child would not operate with the abstract idea of 'God', if s/he were to do so, their faith might be summed up as 'God is like my mum and dad'. *Affiliative faith* reflects a need to belong, to love and to be accepted, and might be characterized by a slogan such as 'I believe what my peers/the church/my family believes'. *Searching faith* asks different questions: Who is God and who am I? Can anyone make sense out of it all? Doubt might be encountered as a necessary part of establishing what faith is. Then there is *Owned faith*, which says, 'This is how it looks from where I am. I don't have all the answers, but I'll stand up for what

I believe, and continue to explore it from as many different perspectives and experiences as I can identify.'

The diagram is intentionally circular, with one ring inside another, and each stage working out from the centre, because the growth of faith can be compared to the growth of a tree, which adds new rings to the outside as it matures. This is a helpful analogy, which highlights four significant factors in relation to the nurture of a child's faith:

A young tree is a real tree. A sapling is truly and completely a tree: as it grows, it does not change its essential nature, it just becomes more sophisticated. The faith of a child is 'real' faith. There is nothing wrong or inadequate with a child's faith, though it needs to grow to maturity.

Trees grow in the right environment. They require appropriate amounts of sun, water, soil, and so on. Faith is the same: it develops in response to our experiences in the world. Without the right environment, a child's faith will wither.

Trees – and faith – grow in a slow, orderly way. New growth builds on previous growth. In a tree, rings are not lost or missed out. Each ring depends on the ones before and after it. Mature faith is not different in character from faith at its beginning – it is not 'greater' faith, but 'expanded' faith.

A previous chapter has highlighted the strengths and weaknesses of developmental models of family life: while they can help to identify specific aspects of growth, they are not always directly applicable to every family or individual. The same is true here. Though the starting point is the nurture of children's faith, and the stages are therefore intrinsically age-related, their developmental dimension does not automatically match the actual experience of all members of faith communities. Arguably, most western Christians might be characterized by 'affiliative faith'. They believe what their church believes, and are not interested in working things through for themselves, and so never engage with either searching faith (potentially too painful) or owned faith (potentially too demanding). Some researchers have suggested that believers go in and out of these different faith positions at different points of life, and faith development is therefore cyclical rather than linear. There is also the challenge of people with learning difficulties, or dementia sufferers, who either stick with experienced faith throughout life, or regress to that stage as a result of their illness. How can the faith of these people be understood? These are important questions, to which there is as yet no obvious answer. But to address them would divert attention from our focus here, which is the spirituality of children.

Regardless of how the place of children in the church might be theologically explained or justified, a central element in the church's problem with nurturing the faith of children is the tendency to define 'faith' in cognitive and intellectual terms. Debates in some churches over whether children should receive communion, or whether people with learning difficulties can become members, highlight this propensity, as the real questions are not about communion or membership but about whether individuals have reached a satisfactory level of cognitive understanding of the doctrines of the Church. Yet the idea that faith can be 'given' to people as a pre-packaged collection of ideas is both educationally unrealistic and spiritually inept. What we can do is to influence the character of the faith that children (and others) already have by the way in which we behave with them. Our actions influence their perceptions, and frame what they will experience – which is why it is important for those adults who want to nurture children to be aware of the fact that they too are in a process of faith and personal development. We are all becoming somebody, and that means faith development will, for all concerned, involve sharing and receiving, as well as giving.[4]

Partners on the journey

The image of spiritual nurture as a road along which children and adults travel together, learning from and supporting one another, is not only true to life but is also a biblical model. In the last chapter we highlighted the way the Bible acknowledges the endemic nature of family dysfunction. But the dysfunction is so noteworthy only because it stands in opposition to other, more positive images of family spirituality. The ideal in ancient Israel is not reflected in stories of violence and abuse, but in festivals such as the Passover, at which children played a major role in the retelling and re-enactment of the stories of their nation (family), as they and their parents together committed themselves afresh to the love of God and neighbour which was central to the Old Testament story. This sense of partnership also features strongly in the teaching of Jesus, as well as in the life of the earliest Christian communities, in which children clearly played an equal role along with adults.[5]

What can children teach adults about God? Having come into this world more recently, it might be imagined that children would intuitively be closer to God, and some aspects of a child's natural behaviour seem to support that. Recent studies have identified several characteristics of the innate spirituality of children.[6] Children instinctively have a sense of awe and wonder, and an open and welcoming nature. They have an innate trust in ultimate goodness, and the value of relationships. They are, in that sense, bearers of grace. They also live for the present, and take only as much as they need at any given moment. They employ imagination and fantasy to understand things. Children's perception of time is quite different from adults; indeed some psychologists think their view of life focuses on what will happen in the timeframe of the next ten minutes. Do churches make faith inaccessible by offering children too much to wrestle with? They certainly have no need to be analyzing things all the time.

The other side of that picture is that it is going to be very easy for adults to damage children's innate spirituality, if they try and make it conform to their own images of how it ought to be. An environment with no obvious beauty, whether in housing, public buildings – or church buildings – makes it hard to believe in goodness. When feelings are dismissed as either wrong or untrustworthy, it is difficult to believe in yourself. And when belief is turned into complicated cognitive concepts, or abstract generalities like 'sin' or 'salvation', then it is harder to connect any of that with the experiences of real life. Sometimes, it seems necessary to challenge the natural optimism of a child – as, for instance, when parents have to insist that 'you shouldn't trust strangers'. No wonder that, in their study of *The Spirituality of the Child*, David Hay and Rebecca Nye entitle one of their chapters 'The Social Destruction of Spirituality', and suggest that by the time a child is ten or eleven years old, their innate spirituality has largely been crushed through what they experience at home and school, and, if they encounter it, in church as well.

How can parents repair – or avoid – some of the damage? It will be important to take a child's world seriously. What are the things that concern them? To a remarkable extent, the same things that bother adults: loneliness, friendships, promises, death. We also need to learn to listen. Grown-ups do not have an automatic right to speak, just because they are adults. The lack of either an ability or a willingness to listen on the part of parents is a major source of conflict in family life. The same when adults fail to operate holistically by insisting that everything must have a logical cause and effect. This can be a particular challenge for highly educated parents, who believe that everything can be sorted out rationally, and who have been encouraged to bury their own emotions. Children naturally operate within a wider frame of reference in which feelings, relationships, and bodies can be more important than ideas. They need to be valued, listened to, and accepted unconditionally. That is not the same thing as accepting everything they might do, but they should be shown unconditional love.

When you think about it, these are all things that adults are also longing for. In spite of that, they have not been well represented in the way that churches, as well as individual Christian parents, have traditionally sought to nurture faith in their children. Many parents have no idea what their children are doing, or how they experience the world. To help children, we need to learn to see things from new angles. In theory, that should not be difficult because growing maturity (personal and spiritual) should result in a greater willingness to question things. In practice, as most adults get older they tend to prefer the safety of what they know. But the journey of faith is never 'safe'. By understanding our own journey up to this point in time, we should be able to recognize that we sometimes place expectations on children that limit their freedom to do things their way – for example, by insisting they always sit still while we speak to them, because that was our own childhood experience. This is a particular challenge within the church, where adults might be familiar with Scripture or tradition and assume children are too – or if not, they ought to be. The words of old hymns can be mystifying (how many children have thought that the 'terrestrial ball' of 'All Hail the Power of Jesus' Name' is some kind of grand dance, rather than the world?), while the lyrics of modern worship songs can be just as meaningless (what does it mean to pray that 'we might be trees of righteousness' (as in the song 'He Gave Me Beauty for Ashes'), or for 'a hope' to be 'gone through the curtain' (as in 'Jesus Is King')?).

The whole matter of communication is one that the church ought to address for people at large, not just children. But for kids in particular, an effective message is always going to involve more than speaking. Simply 'telling' the story doesn't mean that anything has been communicated. In his research on the way messages are communicated, Albert Mehrabian discovered that words account for only 7 per cent of the total impact of a message, with vocal signals such as tone of voice accounting for 38 per cent, and non-verbal signals ('body language') a massive 55 per cent.[7] For children, learning by seeing and doing is especially important: they remember 90 per cent of what they do. Moreover, they do not separate their thinking and their feeling, any more than they divide off the 'secular' from the 'sacred'. Some readers may be wondering why a chapter on spirituality is saying so much about physical or psychological matters rather than more obviously 'spiritual' ones. But that is just the point, for children intuitively see all things as interconnected, with no one area of life disconnected from any other. We should not delude ourselves about the major shift of emphasis that will be required if we are to take all this seriously in relation to the nurture of our children. Most church programmes tend to emphasize the learning of Bible stories, or knowledge of doctrinal or historical facts about the Church. But children never automatically make the leap from story as ancient history to story as spirituality. Actually, adults don't either, which is why effective use of the Bible will always be rooted in real-life experiences. That is not to say that familiarity with Bible stories need not be an important part of the Christian journey – but imparting knowledge of the text is not the same thing as nurturing spiritual development.[8]

Support from the church

Churches love to buy ready-made packages – partly because they are available, and marketers create the impression that any church wishing to be successful needs to have this or that programme, but also because churches love to create a dependency culture in which they do things for people. Human needs, however, are too diverse for one size to fit all: both the needs and the acceptable ways of meeting them will vary from one cultural context to another. What works well in a suburban middle-class church may not be relevant in a working-class or inner-city neighbourhood, and vice versa. Ministering to people must always begin and end with being sensitive to who they are, and that also means being realistic about who we are ourselves. Whatever context we work in, though, supporting and nurturing families will not be the same as doing things for them. Jesus always worked alongside people, creating safe spaces where they could explore their own possibilities for themselves – and this is how we ought to work with families.[9] The possibilities we spell out below are neither exhaustive nor prescriptive, but are more in the nature of a rough sketch of some of the key needs experienced at different stages of family life. While we offer general indications of the sort of things that can be helpful, the details will vary in different circumstances.[10]

Becoming a parent

To be entirely responsible for the life of another person – especially one as vulnerable as a young baby – is an awesome responsibility, and new mothers in particular can be very vulnerable at this time. Knowing how to support them, however, is not always easy, and is largely going to consist of being available and ready to offer whatever help may be welcomed. Enterprising churches will not wait until a baby is born to offer such support. We recently visited a church which had a regular group 'for bumps and bundles', which provided a place where pregnant women and those with small babies could meet for mutual support and sharing. The few weeks immediately before a birth can be very special. For some women it will be their first experience of not being in full-time employment, and even if they are planning to return to work soon after the baby's arrival, it can still be disorienting. As with so many other aspects of family ministry, the help offered within a group of people with shared experiences is invaluable here, and can be a good way for people to make new friends, and to talk informally about matters of common concern. Loneliness is a major problem for many new mothers (as distinct from fathers), and anything the church can do to introduce them to others in the same situation is bound to be positive and helpful. It is amazing how many lifelong friendships are forged through contacts made in ante-natal classes. Remember also that any major life change usually raises questions of a religious or spiritual nature, and many women report that giving birth is a spiritual experience.

Can I handle it?

Not every pregnant couple wants to have a child. Despite the widespread availability of contraception, people still end up facing tough choices. A few years ago, a close friend welcomed us home from an overseas trip with the news that she was pregnant, which for her at that moment was not good news. She already had several children, and wondered whether she would bear another healthy child. She was contemplating an abortion – encouraged by her husband, who saw this as an easy way out of the situation. They were both keen Christians, and some of their church friends insisted they should not choose that option. When faced with matters that evoke intense moral debate, it will always be tempting to try and dictate answers to other people. But we can never make decisions on behalf of another family. We might think we know what we would do in the same circumstances, but unless we have ourselves been there it is impossible to be sure how we would react. If we want to be able to help a family on a longer-term basis the priority will always be to enable people to get the appropriate information, so they can decide for themselves. Equally, it is never helpful to leave people floundering, and in this particular instance we encouraged our friend not to make a decision through indecision. But it was not our business to be directive, and we were most help by being open, listening, and praying through individual aspects of her situation. It emerged that her uncertainty about pregnancy was just one expression of doubts about other relationships, particularly with her husband. Had we tried to move her in one particular direction, then regardless of which direction that was, the space for further personal growth would have been closed off. As it was, she made her own decision. She had her baby, which was probably just as well as she and her husband split up not long after and she had plenty of other guilt to work through without having an abortion to worry about as well.

'Can you "do" my baby?'

It might seem surprising for us to mention baptism, after what we said about the church's failure to turn it into effective nurture for children's faith. But parents tend to see it more as a natural rite of passage than a theological issue, and may not even know what to ask for – hence our sub-title. However ill informed such parents might seem, in terms of practical care the request to 'do' their baby should always be seen in the context of the church's mission. Otherwise the church can appear hypocritical – proclaiming its belief in the family, but unwilling to welcome parents and their children at their point of need. For people who are completely unchurched, actually breaking into the alien environment of church culture to make such a request takes such an enormous effort that this in itself can be a significant statement about their own spiritual search – especially when they could easily go to a secular celebrant for a naming ceremony. When people come knocking at the church door of their own volition, this is not the point at which to turn them away, and certainly not on the basis of a theological argument that will mean nothing to them and may only serve to reinforce the impression that church is an unreceptive and threatening place for ordinary people. Bishop John Finney correctly observes that 'Whatever the theological implications the evidence suggests that in practice parents need to be shown total welcome and also a way in which they can find out more about God in their own time.'[11]

Lay people can provide the most user-friendly line of communication with new parents at this point. If, as we suggest below, effective family ministry involves a parenting group, then members of such a group are likely to be ideally placed to share their own experiences – of faith as well as family – and to offer friendship and support in a relevant way. Many denominations have produced good resources for use with parents at this time, including videos which can be left with a family to watch and discuss at their own convenience. But in our experience, one of the most valuable things you can do with a family is to pray. Strangely, this is one of the things that western clergy (especially men) find very hard to do in anything other than a self-conscious way. Yet prayer is the natural starting-point of a spiritual journey for so many who are coming to faith today. Nurture of a family does not need to begin in the church building, and it can be some considerable time before they feel easy about attending a service. Some may never make it, for a variety of reasons.

Parents and toddlers

Toddlers need the company of other children in order to develop their own personalities. Groups are not just for the benefit of parents: with the shrinking size of the family, they also play an increasingly important role in the socialization of our children.

It is worth spelling out a few definitions here. Parent and toddler groups are exactly what the name suggests: parent and child are there together all the time. While all the adults and all the children present obviously interact with each other, no adult takes responsibility for someone else's child. It is important to differentiate between parent and toddler groups and nursery care. Though requirements vary from one country to another, under most western legislation the laws that govern the two sorts of provision are quite different, and once children are being left in the care of another person there are statutory requirements to be fulfilled. A crèche is therefore also a different entity from a parent and toddler group.

There is a widely acknowledged need for good quality child care while parents are at work, and some churches may well find they have suitable premises that could be used for this purpose. With the employment of properly qualified staff this is one area to which far-sighted churches should be giving some attention. Key considerations for churches thinking of this are quality (it needs to be an enriching experience for children) and accessibility (it should not be too expensive), as well as the various statutory requirements in relation to the premises themselves. One thing that a church could take account of, which is not always the case in regular nurseries, is the possibility of including the children of non-working mothers from traditional patriarchal families, as well as those who have chosen not to work for a period of time. Depending on local circumstances, a child-care initiative could provide an invaluable practical resource for the community, as well as being a part of the church's mission. But to do this demands a considerable time commitment and financial investment, and needs careful planning, which is why the parent and toddler group is going to be a more realistic option for most congregations. Many churches have had such groups for a long time, though some seem to restrict them only to 'mothers and toddlers'. Better to have one for both fathers and mothers, otherwise the church can find itself reinforcing the impression that neither parenting nor church is for men. The fact that growing numbers of fathers attend parent and toddler groups today is something to be welcomed. It is good news for mothers, who in this generation are able to share the parenting role instead of it being their sole responsibility. And it is good news for the children, who are being given a role model for parenting that will prepare them well for being parents themselves.

So far, so good. But as we all know, it is one thing to have a parent and toddler group meeting on church premises – quite another for it to function as an integrated part of the church's ministry. Sometimes there are good reasons why this never happens: the church does not really want it as part of its ministry. It can be hard to make space for babies in church. They are messy, smelly, and noisy. This explains why some churches accommodate them in the least attractive parts of their building, maybe surrounded by ancient posters of Jesus sitting with children who look quite different from themselves. One toddler we knew screamed every time he was taken to the church crèche. His parents eventually discovered that he was terrified of the premises, and to be left there was not a good experience. It is nothing new for small children to be problematic to the religious establishment: Jesus was born in a stable. But they are more important than that to God. And in any case, they rarely make more mess than adults: they just make a different kind of mess.

There are plenty of good resources with ideas on how to run a successful parent and toddler group from the church. But how can such a group be a genuine part of the church's mission? An important starting point will be for the organization and structure to be based on a genuine partnership formed from among those people who are part of the group. Successful and spiritually worthwhile groups are not run *by* churches *for* parents, but *in* churches *by* parents. There is a difference, and it relates to ownership and accountability. Church people like to control things, especially events attended by unchurched people. But when 'insiders' take all the responsibility, other people never feel they belong. And when people do not belong, they have no commitment. A parent and toddler group should be one of the easiest things to facilitate, but difficulties can arise in the minds of some Christians when others are given power to make decisions. This is an unproductive approach, for several reasons.

First, in terms of the church's mission, it is a fact that successful evangelization most often happens through partnership and not through confrontation.[12] Second, a young parent with no connection with church apart from a parent and toddler group is bound to have a better idea of what will suit the group than an older church member who is well meaning (and can still play a useful part), but out of touch. And third, any group in the church ought constantly to be modelling open sharing relationships. If we cannot work together showing unconditional acceptance to other people, regardless of who they are, then our relationships will not be helpful for inspiring their own family life. Showing unconditional acceptance is not the same as doing things for people: it is about helping everyone to find their full God-given human potential. A major problem in many church groups is that there is always the ulterior motive of trying to get people to 'come to church', instead of being interested in them for who they are.

To show this level of concern, some basic information about people is obviously necessary. An easy and non-threatening way to form a membership list, and to keep people in touch, is to ask people to supply their email addresses. Additional information that might be useful would be names of other family members, birthdays, phone numbers, and street addresses. But gathering such information needs sensitivity. In one parent and toddler group we know, people were reluctant to divulge their addresses.

Experience had predisposed them to see the church on the side of the establishment, and they needed to be convinced that the information obtained would not go straight to social work agencies. For them, there seemed a good chance that the church's parent and toddler group was some sort of undercover operation to pry into their lives. It took time to break through this understandable prejudice – helped by an older granny, who knew all this information anyway because she lived in the same streets as the parents, and who was able to take the initiative in a low-key way because she was trusted and known.

Expressions of faith can play a significant part in parent and toddler groups, but this also needs sensitivity. Creative play and storytelling are likely to be more useful than singing Christian choruses. The changing seasons offer particular opportunities for celebration, and the possibility of short reflection times (though slimmed-down versions of traditional services are almost never appropriate in such a setting). In the course of our research for this book, we were surprised to discover how few clergy ever visit parent and toddler groups meeting in their churches – and that unchurched parents in these groups find that just as strange as we do. Some of us have become so defensive about our faith that we seem almost embarrassed to mention it to anyone else at all, or even just to be ourselves. But when unchurched people are in a church building, they expect to encounter something to do with religion, and are surprised when they don't. That doesn't mean ministers should take things over in a pompous and paternalistic way, but conversations over coffee and toys can be a far more useful way of forging relationships than preaching any number of sermons. Small talk is no problem: most parents love to talk about their offspring. You don't need to go to every meeting of the group, or for the whole time. But a casual visit, speaking to everyone – not just church members – and taking the initiative to introduce yourself rather than waiting for formal announcements, can be a significant pastoral opportunity. If you have never tried this before, then prepare to be amazed at the number of requests for prayer you are likely to receive – and be ready to meet them!

Special events

Not every church has the resources to run regular groups. But a seasonal event might still be possible – for instance, a story-telling or mime/movement/music group for toddlers during Advent.[13] City-centre churches or those located in and around shopping malls might easily find that parents are desperate for a break from shopping, and the combination of a coffee bar with activities for the toddlers may be just what they are looking for. One church we know runs a year-round city-centre shoppers' crèche, and is not only providing a valuable service (for which parents pay), but also extending its own networks into many parts of the community.

As the statutory provision of pre-school facilities improves all the time, so the opportunities for churches will change. But one thing that is likely to increase in popularity is a story-telling session. The *Harry Potter* phenomenon seems to have taken adults by surprise. Yet children love stories, and all over the world today there is a great rediscovery of the value of story-telling, not least because we are realizing how much we have lost in the west, by comparison with those communities which have preserved their oral traditions. Parents also love stories, and as children move just beyond the toddler stage a natural extension could be into book-borrowing facilities. Some churches have their own, others work in partnership with local libraries or schools. As governments provide ever fewer educational resources, there will be increasing demand for community groups to offer such learning experiences. Parents, of course, make good story-tellers, and encouraging them in this can also enhance their experiences as parents, because all young children love to have a story read to them, and the physical closeness as a child sits on a parent's knee can play a key role in the development of a good self-image.[14] The creative and expressive arts are more popular than ever, and given the kind of premises that most churches have, it ought not to be too difficult for churches to help service this need.

Care after school

As children grow, so their needs change. Most parents are still at work after school has ended for the day, and not all schools have their own after-school groups. Here is another opportunity for voluntary organizations to support family life. The image of the latch-key kid is a familiar one, and though it can be good for older children to have some home responsibilities after school, being alone can also provide the opportunity for all kinds of negative social experimentation. In any case, most countries have legal requirements regarding the age at which children can stay at home unattended, though they are rarely enforced unless other circumstances draw a child to the attention of the authorities.

The provision of appropriate after-school care need not be a drain on church finances, as parents are prepared to pay for this kind of service. Beyond the obvious advantage of keeping children out of mischief and danger, it can also provide useful outlets for the talents of older people, many of whom would welcome contact with youngsters once their own families are grown up or have moved away. Just being available to sit down and hear a small child reading could make a big difference to someone who is a slow learner, or whose parents are too tired when they get home from work, or it is too late. An after-school group needs a clearly defined aim, and for many children the provision of a space to do school homework can make a big difference to their future prospects. Children living in cramped homes often fail to reach their full potential for that reason, while others with no access to computer facilities are also disadvantaged. The provision of Internet access in a supervised environment has obvious benefits. One group of this kind operates in a very deprived area, and kids go in after school not only to do homework, but also to learn basic domestic skills. Part of their time is spent cooking an evening meal, and then when their parents collect them after work (mostly lone mothers in this case), parents and children eat their meal together in the church, before going home. That is a really valuable contribution to family stability, providing practical support in the form of food and skills training, all of which helps parents and children feel worthwhile and valued – while just sitting at a table together creates a space for conversation that otherwise might not exist in many of their homes. In addition, all this is identifying the church as a good place to be, and thereby making a contribution to the church's ongoing missionary task in that community.

Such schemes will require some commitment from a church, but it is easy to start in a small way. The venture just described was the brainchild of a woman in her fifties who saw a need and got it off the ground by investing her own time, and some of her own money. As in all other aspects of our work with children, the child's safety must be a key concern, not just from accidents (the premises need to be safe and secure) but also from adults who might misuse their position of trust. Even in countries where there is no statutory requirement for it, all workers should be thoroughly vetted and clearly understand the boundaries of appropriate physical contact with children, and everything that happens must be in the open and above suspicion.

Parenting groups

When things go wrong, the most we can do is to help minimize the damage. Far better therefore to recognize that parents need support all the time: no matter how much experience they might have, they are always travelling a new road. No two children are the same, not even in the same family, and with each one there are new lessons to be learned. At such times, it is of enormous value to be part of a group, in which parents can learn from other parents as they share their stories of life in the family. The more diverse the experiences in the group, the greater the learning is likely to be.

We co-ordinated such a group for several years, meeting once a month on Friday evenings. Several church parents were struggling to reconcile what happened in their homes with what they imagined a 'Christian family' should be. Some had spouses who were not Christians, which seemed to be an additional factor creating tensions within the home, but there were also some lone parents, and others in second or subsequent marriages who had parental responsibilities towards children living separately from them. Just about everybody brought a huge burden of guilt – not the ideal basis on which to establish any sort of group, but almost inevitable in one related to the family, because most parents seem to be more aware of their failures than their successes.

A well-meaning individual generously offered to buy an extensive set of videos and study books produced by a Christian organization specializing in family matters. This had no appeal for us. Parenting is not a set of techniques that can be learned, but depends on a particular human identity. So we invited people to come along just to meet others with similar concerns to themselves, to socialize and to talk. Some other church leaders regarded this as a very weak agenda, but it appealed to those with the questions, and at the first meeting just under twenty people turned up. Apart from the lone parents, everyone came with a partner, including those spouses who did not attend church. We started with drinks and snacks, and then explained how we wanted the group to set its own agenda. But first it was important for us to share our own story of family and home. Church leaders are not good at revealing their own weaknesses, but people will never be open with us if we are not prepared to be honest with them. We just described our own family, and spoke candidly about our strengths and weaknesses as we saw them. We mentioned the things that had not worked, as well as those that had. We also spoke about our faith, and of the struggles we had when our second child unexpectedly died – of how we were angry and impatient with the church, and of how, even years later, we were still puzzled and frustrated by the experience.

After that, each person said as much or as little as they wished. One thing struck us right away: the men especially were saying things that their partners had never heard them say previously! Some men seem unable to speak openly on a one-to-one basis with their partners, but are happy to discuss quite intimate details in front of a group, even one which includes their spouse. In no time at all the group had an extensive agenda of shared concerns. We had been wiser than we knew in declining to use a pre-packaged programme that offered all the 'right' answers – because none of these people were asking the 'right' questions!

Some matters required the insight of experts – and for those, we invited knowledgeable people to meet with us (but only with the agreement of the whole group as to who should be invited). At other times, we enlisted the help of older people whose children had grown up, and learned from their experience. But mostly we tackled things by sharing our own respective stories.

What do people get out of groups like this? First of all, a chance to escape from the home and immediate demands of children. It's surprising how many parents literally never get the chance to go anywhere together. The cost of going out can be one reason; lack of reliable babysitting can be another. Parenting groups are not costly (though don't fall into the trap of providing everything for people: that only devalues them); and church should be a good place to recruit babysitters. The chance to make new friends is more significant in the lives of parents than we sometimes appreciate. Encouragement is another important benefit: as people hear about the struggles of others, they discover that they are not alone, and it is not true that they are the worst parents in the world. There is the further realization that we all have something to share. Whatever our experience, it will be valuable to someone else. Christians can be surprised to find that non-Christians make very good parents, and they might actually learn from them. And non-Christians can be encouraged by the realization that church people have just as many struggles with families (and faith) as they have. Women who have taken time out of work for a few years to raise children are often afflicted by the 'I'm only a housewife' syndrome, and the discovery that their insights can enrich the lives of others gives a boost to their self-confidence. Mutual sharing helps us all to see that we are worth something, and that being a parent is a role of great value. Parenting groups are also the place where people might start to come to terms with their own childhood. Group leaders need to be ready for this to happen, as it can take a distressing, even violent form. As adults talk about their children, they regard their own childhood in a new light, maybe understanding for the first time the reasons for lost opportunities and broken relationships. When this happens, listening (as opposed to speaking) becomes even more important than usual.

Knowing how to include a faith dimension can be a problem

for some church groups, where there can often be no concept of how to run any meeting unless it begins with a hymn and a prayer, and probably a Bible reading. If you want to kill a parenting group stone dead, then that is the way to do it. On the other hand, we are strongly of the view that faith should play a part. The precise form this takes will depend on local culture, and the personal disposition of group members and leaders. Different things will apply in different places, and it would be wrong for us to be prescriptive. But anything involving movement has enormous potential not only for fun, but also for personal healing in such groups. Things like parachute games can be a great way to cement relationships. On more than one occasion, and in different countries, when we have used circle dancing focused on some kind of reflective theme people who have been the victims of sexual abuse or violence have found it addressing their personal needs in ways that other kinds of therapy seem to by-pass. Thinking of fun, we have also used mask-making in groups like this – dividing into pairs and making a plaster mask on one another's faces, then talking about the experience afterwards. This is another valuable tool for coming to terms with our own identity, and the way we relate to others. Some people describe the experience as like being born, others talk of being released, cleansed, or totally transformed. One woman became enraged by it, only to come back a day later and begin to address unfinished business relating to the death of her father. But we cannot emphasize too strongly the necessity for group leaders who plan to experiment with techniques as powerful as dance or mask-making to work through the possible consequences for themselves and others in advance of using them with a group.[15]

Though we would be unlikely to introduce formal prayer into a parenting group, there is great value in making space for this possibility. You might easily find that unchurched people are more receptive than church members, especially if you create spaces for non-verbal forms of prayer. Parenting groups can also play an important part in the church's mission. A friend of ours began a group with eight couples, with the idea that after some time they in turn would network with other couples and be available to run groups themselves. These groups had a snowball effect and proved so popular they found themselves invited by the local school board to run them in the school as well as the church.

Some churches run groups for parents who are divorced, and working through how to be good parents when children live with former spouses. Others have groups for those struggling with the demands of being an acceptable parent in a blended family, or for lone parents, victims of abuse, families in conflict with the law – or for men seeking a new identity. Variations on the theme are endless. Sometimes it makes good sense for just one group to include people from many different parenting situations, but quite often – either through prejudice or because of the need for specialist help or just because of sheer numbers – separate provision makes more sense. The crucial thing is to be flexible. Groups should be in a continual state of change anyway, because hopefully the needs and concerns of the people in them will change. And eventually, all groups will need to reconfigure themselves.

In any group situation, it is important for facilitators to remember that they are just that: they are not counsellors. They need to be open and sensitive to other people, and know where to find specialist help for particular individuals as and when that may be needed. Training for group facilitators is obviously important, and can be done very effectively not by hand-picking people who seem to be natural leaders, but by offering it to everyone. A course in reflective listening can be particularly useful, and the skills picked up during such training might actually be the very thing many people are lacking in their own family relationships. The more people who have these skills, the more effective the group will be anyway.

Some Christians seem to imagine that just being a Christian empowers people to handle every conceivable eventuality in life. But parenting skills need to be learned. Few of us are naturally well equipped, and we generally pass on the sort of parenting we have received. Most people want to be good parents. No one plans to make mistakes. But stresses along the way often mean that is what happens. It can be difficult to change, even if we want to. Parenting groups will not prevent all the mistakes, but they will enable people to change some things, and above all they create a safe space for parents to admit they need help – and to find it. That is probably the single most valuable contribution that any church can make to family support.

Other possibilities

Parents who have divorced face particular difficulties, especially fathers, who are usually the ones who end up living separately from their children. With the best will in the world, it is not easy for fathers in that situation to keep up with their children and to continue being good fathers. Western society has simply not thought through this issue. While court judgements restricting access by fathers to their children are often made for good reasons, especially when violence and abuse have been involved, to imagine that adequate fathering can take place in just a few hours at weekends flies in the face of all the facts. Around 40 per cent of all divorced fathers just give up on it, and no more than about one in six of fathers who are entitled to regular access actually take up the option. Even those who stick with their kids easily become a caricature, indiscriminately spending money to give them treats that make it even more difficult for the mother, who is responsible for the day-to-day parenting. Working out how to help absent parents to be real parents who offer constant advice and discipline is not easy. Some churches have begun to explore this area, through providing a safe neutral territory on which fathers can meet their children. Particularly in cases where abuse has been an issue, there may be a legal requirement for supervised access. That is a good start, but this can be progressed further by the development of fatherhood groups, at which fathers and their children meet with facilitators and do things as varied as sports or trips to the cinema or countryside. Doing things in a group is itself a good experience in learning relational skills, and can make a difference to other social problems afflicting the lives of lone parents, such as unemployment, alcoholism and drug addiction.

There is a similar need for safe places in which families that have suffered abuse can learn to be together again. Public agencies have limited resources for such provision, but a warm, comfortable space where families can sit and play, as well as cook a meal together, can make a major contribution to family healing. Sitting and talking at such a time can be very difficult: doing things together can start the process of a return to normal relationships. This is something that would need to be done in collaboration with statutory social work agencies, but they are generally very welcoming to approaches from churches along these lines.

Many parents are concerned about how to protect their children from sexual abuse. Several organizations offer useful material in this area, though in the Christian sphere there is nothing to touch the courses developed through the innovative work of the Revd Marie M. Fortune at the Center for the Prevention of Sexual and Domestic Violence in Seattle. It was first published in 1989, but her course for 9–12 year olds, packaged and intended to be used in the same way as traditional holiday club materials, is still well out in front of the field (whether religious or secular) and could be offered with great advantage.[16] There is an opportunity here for churches with vision and imagination to provide a resource that would receive strong support from many other non-church organizations, and which could provide yet another point of bridge-building into the wider community.

Problems over drug abuse and experimentation should also feature on the church's agenda, because part of our responsibility to children is to ensure that – without causing them undue fear – they are well informed and know how to handle the kind of difficult situations which some will meet even in primary school. Partnerships with schools could easily be the way to work in this area: many schools have insufficient resources to handle all the problems, while many teachers themselves have no idea what to say. The local situation will determine the way forward, but Christians certainly have a contribution to make. Here, as elsewhere in ministry with families, prevention is better than cure. In most pastoral situations, churches tend to be reactive, waiting for a crisis to occur and then trying to pick up the pieces. We are often quite good at doing this, but to be of maximum usefulness both to our own members and to the wider community (of which Christians are also a part), we will need to give much higher priority to taking initiatives that will sustain and support family life before real problems arise.

8 The family and the church

All families encounter stresses and strains as they wrestle with the everyday realities of living harmoniously with other people. Sometimes things go wrong, and disaster ensues. Families crumble, individuals are deeply hurt – and this is often the point at which church leaders become involved. But those of us who work in ministry with families need to appreciate that the provision of counselling in times of crisis – though essential – will not necessarily be the most effective way to help those families who are already in the church, or to reach out to those who as yet are not. More than anything else, what families will value is an ongoing atmosphere of support that can engender the positive development of wholesome relationships in the home, and help to integrate faith with the rest of life. When Christians say, 'We believe in the family', what they often mean is that they are committed to preserving relationships that have fallen on hard times, and keeping families together regardless of the consequences. It is our opinion that if more energy was invested in the creation of positive attitudes towards relationships, we would create a more secure emotional future for ourselves and our children, as well as helping people avoid some of the more obvious causes of breakdown in family life. If the church does not take this need seriously, it can actually create dysfunction for those families associated with it. Before we can minister with integrity to families in times of crisis, we have to create churches that are themselves family-friendly.

A place for children

The one thing that families need more than anything else is support. Yet people wrestling with changing family circumstances can find it hard to identify the church as an obvious source of such support. Many churches feel they have done all they can just so long as there are networks of pastoral care into which people with difficulties can be integrated. Personal relationships are important, but being a family-oriented church requires much more, and involves reappraisal of the actual structures of the church so as to take account of the needs of families. Though families – and churches – are more than children, they are likely to be fairly central in this concern. Churches sometimes see a conflict between this and being available to single people, but this is a false dichotomy created by a general lack of understanding among Christians of the nature of singleness in today's world. Churches still generally operate with a view of the single life that derives from the nineteenth century, if not earlier, limiting its definition to people without intimate relationships. But as we indicated in chapter 2, this no longer matches the reality. There is undoubtedly a major challenge for the church here, which will require some far-reaching reflection on the nature of sexuality in particular in order to connect with the concerns of the one age group that is most committed to a diversity of single lifestyles (25–35). But it is a false dichotomy to contrast the needs of single people overall with the concerns of families. Very large numbers of single people have children, and in the absence of a second full-time parent the church can be a helpful social environment. Many of those churches that are growing do so because of what they offer to parents of all types who are looking to provide their children with values as well as networks of friends in the wider community. If the needs of families and the needs of singles conflict with one another in a particular congregation, that almost certainly means that the single people there are not at all representative of the wider population. That is an invitation to create specialist ministries that will connect effectively with different types of single people. Being pro-singles does not entail being anti-family, or vice versa. The recognition that, in ministry as in everything else, one size does not fit all, is an obvious corollary to our recommendation that special groups can help parents or teenagers.

Sunday services are the one thing that all churches most obviously do. So how does the average church shape up in relation to such people? Here is a typical scenario – like others, it is a real-life story drawn from our own experience. Donald (not his

real name) was in his mid-thirties, and father to two young
children. He and his wife both had demanding full-time jobs,
so weekends were their main opportunity for nurturing family
relationships. Neither of them were Christians, but they recognized the contribution that spiritual and moral values could
make to family wellbeing. Moving to a new house in a medium-
sized village provided the opportunity to explore what the
church had to offer, and so one Sunday morning Donald, along
with his family, ventured into what for him was somewhat
threatening and alien territory. But he knew the Christians in this
particular parish were saying rather loudly that they believed in
the family, and since he could identify with that he thought it
might be worth seeing what they had to offer. In spite of his
own positive predisposition, and his impression that the church
shared his concerns for the family, it was not a good experience.
Though the church said, 'We believe in the family' he and his
wife found its structures operated in ways that they felt undermined their priorities for the weekend. Quality time for them
meant being physically present with their children, and it only
dawned on him that the church had a different agenda when his
two-year-old was taken off into the crèche by a stranger whom
he had never met before. Then his six-year-old was shunted into
a different children's group, again to be placed in the care of
strangers. While Donald created a mental checklist of all the
potential dangers that could confront his children in such circumstances, his wife was cornered by other unknown, if well-
meaning people who tried to sign her up for groups and clubs
that, they assured her, were especially – and exclusively – for
women. Within a matter of minutes of getting into the church,
Donald was wondering why he was there. For him the starting
point of good relationships was actually being with his family –
and that was evidently the one thing he could not do in church.
It was hard enough being apart from them all week, without
volunteering for it on Sunday mornings. In conversation later,
his wife confided that she felt equally out of place. As a successful
manager, she thought she could perhaps make some useful contribution to a voluntary organization like the church – especially
if it empowered her as a parent. The other women who spoke
to her had identified plenty of things she could do – but they

were all about coffee rotas, flower calendars, and other activities that just did not match who she was, and the talents she thought she could offer. Sadly, they decided together that, if they were to be serious about their family life, going to church was one thing they could do without. That experience is not far-fetched or unusual, but is being repeated in western churches of all denominations every Sunday in the year.

At the bottom of this is a clash of cultures. Traditionally, churches have invested heavily in the provision of special facilities for children, with crèches, Sunday Schools, and so on. A couple of generations ago, that matched the needs of families: they had spent the entire week in one another's presence, and attendance at a church service with good child-care facilities was one chance for parents to relax without worrying about their kids. Today, the situation is quite different. Apart from early morning and bedtime, many parents never see their kids midweek, and the last thing they want or need is to spend yet more time separated from their partners and children at weekends. Those who are bothered about giving their children some sense of values and spirituality (and there are still plenty) will not thrive in the individualistic atmosphere that pervades many churches. They will instead seek out experiences that offer quality time with their children, and that facilitate the building of community rather than imposing more of the fragmentation that is all-pervasive in the rest of life. To be serious about family ministries, churches may need to change some of their structures. For if a church is not family-friendly, then why should anyone expect families to come?

A family-friendly service is going to be a child-friendly service, but it will not be a children's service. In the 1960s and 1970s many British churches experimented with what they generally called 'family worship'. More often than not, what they did on such occasions was not family worship at all: it was children's worship, at which adults happened to be present. It is not hard to find churches that still operate that way. Everything is reduced to its lowest common denominator, which seems to be the level of a three-year-old – or, more often, what well-intentioned but out-of-touch adults imagine would appeal to a toddler – and adults and older children end up feeling uncomfortable by being invited to do childish things. In addition, such 'family services' are quite often used to endorse the image of the industrial nuclear family as the ideal way of being a 'Christian' family, which only serves to reinforce the isolation of single people (whether parents or not) as well as childless couples.[1]

Creating community

People need other people. To be truly human, we need to belong somewhere, to be accepted and affirmed by others in relationships of openness and unconditional love. At one time, the family provided that, but this is no longer universally the case. A major reason why many younger people find relationships difficult is that they have no models to aspire to. The fragmentation of relationships at all levels highlights this, and if somebody could package a community in which people of different dispositions and outlooks interact harmoniously, working through their differences in a spirit of mutual respect and humility, they could make a fortune. Arguably, the single most valuable thing the church can do for families today is to model life in that sort of community. Openness, acceptance, the creation of safe spaces where we can be ourselves, sharing our weaknesses as well as our strengths – these are all hallmarks of the kingdom of God. Relationships are the all-important thing for families today, and Christians must face the challenge of moving on from merely talking about them, to actually demonstrating them. People are searching for new ways to belong, and when the church models good practice in relationships it not only encourages and empowers those families it already knows, but will increasingly find itself fulfilling the evangelistic mandate to share the good news more widely through the quality of human love (John 13:34–5). When you think about it, the church is just about the only place left in western society where people of all generations can naturally meet and work out what a truly intergenerational community might look like.

Those churches that surround themselves with strong boundaries of belief and only accept people once they have signed up to some doctrinal statement will find it difficult to create this kind of open, inclusive community. That sort of exclusivity is not only bad mission strategy, it is also poor theology. The last two or three centuries have seen the balance between beliefs and experience disturbed in such a way that dogma has been elevated at the expense of discipleship. This is to get things the wrong way round. Theology in its most pristine form starts not with rational reflection, but with discipleship. We are called to follow Jesus, and 'theology' is what emerges as we reflect on the meaning of the experience. The earliest disciples followed (and were, therefore, 'real' disciples) long before they had any 'beliefs' about Christology, salvation, the sacraments, or indeed any of the other things we imagine to be so central today (Mark 1:16–20).[2] Jesus consistently invited people to journey with him first, and to reflect on the meaning of faith in the process of journeying. Belonging really did precede believing. When we ignore that, it is virtually impossible for the church to be a gospel community.

Worship

We have both argued in other books that worship is central to the church's life and witness, and what is true of mission is no less true when it comes to nurturing families.[3] Experiences of authentic worship will both contain and communicate the whole gospel for today's families. But what do we mean by worship? A phrase we have often used in workshops is that worship is 'all that we are, responding to all that God is'. When we consider 'all that we are', we can begin to see some ways in which our worship might address the needs of families. It can be a very useful exercise to take that phrase and invite a congregation to describe who they think they are (which could be quite different from the opinions of clergy and other leaders). Then ask how what you do in worship reflects the spiritual concerns of that varied group of people. Repeat the exercise and extend the list by reflecting on the people you want to reach in the wider community, and their needs. And keep doing it, because corporate worship easily comes to reflect the concerns of only a small group of people. By acknowledging the richness of the human community, and actively creating a space for everyone, we can make a major contribution to the development of an experiential model for family life: the ability to love and be loved, in a warm, accepting, and caring community of women, men, and children.

One group which did that discovered that even in their prayers they were reflecting a very narrow band of human experience. Whenever families were mentioned, they seemed to be ideal stereotypes, with children and parents who were too good to be true. And while the poor and destitute of far-flung corners of the world were regularly prayed for, those being abused in their own community were mostly ignored. Furthermore, it emerged that specific teaching on relationships had not featured in any sermon series for years, and on those rare occasions when families had been mentioned there had been no serious engagement with the stories of dysfunctional Bible families and the struggle to find faith in situations of pain and personal alienation. Instead of presenting only disinfected and idealized images of the 'Christian family', we should be helping people to engage in a Christian way with the families they already have. There is a remarkable absence of positive teaching on the matters that bother people the most: things like domestic violence and sexual abuse, or even more straightforward matters such as the pressures of parenting and of forming new relationships in the context of blended families. If our churches are at all representative of the wider population (and that, in many cases, will be a very big 'if'), there will be people in our congregations who struggle with these things, but because of the lack of Christian teaching on them are forced to look elsewhere for wisdom and guidance. Even when such topics are addressed, they are sometimes mentioned only to condemn lifestyles that preachers deem unacceptable. For people already struggling with a lack of self-esteem, that is not going to be good news. In the big theological picture, it is true to say that sin is always involved in situations of dysfunction and breakdown. But sin is not always something that people do. It is often something that people suffer: they are sinned against.[4] To people like this, the gospel does not say, 'You are responsible', but 'You can become responsible for your life – with Christ's help you can find healing and empowerment for a new future'. Jesus met with people in exactly these circumstances, and consistently lifted them up in this way, affirming them as people of great value. By encouraging positive attitudes toward relationships, we can help to create a more secure emotional future for both parents and children, as well as assisting people to avoid some of the more obvious causes of breakdown in family life. Conversely, when the church fails to take this need seriously, it can actually create dysfunction for those families associated with it, including increasingly members of its own full-time staff.

Family-friendly churches will also reflect on the sort of language they use. Three aspects are worth thinking about. First of all, there are words describing the church itself. Some churches call themselves a family, maybe qualifying it as 'the family of God'. This is not good practice in today's context. For one thing, calling the church a 'family' has no roots within the historic Christian tradition. More importantly, perhaps, relationships in a community like the church have different constraints than in a family. There are different boundaries for physical intimacy, between both adults and children: parents and children can touch one another in ways that would be improper between children and other adults. Family-style names (honorary 'uncles' or 'aunts') may be traditional in some church circles, but they are inappropriate for today's families, where abusers are often a child's own uncles and aunts. In this context, a safer environment is created when children are on first-name terms with adults, in which the language identifies the boundaries. It may be regrettable that it is necessary to safeguard children in this way even in the church, but that is the reality. The church is not a family: it is a community. Words for people are also important. The use of male-dominated language ('men', 'mankind', and so on) is now widely discouraged in the culture at large. This is more than mere political correctness: the way we use language has changed, and when people hear the word 'men' today they connect it with males – so if you are a woman and the church only talks about 'men', why would you want to be a Christian? Hymns regularly offend at this point, and newer 'worship songs' are sometimes worse than older ones. If hymns are to be spiritually uplifting, everyone needs to find themselves in there – especially those who have already been marginalized or excluded from the life of the community in other ways. The same is true of the words we use for God. Since Christians have always affirmed that God is beyond sex and gender, and the Bible itself uses a mixture of both male and female imagery for God, it is surprising how much heated debate this can generate.[5] But in terms of supporting families, using exclusively male language for God is unhelpful. It reinforces unchristian patriarchal attitudes, and can actually be a stumbling block for people sexually abused by their fathers, for whom the notion that God is a father (even a very perfect one) makes no sense at all, and is a distortion of a proper Christian understanding of who God is.

Times and places

Traditional liturgies describe worship as being 'for all people, at all times and in all places'. The reality can be rather different: it is accessible only to some of the people, at very limited times and in sometimes inhospitable places. Sunday services at traditional times are becoming increasingly problematic even for those people who belong to the church, never mind those whom we might be wishing to reach. All families develop their own habits, especially at weekends when many have more opportunity to design their own schedules. Different stages of family life make different demands, and the timetable that suits parents of small children is unlikely to match the lifestyles of teenagers. No one time will suit everyone, which is why churches with multiple times of meeting have an advantage over those which gather only once on a Sunday. Individual congregations should consider the needs of those whom they want to reach. Parents of small children might well find early morning fits in with their feeding and sleeping patterns better than mid-morning (by 11 a.m. they might already have been active for five or six hours). Families with older kids might find that late afternoon suits them, after they have taken a long lie-in, done the shopping, and visited friends or grandparents. For others, an opportunity to worship in the evening might be more useful, especially those who work regularly on Sundays. Actually, the only people for whom traditional times like 10.30 or 11 a.m. are really appropriate may be traditional churchgoing families, who have grown accustomed to doing things at that time. It may be that some – for example,

parents who are divorced or separated and only get to see their
kids on Sundays – will never make it on Sunday, but could
connect with church midweek.

The changing shape of the family, and the growth in weekend
leisure activities – not to mention the need for many to do their
shopping then – are all key reasons why churches must go back
to basics in this way if they are to maximize opportunities to
work with all sections of the community. Some Christians react
very negatively to this sort of cultural change, regretting the
passing of the traditional 'Sabbath' and even trying to turn
the clock back. Right now, at the time of writing, we know one
family which prohibits its children from watching TV on Sunday,
and in other ways tries to recreate a Victorian Sunday. Churches
with that sort of mentality will struggle to connect with anyone
in the real world, whatever their family type may be. Today's
families are not like that, and what is required is more lateral
thinking to connect with the way we live now. At an earlier stage
of our lives we were involved in a Chinese church. The church
members were a mixture of students and workers in restaurants,
concerned about reaching out to non-Christian families, as well
as ministering to their own. Restaurant workers in particular got
to bed very late on Saturday nights, and there was no point
trying to have a Sunday morning service: no one would come.
But they did have a class for children at that time, at which the
students taught Chinese language and culture. Then in mid-
afternoon the parents of these children would join them and all
ages would have a time of corporate worship. Next would be a
community meal, which could take them through to 6 or 6.30
p.m., following which the young people would play table tennis
(this being a game with particular appeal to Chinese people), or
just sit around and chat and play music, while the adults would
spend time in groups talking about faith, or discussing other
matters of mutual concern. That church was well ahead of its
time, because what we describe took place over thirty years ago!
While the details will obviously differ from one place to another,
it may well be the sort of pattern that will suit ministry with
today's families. Instead of just holding services, a church like
that is intentionally creating community. The atmosphere of such
a gathering creates a different dynamic for worship, and

whenever food is involved there is always a place for everyone to be fully included in what is going on, regardless of their age or marital status. Increasingly, growing churches in many countries are moving towards this kind of pattern of worship and community building.[6] Not only does it match contemporary lifestyles, but it also mirrors the way the earliest Christian communities met, and can offer an important sign of the kingdom for today's world, calling people to follow Jesus as well as creating churches that will facilitate spiritual growth in families of many different shapes and structures.[7]

Teenagers and church

The process of spiritual growth outlined in a previous chapter assumes that 'searching faith' will be just that, and further implies that doubt and faith are probably two sides of the same coin. So we need not be surprised when young people question the value of the church: mature individuals always have done. But the situation today is of a different order altogether. Throughout the western world, the children of Christian parents are leaving the church at ever younger ages, and rarely return. The reasons for this are complex, but there is no question that if kids do not feel they belong, then they will not stay. Why should they? Kim Philby was one of the most damaging double-agents in the British intelligence service during the twentieth century. Years after selling his country's secrets, and defecting to live in the old Soviet Union, he was asked why he had done it. His answer was simple, yet revealing: 'I never really felt I belonged in England'. Those churches which as a matter of policy cannot accept children as real members, or exclude them from selected aspects of church life, face a real challenge here, for how can you with integrity say that they are part of the faith community if the rules exclude them? The majority of children, though, never have any meaningful contact with the church at all. Church is regularly dismissed as boring or irrelevant, though today's young people are, if anything, more spiritually concerned than ever. Increasing numbers of them are turning to Wicca and other nature-based spiritualities, especially girls. So what is their problem with the church? Several factors immediately suggest themselves:

Inaccessibility. The times and places of meeting do not make it easy for even those who are committed to connect with the church. Sunday is the only day some get to see one or both of their parents, while many more will be occupied with sports activities, homework, duties in the home, or (for older teenagers) part-time work or just staying in bed. If the times of traditional church operate in a different world from their parents, then for teenagers they might as well be from another galaxy. The rhythms of a young person's life today are completely different from the way most churches organize things.

Irrelevance. Church seems to have little understanding or awareness of today's cultures and lifestyles, in matters ranging from dress to sexual behaviour. It appears to proceed on the assumption that nothing has changed, whereas the reality is that just about everything has changed since the parents of today's teens were teenagers themselves. Those young people who start off connecting with the church, and then leave it, do so not out of ignorance (as church leaders tend to think) but based on their experience: they know what it is about, and it has no meaning for them. They are not necessarily against it in any significant way: it simply does not touch their lives in any relevant sense.

Lack of concern. By this, we mean that the church seems not to be bothered about anything or anyone outside its own limited circles. Teenagers are increasingly concerned about their future – whether they will have one, or whether older generations will destroy the world as we know it before they have a chance to grow up. Many teenagers know others who have committed suicide, or harmed themselves in some other way, or who are victims of fragmented families. To them, a church that is pre-occupied with its own internal concerns – money, buildings, issues of power and control – is not perceived as a helpful organization. Dietrich Bonhoeffer wrote from prison that 'the church is the church only when it exists for others'.[8] Many young people would agree with him – and would connect with that kind of church.

No real community. Teenagers need support. They need to be accepted in the church and taken seriously by other adults. In this respect, they are no different from any other age group, except that in adolescence the need to belong and be accepted and affirmed in one's new, emerging adult personality is much stronger than it is at almost any other time of life. The more fragmentation there is in family life, the more urgent this need becomes. New religious movements thrive because they address these issues by offering friendship and acceptance. Young people will connect with the church when they find acceptance, friendship, and support. This is far more important than trendy services or any of the other gimmicks that older Christians sometimes imagine to be necessary.

Too 'educational'. Church can be just like school, especially in the kind of activities that are offered to young people. This goes back to what was said earlier, about a preference for dogma over discipleship. Some (a diminishing minority) like a bookish approach, but this is not generally a characteristic of today's post-modern culture, in which even young people are more likely to be looking for the healing of their emotions than the enlightenment of their minds.

A sense of belonging can be encouraged in many different ways, some of them obvious. For example, if teenagers never hear people like them referred to in the prayers in church services, they can be forgiven for supposing they do not belong. Yet this happens only infrequently. If people of their own age never take part in the service, then it should not surprise us if they fail to attend. On the other hand, when they are recognized and their skills are used, they will be there. Teenagers can do many things very effectively. Some things they can do better than adults, such as operating the PA system, or providing the regular musical accompaniment, or creating computer visuals to illustrate the liturgy. They can also have a relevant input into the leadership structures of the church. It can be depressing to hear of church committees searching for young people to join them, and defining 'young' as people in their late twenties or thirties – or older. Of course, young people are not necessarily going to be available to attend meetings at the times that suit older people – and they will certainly be unlikely to make church committees a major priority at this stage in their life. But churches that do not share decision-making and responsibility with young people need not be surprised if they lose them. Teenagers will be in church when they know they are needed.

Parents are not the only ones who can be helped by being part of a support group. If anything, the company of peers is even more important for teenagers than it is for their parents. But teenage is not just one single state of being. In time, the teenage years are relatively short, and only last from thirteen to nineteen. But they span a colossal range of human development, both physical and personal. Most sixteen-year-olds feel they have little in common with fourteen-year-olds, while someone of nineteen is entirely different from a thirteen-year-old. They need to have the opportunity to be with others of the same age and not be pressurized by the questions of those who are either younger or older teenagers. Then there is the phenomenon of so-called 'tweenagers' – too old to be children, but not yet teens. To accommodate this, the most effective youth groups will be changing all the time, as different ages and stages predominate in the life of a particular congregation. But there are some general considerations that apply at all stages of teenage.

As with any other kind of support group, the choice of leaders is crucial. It is always important to have more than one leader, including both women and men. Churches sometimes choose youth leaders because they are interested in music, but people skills are far more important. The way leaders relate to each other will provide an important role model for teenagers, and in some circumstances one or two young couples can be ideal. Some of the very best youth groups we know are run by people like this. On the other hand, so are some of the worst. Churches can impose unfair responsibilities on couples who are themselves at a formative stage in their own relationships, and that is counter-productive both for the group and the couple. In addition, many of the people who fall into this category are pursuing demanding careers, and need to maximize their own opportunities for rest and relaxation. Couples without children also have the freedom to make spontaneous decisions about how they will spend their leisure, and doing so does not always work to the advantage of teenagers with whom they may be involved. When a youth group is focused around the leaders' own lifestyles, then teenagers (who of course can be notoriously fickle themselves) will feel let down. In such demanding work, flexibility needs to be combined with a serious level of commitment. It is a time-consuming business to be available to teenagers, and those who take on such work need to be prepared for that. In the end, though, commitment is far more important than age. Some of the best youth groups are run by people well past mid-life, though if older people get involved it is important that they be themselves, and do not try and use a youth group as a way of hanging onto the last vestiges of their own youth. There is nothing worse than a group for teenagers run by fifty-year-olds trying to be trendy. Incidentally, always remember that young people can minister to young people. One church we know has a system that encourages teenagers to pair up with someone else who is only one or (at most) two years older than themselves. They befriend one another, go places together, learn new skills together – and encourage each other in faith and growing up, as they share what they are learning.

We have already highlighted the importance of church not becoming an extension of formal education. In the ideal scenario, perhaps we should aim to offer different kinds of activity within each of the adolescent age bands we have identified: one group for fun and friendship, and another for learning and discipleship. School does, however, occupy a large chunk of a teenager's life, and this can easily develop into a friction point between church and home. Responsible parents will not appreciate it when the church always holds youth events late on Sunday evenings, thereby making it more difficult for teenagers to get up in good time for school the next day. But with an imaginative approach, the integration of school work with recreation can provide useful opportunities for the church to support teenagers. Many American and Australian churches (and some British para-church organizations) run special revision camps for their young people, in the school holiday immediately preceding the main annual examinations. The kids take their work to camp, and have organized times to do exam preparation, backed up with skilled assistance from Christians with specialist knowledge of particular subjects. Having a structure helps them get more work done than if they were at home by themselves (and overcomes the loneliness of study), while it also provides space for play and relaxation as well as faith building. The kids like it, their parents are willing to pay for it, and older generations of church members find a useful outlet for their talents. In the process, teenagers are exploring at first hand a collaborative model of working that can only be enormously beneficial to them. The residential model may not work everywhere, but the needs of teenagers for space to do their school homework is just as pressing as the needs of younger children.

The ideas shared here merely scratch the surface of what is possible. Underlying them all, however, is one essential conviction. Our churches have rich resources which, with imagination and vision, can be used to empower and renew the family. Buildings are part of that resource, just as a home is an important asset for a family. But people are the most valuable resource of all. The one thing we all have in common, at whatever stage of life and family experience we may find ourselves, is our humanity. In his book *Living the Faith Community*, John Westerhoff remarks that 'we commonly think of Christian life from an individualistic or, at best, an organizational perspective, but rarely from a communal perspective.'[9] In that respect, we share the weakness of our culture, where individualism and rationalization have taken over, and the result is a lot of lonely and battered people. It is no wonder that families are struggling to be communities, because we are presenting them with so few viable models. When the church displays new ways of living and relating to one another in an inclusive community that spans all generations and has space for all kinds of people, that may be the most valuable contribution we can make to the revitalization of the family in our generation.

9 Families in times of crisis

Family crisis occurs for many different reasons: illness, death, divorce, disability, accidents, addiction. The list is endless, and to cover all such eventualities would need another book to itself. But some types of crisis arise out of the dynamic of family life itself, as one person tries to manipulate relationships in the home for their own advantage. Violent abuse within the family is a major problem, and even the smallest church is likely to have people who have suffered this way or who will do so at some stage of their life. It can create real problems for the church, especially when it involves Christians. Part of the difficulty is that church structures offer insufficient open spaces within which people can easily share their experiences with others. That tends to create a conspiracy of silence, so that by the time an issue relating to domestic violence surfaces in the church it is likely to have reached serious proportions. It is therefore especially important that church leaders know in advance how they will respond, and have procedures in place to offer immediate help in such circumstances. That includes knowledge of the legal requirements and appropriate local contacts, as well as some basic insight into the situation itself. Prompt action can be essential, and it only makes things worse if something happens and no one knows what to do.

Working in partnership

Problems in this area can only be tackled by the church in partnership with other agencies, particularly when illegal or criminal activity is involved. The specific agencies vary from one country to another, and churches that are serious about family wellbeing will be in contact with them in advance of actual need. Christians often imagine that secular agencies are not interested in working with religious groups, but our experience shows the exact opposite. Resources are always insufficient to handle family problems satisfactorily, and the more people who are prepared to make a contribution, the better. Unfortunately, Christians can give the impression that they have all the answers and are intent on either correcting what they see as wrong approaches on the part of social workers, or assuming that the church knows how to do it because Christians are not implicated in this kind of family dysfunction. Several high profile cases have shown that to be untrue, and everyone knows that in some cases religious factors can make healing for wounded families more difficult, not easier. Christians with slick answers and intransigent attitudes are unlikely to be of much help. There is no magic wand that can be waved to transform dysfunctional situations, and anyone who thinks there is understands nothing about human emotions and relationships. Moreover, the gospel does not offer a quick fix, but points to the possibility of resurrection after pain and suffering – calling those who are wounded to take up their cross and follow Jesus.

At the same time, Jesus provides us with many instructive models for lifting up those who are broken, as well as encouraging the acceptance of all whose values match those of God's kingdom. That certainly includes social work departments and other statutory and voluntary agencies working with families, and we should therefore approach these bodies as potential partners, working in the same community and with a common concern for the wellbeing of the same group of people. Starting a dialogue can best be done by a key worker from the church (not necessarily clergy) approaching whoever is in charge of the respective organizations. It may take a bit longer to arrange a meeting with the person at the top, but doing so shows a seriousness of purpose. A social worker who happens to be a church member will not necessarily be the best person to do this. It is unwise to generalize, but Christians who are social workers sometimes have a different personal agenda than the service as a whole, and can be held at arm's length by their colleagues for that reason. Taking that route can result in the church being unhelpfully labelled before a conversation has even started. It will always be more effective for a church to approach social work through official channels, and then the relationship starts with a clean sheet.

At a meeting, be more willing to listen than to talk, but never be afraid to mention that you are a Christian. There is a growing awareness of the importance of spirituality for the healing of broken relationships, and secular agencies often find themselves utilizing so-called 'New Age' therapies because no one else seems to have anything to offer. You could also exchange information about areas of common interest, and the resource the church can offer (people as well as buildings). This is the time to ask for the information that you would like to have available to support your own dealings with families – things like the number to call if someone discloses personal abuse, or the emergency number that can mobilize a team to attend episodes of violence at any time of day or night. Get to know how social work agencies and the police operate, and what the correct procedures are. Well-meaning amateurs can unwittingly make things more difficult for statutory agencies, and they will respect the fact that you want to follow the proper guidelines (many of which are, of course, legal requirements). Ask if there are any needs in the community which the local social work department is aware of and with which they feel the church might be able to give some assistance. Trust needs to be built up for anything significant to happen, but one church we know went down this route, and found itself as a partner in an advisory service which was jointly sponsored by the church, the local government social services department, and a charity. At the very least, if you have a relationship with such bodies it will make an enormous difference when you are faced with a real-life crisis situation.

Violence in the home

Before the late 1960s, domestic violence was scarcely an issue at all, and it was not until Erin Pizzey (founder of the world's first shelter for battered women) published her ground-breaking book *Scream Quietly or the Neighbours Will Hear* that it was at all widely recognized.[1] Her follow-up study, highlighting the fact that violent behaviour in the home was not restricted to men, was less well received and became unavailable almost as soon as it was published.[2] Today, it is undeniable that men and women both fall victim to domestic violence, while there is a growing trend of children terrorizing their parents. In a study published by the UK government's Home Office in 1999, authors Catriona Mirrlees-Black and Carole Byron analyzed figures from the British Crime Survey for 1996, and found that exactly the same number of men and women (4.2 per cent) had been assaulted by their partner in the previous year (1995), though overall male violence against women still predominates, with 23 per cent of women being assaulted at some time, compared with 15 per cent of men.[3] Figures from the US and Canada highlight the same situation.[4]

There is a tendency among Christians to assume that violence is not a problem in church families. As part of our research for this book, clergy were asked how they would react to an incident of domestic violence involving members of their congregation, and almost all of them denied its existence. One minister in a small, economically oppressed community said that in the fifteen years he had ministered there he had not come across one single incident in his congregation. But if we were to list families known personally to us where domestic violence has been an issue, it would read like a roll call of household names in the Christian world. Christian families are no different from other families, and violence occurs among people from all walks of life, regardless of class, ethnicity, or religious involvement. Unless we are prepared to recognize this, then obviously we are unlikely to do much about it. Part of the difficulty is that churches are still largely male-dominated institutions, even where there are women in ministry, and their structures reflect a male mindset and style of doing things. For men, violence against women is not a pastoral problem that can be kept at arm's length, but is personally threatening, and natural defence mechanisms are bound to play a part in ensuring that the subject is taken less seriously than it deserves.

Defining violence

Violence can take many forms, of which physical injury is only one. Psychological and emotional violence can include the withdrawal of normal love and affection, as well as verbal abuse. Christian men might try to avoid physical violence, but use words instead. People whose world is dominated by words can find verbal violence just as satisfying as physical assault, and (unlike physical violence) it has the added advantage of leaving no visible scars. One of the most insidious aspects of domestic violence is the ease with which it does become invisible. Even when its existence is obvious, there is a built-in tendency for all concerned to close ranks and deny it.

Violence thrives most readily when the family is already dysfunctional in some other way. Women who have been taught that 'submission' to their husbands is an intrinsic part of Christian discipleship are particularly at risk in this respect, for they can interpret physical attack as 'punishment' from God, brought about by some great sin in their lives. If that sounds far-fetched in the twenty-first century, we would refer back to the discussion in chapter 6, as well as countless recorded episodes of such attitudes, especially among conservative Christians.[5] Holding the belief that anyone should submit to another is the first step on the road to physical violence: the one is a logical development from the other, and is an open invitation to abuse of all kinds.[6] Church leaders should be far more proactive in challenging such attitudes, but our own research has indicated that there are still many who regularly advise women in abusive relationships to return to their husbands, either for the sake of keeping their marriage intact or for the sake of their children. Others offer simplistic solutions by suggesting that victims just need to live with the situation and pray about it, and things will somehow work out.

Helping the victim

It would be wrong to suggest that all church leaders – or even a majority – promote these ideas. So what about those who want to be more helpful? What can we now do? Part of the answer lies in our repeated emphasis on the need for the church to be a genuine community of caring people, which will be a refuge for those who are hurting. More than anything else, people need to feel confident in turning to the church for comfort and healing. But there are also a number of specific things to consider.

As well as knowledge of the support offered by different agencies, we also need to promote general awareness of the issue within the congregation. This will include reflecting on the messages we communicate from the pulpit and in our Bible study groups. Do we side-step things by making vague statements about authority within the family, which then leave people struggling with the questions we described through Clare and Martin's experience in chapter 6? We can also encourage the whole Christian community to be a place of hospitality and healing for the survivors of violence, and make special provision for the recognition of their predicament during services of reconciliation and healing. It is also helpful to have materials available that will highlight these issues. Though reading a book will never resolve a deep personal crisis, we should have suitable literature available for victims to take, or to be given to them when they come looking for help. Though almost twenty years old, Marie Fortune's small booklet *Keeping the Faith: Questions and Answers for the Abused Woman* is still an outstanding resource for this purpose.[7]

We also need to be realistic about how violence is likely to come to our notice. People will often approach pastoral workers or friends with some general question, rather than announcing that they are being assaulted by their spouse or children. They need us to be sensitive and give them space to address the difficult matters that may be hidden beneath the surface. Battered women do not easily share any of this with a man, and victimized men will be even less likely to admit it to a woman, while children will find it difficult to talk to any adult. The precise way in which any of that happens will also differ from one ethnic group to another. This just underlines the need for churches to employ staff who are different from one another, reflecting the diversity of the wider population, so that the pastoral support network can be accessible to all.

It may seem elementary, but once the communication barrier has been broken it is crucial that we believe what we are told. If the person being accused is a Christian – especially a key worker or minister – it might challenge our preconceptions, but it is exceedingly rare for people to invent stories of violence or abuse. When that does happen it is almost always done by a person who is seriously disturbed in some other obvious way. Victims are more likely to minimize the extent of their suffering, which means that no matter how horrific it seems, what we are being told will probably be only a tiny fraction of the full story. We should also be prepared to challenge the violence without backing down. Some violent people actually want to change their behaviour, and all they need is for a third party to challenge them to do so. But there are many more who will react by denying what is going on, and it is important not to do anything that might make the victim's situation worse. It is essential, first, because any confrontation with an offender can put their victim in even more danger. But second, people who are regularly beaten have a very low self-esteem. They need to know that there is nothing more shameful about being assaulted than about being run over by a bus. They need to be lifted up and affirmed, and assured of their special value. That includes empowering them no longer to be pawns in someone else's game, but to take responsibility for themselves. Be realistic about the fact that people in crisis often need prompt action if their situation is not to deteriorate rapidly, and may be so confused and uncertain that they are incapable at that moment of making good decisions. Though pastoral workers should generally never act without consent from their clients, this can be one of those few occasions when it is helpful to have another person take control of things, but always on a short-term basis.

When violence is between partners, whether married or not, then the victim will need to consider whether a relationship that is so dysfunctional has a future. Breaking up is never easy, even when it is caused by such experiences. Christians are right to stress the importance of commitment, but people hardly ever break up for trivial reasons. Commitment involves mutual accountability, and marriage vows are denied just as effectively through violence as through adultery.[8] Clergy are sometimes inclined to suggest relationship counselling for couples locked in a cycle of repeated violence. That implies that both partners need to change, and can send a subtle message to the victim that he or she is to blame for what is happening, while assuring the perpetrator that his or her actions are not so bad after all, and may even be excusable. But violence is always the perpetrator's problem, and not a relational problem. There are also other reasons why counselling should not be the first line of approach. The immediate goal must be to stop the violence. Unless that happens (and it usually involves some form of treatment or therapy for the perpetrator), counselling will, at best, be a waste of time, and might even add to the violence by offering yet more excuses for it. In the meantime, if the violence is life-threatening, the victim will need a safe place to live, and help to rebuild their damaged sense of self-worth. Living alone may not need to be the long-term solution, but until victims know that they can do it, it will be an uphill struggle to redesign relationships with the same partner.

The cycle of violence

Domestic violence operates in a complex and cyclical fashion, but its underlying roots are similar for both men and women, and starts with anger. Something happens that triggers the building of tension. It can be absolutely anything, but is usually related to feelings of anxiety or powerlessness. Facing these deep feelings may be too difficult, and it is easier to be angry. As such, it is a natural emotion which may or may not be justified – but the important thing is how people handle it. Channelled in an assertive way, anger energy can be used productively to solve problems. Used aggressively, it erupts in violence which only makes things worse. In the home situation, something as trivial as a meal not being ready or the TV being on the wrong channel, can push people over the edge into what has been called 'volcanic violence'.[9] In the past, domestic violence was almost always perpetrated by men on women. Today, with women needing to adopt aggressive attitudes in order to be sufficiently competitive in the workplace, there is a discernible increase in violence perpetrated by females. Women have always had the same capacity for anger as men, but the sexes traditionally dealt with it differently. Men – for reasons connected with society's expectations and media images rather than with being male as such – tended to explode, spreading the fallout of their anger far and wide. In public spaces, such explosions are normally confined to verbal arguments, screaming, pacing up and down, and so on, but in the privacy of the home they more easily boil over into physical violence. Women – who traditionally stayed at home, conscious of not having the same recognition in the outside world – were more inclined to deal with anger by suppressing it ('imploding'), encouraged by society's image of them as 'sugar and spice and all things nice'. Imploded anger is not hidden, but tends not to be physically violent, manifesting itself in sulking, bitterness, resentment, sarcasm, sadness, disappointment, and so on. It can also induce health problems such as depression, headaches, skin disorders, and in some people even reduces the effectiveness of the immune system and triggers heart disease.

Why do people behave like this? A minority of violent people are psychopaths or suffer from other personality disorders, but most perpetrators of domestic violence appear to be otherwise quite 'normal'. Stress is bound to be one key factor. Many women have found that having it all often means they have to do it all – working inside the home as well as outside it – and there is a proven link between high levels of stress and violence. There can also be the additional physiological pressures created by premenstrual syndrome, something that most men fail either to recognize or understand. Men are also stressed, but in different ways, especially related to male identity. They have already seen their prospects in the workplace diminished by the expansion of opportunities for women, and are becoming increasingly irrelevant even for fathering children, as scientists are now claiming that it will be possible to create babies without any male contribution at all. It has long been recognized that violent people have often grown up in violent homes. But violence in men also seems to be related to cultural norms about what it means to be male or female. The emergence of the industrial nuclear family created the consistent expectation that to be a real man is to be in control – a belief that, in the Christian context, was historically supported by a selective and culturally conditioned approach to Scripture.[10] Moreover, until relatively recent times western culture tended to elevate the rational and downgrade the emotional. Today, we send out mixed messages about this. On the one hand, we are bombarded with messages telling us to be in touch with our inner selves, but on the other the workplace in particular still operates on an exclusively rational level. While men are encouraged to uncover their 'feminine' side, women find it essential to behave in a macho 'male' way in order to make progress in employment. When we feel vulnerable in any of these respects, anger is never far beneath the surface – and when we do not know how to deal with our anger, violence follows close behind. Ten years ago, anger management therapists were few and far between: today, it seems that every celebrity has one, and the rest of us are joining them in increasing numbers.

Some persistently violent people will need specialist help if they are to change, and church leaders should never hesitate to refer such people to appropriate professionals. But the church should not expect to hand over all responsibility to other agencies. We have consistently emphasized the need for the church to take a positive lead in active support of families, particularly by modelling a Christian understanding of community. Whole people do not create dysfunctional families, and the gospel is supposed to be about helping people to be whole. Healing of the emotions, and the discovery by both women and men of what it means to be made in the image of God, will be at the heart of a truly Christian understanding of the family. People need a safe space – psychological as well as physical – to help them find complete healing. Think of the woman mentioned in Luke 8:43–8. She had not been physically assaulted, but she was untouchable. No one wanted to know her. She was victimized, and she felt ashamed. What did Jesus do for her? He noticed she was there, and accepted her as she was – and out of that she found healing. One invaluable thing that Christians can do is to acknowledge people's suffering, instead of feeling uncomfortable about it.

Abuse of children

In homes where parents fight one another, children are likely to be more at risk than in other homes. The underlying causes of domestic violence and child abuse are often very similar. But it is not just parents who abuse children: it is often other close relatives or people living in and about the same house. That makes children especially vulnerable, because they cannot necessarily count on any adult in their family taking their side. Moreover, their size and relative physical weakness puts them at a disadvantage in any dealings with adults.

Varieties of abuse

Children suffer in many hidden ways, but there are several common identifiable forms of abuse. Physical assault includes any non-accidental injury, and its causes are broadly similar to the factors that lead men and women to be violent: stress, inadequate anger management, and the perceived need of parents to be in control of the family situation. Because of the way it can be linked to beliefs about discipline, it requires some careful handling in the pastoral situation. Expectations vary, and what some might regard as a harmful form of discipline can seem perfectly normal to others, especially where different ethnic groups are involved. But everyone accepts that anything resulting in physical injury (bruises, cuts, broken bones) is unacceptable. A variation on physical assault of the child can be the wanton destruction of property or pets that are important to the child. This can be just as hurtful as being beaten, and is sometimes used as a form of discipline by parents for that very reason.

Psychological or emotional abuse is also common. Children are threatened with the withholding of love and affection or are constantly teased or degraded in some way. Children may be constantly criticized in front of friends or siblings: their clothes are never as tidy as someone else's, their hair is not properly combed, they never say the right thing, and so on. This kind of abuse is widespread, especially among church families.[11] Specifically religious abuse might involve threatening a child with Bible verses that seem to condemn their behaviour, or making God's acceptance of them dependent on certain forms of permissible behaviour.[12] It can also involve repressing their emotions ('I don't want any crying') – something that can have catastrophic consequences for future generations of families as well as the individuals concerned. Calling children names, and manipulating them to do what parents want, or refusing to speak at all until they conform, are all techniques of emotional blackmail that parents can use to control their offspring. Another variation occurs when parents try to work out their own unfulfilled ambitions through their children. From an early age, Olive was told that she was destined to become a missionary. Her mother had herself been inspired by tales of missionary adventurers, and regretted she never had the chance to be one herself. The next best thing was to live it out through the coming generation, especially through a child whose birth could be made to appear the reason why the parent's own dream had never come to pass. In the long term, of course, manipulation rarely achieves what it was intended to do. Instead, it leads to a breakdown of relationships between children and parents, and stores up problems for the future if the child in adult life then tries to manipulate other people.

Neglect is another form of child abuse. Here again, there can be a clash of cultural expectations, and what seems reasonable in one context may be thought harsh somewhere else. Some families might regard depriving a child of food for a day as brutal, while those who do that might have the same opinion of parents who expect a child of five to sleep in a room alone at night. But neglect can generally be defined as the lack of provision of basic needs of food, clothing, and shelter. It can also include circumstances in which a young child is expected to take responsibility for other family members. The misuse of alcohol is often a factor here. Sexual abuse covers many different things, including incest, rape, having intercourse with children, taking indecent photographs of them, encouraging them to become prostitutes, and a collection of other practices generally subsumed under the legal terminology of 'lewd and libidinous behaviour'. However, defining the phenomenon is the easy part: proving that something has taken place, and if so what, is by no means straightforward.

All these forms of abuse are similar, especially in terms of their pastoral consequences. It is impossible to predict in advance which children are going to be most at risk from which types of abuse. Abusive parents do not always abuse all their children. Sometimes one child is singled out as especially disruptive or difficult, and once the cycle is established, then both parents and child take it for granted that this child is the problem.

Recognizing abuse

It is easy to give checklists of the signs of possible abuse, and many books on the subject do so. There is no doubt that a child's behaviour can reveal a lot about what is going on. When patterns change without any other obvious reason, it will be natural to look for some other, perhaps hidden, explanation. Some children who are abused in the home become shy and introverted, while others become hyperactive. Some become aggressive and angry, while others become very domesticated, as if they are trying to take the home over and correct things so as to compensate for the immaturity of the actual parents. Many develop problems with sleeping, wetting the bed unexpectedly or having constant nightmares. Abuse can lead to the development of eating disorders. Other children become chronically withdrawn, depressed, submissive, and fearful. They are reluctant to go to certain places, which can sometimes include home (many kids who wander about the streets do so because that seems to be safer than going home). School work might also suffer. History or mathematics seems less important when your whole life is being turned upside down. Some therapists have developed more specific indicators. For example, it has been claimed that a child who is sexually abused will tend to draw people with no hands or feet. Others point out that an abused child can find it difficult to walk alongside an adult, preferring instead to walk behind in a submissive posture. It is possible to make too much out of such things. There is no one set of behavioural signs that necessarily indicate a child is being abused, nor is the presence of one or more of these necessarily a sign of abuse. Perhaps the one exception is when children make sexual advances to other children. Children who show evidence of explicit sexual knowledge, and who are prepared to act out what they know, are almost certainly going to be victims of sexual abuse.

It is more common for those who work a lot with children to develop an intuition for such things. Olive recalls an incident in Jamaica as she was leaving a church with a group of clergy. As they walked down the street, the group passed a child who just looked very sad. No one gave her a second glance, except Olive and one other person. They both had extensive experience of abused children, and though only one of them was in their own cultural context there was something about the child's body language that instinctively caused them both to ask the same questions. There is a degree of perception which comes from experience. When working with a particular group of children on a regular basis, it is even easier to pick up the hidden signals that something may be wrong. Churches which run activities for children with different teams of people alternating with one another are at a disadvantage here. If adults are to be accessible and user-friendly to children, continuity is important. It is neither possible nor desirable for every children's worker to become a psychoanalyst (and well-meaning amateurs can do more harm than good), but some basic training on this subject, combined with an understanding of stages of faith development, should be built into the church's work among children.[13] In February 2000, the case of eight-year-old Victoria Climbié shocked the British public and highlighted the need for church leaders to listen to children. This little girl had been sent from the Ivory Coast to stay with her great aunt and her live-in lover in order to advance her educational and other opportunities. She was systematically abused (eventually murdered) by them. The case was so horrific that a major public inquiry was established to look into it. It emerged that leaders at three different churches had failed to notice anything wrong, despite being asked by Victoria's own great aunt for help on behavioural problems commonly associated with abuse (some of them identical with those we mentioned above). One of the church leaders told the official inquiry that he had believed the little girl was demon possessed.[14] David Pearson, director of the UK Churches' Child Protection Advisory Service, later commented that 'churches can be very dangerous places for children' – surely the understatement of the century, in light of all that had happened.

Helping victims

As with any personal crisis, effective pastoral support begins with an adequate understanding of the problem, and its likely effects on the victim. One thing is absolutely certain in relation to child abuse: children are never responsible for abuse that happens to them. If a child reveals a situation of abuse to an adult, it is important first of all to believe the child and take his or her story seriously. Despite the constant mention of sexual abuse in the media, in real life there is still a tendency to play it down. But allegations of sexual abuse must be taken seriously. Children who are being actively abused find it hard to share this experience with other people, and there will be a tendency to under-report, rather than exaggerate. The abuser is always likely to be in a position of authority over them, and may offer bribes or threats to prevent them reporting what is taking place. In addition, children may secretly believe it is their fault anyway, and be afraid of being accused of doing something wrong. More-over, children naturally fear that if they tell their story the whole family will fall apart – and it will be their fault. The abuser may already have warned the child of this possibility. Some might be enjoying the special attention they are receiving, even though it is also painful and confusing. If children do disclose sexual abuse, therefore, it is extremely important to reassure them that they have done the right thing, and for an adult to act with absolute integrity that will not betray this trust. If the parents are impli-cated, this means not going straight to them to report what has been disclosed. Too often, children have mentioned things to adults who have not only not believed them, but have then informed the very adults who are abusing them.

In any case of alleged sexual abuse, it is essential that the appropriate authorities are informed, and that this is done quickly, especially if the abuser lives in the same house as the victim. Abuse is not just a moral aberration: it is a crime. But if swift action is not taken, the family will close ranks and deny that anything has taken place. At the same time, the victim is likely to be at even greater risk for having let the family secret slip out. Once a case has been disclosed, what happens next will vary from one jurisdiction to another. In cases of incestuous sexual abuse it is likely to include the removal of either child or abuser from the home, at least on a temporary basis until the situation can be properly assessed. This can present children with a dilemma: if they are the one to be removed, they may feel punished and conclude that they were in the wrong anyway. Either way, a child will probably regret having broken up the family, and may also be the recipient of aggression from the non-offending parent (who will not necessarily know what has been going on). Support for the child and for this parent will be crucial, because their relationship is the one that is most likely to survive on a long-term basis. The kind of support the church can most usefully give is simply by being there and being available. Specialist counselling should be left to those who are equipped for that.

In terms of the development of a child's faith and value system, abuse of all kinds has profoundly destructive consequences. Without help, disturbed children will become disturbed adults. Children who experience nothing but anger and violence from their parents develop a distorted image of God, which in later life typically leads them to give up on faith altogether. 'Because they were betrayed by those they trusted most, victims of abuse have trouble trusting anyone, including God.'[15] They also develop a perverted understanding of love, and the relationship between suffering and joy. Abused children are receiving conflicting messages from their parents: 'they love me, they hurt me, therefore love is the same thing as pain'. Unless this deviant logic is corrected by future experiences of unconditional love and acceptance, they will go on as adults to inflict the same suffering on others, often without any conscious realization that what they are doing is abnormal behaviour.

Helping parents

How to help the parents will depend on whether the child abuse has taken place in the family, or outside. It will be much easier to help those whose child has been abused by a stranger. They will feel it as keenly as if they had been abused themselves. The good news is that 'Children living in homes with secure and reassuring parents who experience sexual abuse by a stranger show little lasting effects.'[16] Still, that can be hard to believe in the midst of the crisis. The parents are also victims, and will need as much reassurance as the child. They will need to know that they are good parents, and they really can care for their children. It was not their fault if a stranger abducted their child in the street, or a neighbour or a friend's father abused them. It may be, though, that there will be an element of truth in some of the things they feel. Perhaps their schedule is too busy, and they spend too much time at work without making adequate provision for their children to be cared for. In that case, they need help to change things and revise their priorities. This will include assisting them to identify appropriate boundaries for the child that will be fair. For example, there will be an understandable temptation to restrict the child's movements, so that he or she is less vulnerable. Adults can see that the child might be safer staying at home, but for a child that can feel like punishment, as if he or she was to blame for what happened all along. There will also be unfinished business to work through with the abuser – and with God. These are things that only the couple concerned can address, which is why reflective listening will be of more help than much speaking. In due course, questions like this might usefully be aired in the context of a support group with other parents.

Helping parents who are themselves implicated in abusive situations is a lot more difficult. We have already said a little about support for the non-offending parent. Helping the offenders will be a tougher business. For a start, they are likely to be subject to some legal restrictions, and may end up in prison. On top of that, they are unlikely to be prepared to face up to what has happened. Incidentally, if someone comes to you to confess to sexual abuse, don't be hoodwinked into treating it lightly. They are probably looking for a quick dispensation of forgiveness, and hoping to avoid the messy consequences of their actions that way. The reality is that sex offenders are devious people. Almost all of them have some underlying psychological flaw, that on the one hand allows them to be very authoritarian people with a strict moral code, while at the same time exploiting their own – or other people's – vulnerable children. Don't be tempted to have too much sympathy for them. Church leaders

are easily hoodwinked into providing sex offenders with a
character reference, or telling a court that, even if they did it, it
was so out of character that they should be given a second
chance. But sexual abuse is addictive and compulsive: once an
offender starts, it is difficult to stop. Enrolment in a treatment
programme may or may not work, but more often than not the
intervention of the law is the only way to deal with the situation.
Anyone who tries to minister to sex offenders needs to be realistic
about the chances of rehabilitation, and under no circumstances
appear to condone or even excuse what has happened. Offering
support to an offender will be a long-term business, and should
always be in conjunction with a recognized rehabilitation programme. Never be tempted to become the front-line provider of
primary care.[17]

Abusive families

Prevention is always better than cure, and the provision of
adequate support for families can play a significant part in avoiding the destructive kind of dysfunction we have considered in
this chapter. There is a general consensus that abusive families
share many of the same characteristics. Like all checklists, this
one is a generalization, but identifying some of the features of a
family at risk can be a major help in alerting the sensitive
Christian to a pastoral need.

Recognizing the signs

Abusive parents have often experienced abusive behaviour
themselves. We all learn how to be parents by watching our
own parents, and unless we take specific steps to learn different
parenting skills we will probably repeat their mistakes. This
includes sexual abuse, for it is widely believed that most abusers
were themselves abused as children (though the reverse is not
true, for not everyone who has been abused goes on to abuse
other people).[18] Abusive parents typically do not understand
children's needs, and lack parenting skills. They are constantly
comparing themselves unfavourably with other parents, whom
they imagine are doing a better job, or are better informed. As a

result of these perceived inadequacies, they feel guilty and inferior, and take it out on their children. They are probably harsh disciplinarians as well, and are likely to understand little about child development. They think of children not as little people, but as little adults, and imagine that children act in the same way and for the same reasons as adults would. Within the Christian community, this outlook may be complicated by the addition of a theological understanding of salvation couched exclusively in terms of an adult experience. In this context, children may be burdened with adult notions of sin and guilt that can adversely affect their own personal development.

Abusive families are also often isolated from neighbours and their own relatives. Friendships are discouraged, sometimes for moral or religious reasons (the parents don't want their children to mix with people with different opinions or lifestyles, which then become not just different but sinful). This in turn creates the impression that their family is special, and probably better than others. When child abuse is introduced into this equation, the abusive behaviour then reinforces the feeling of difference from other families, and strengthens the pressures to be secretive about it and to stay isolated from the rest of society. Abusing families can also find it difficult to allow their members much independence. The natural human desire for warm personal relationships is intensified to the point where the family becomes an end in itself. Parents with emotional problems inherited from their own childhood are hungry for love and acceptance, and compete with one another to see who can get the most. The one who loses out then turns to the children, but since they can never satisfy their needs they in turn become the objects of aggression.

Addressing the problem

Abusive families struggle to accept change. In this, they only reflect where our culture as a whole finds itself. Ultimately, our inability to handle abuse and domestic violence can be traced back to our inadequate social understandings of the family, in particular our over-emphasis on the rights of individuals, with no sense of mutual responsibility. Families that are not genuine communities become battlegrounds for control, whether by men over women, women over men, children over their parents, or parents over children. The sense of powerlessness which this instils in the victims affects them through the rest of their life. One of the ironic things about sexual abuse is that it is not mainly about sexual acts, but about the distortion of relationships, the betrayal of trust, and the abuse of power. The practical problems will not begin to be resolved until we address some fundamental issues about power within the family. Churches are not the only organizations that can provide support for families in crisis, and we have already emphasized the importance of partnership with other agencies. But the spiritual dimension of the healing of broken relationships is important, and should be a significant component of what the church has to offer. Support groups are so valuable precisely because of this, as they offer a chance for people to move on from receiving help to giving it to others. The longer you are in a group the more you see yourself changing from being the person who needs all the assistance to the one who starts to support others. That discovery alone can work wonders for a person's self-image.

Providing opportunity for prayer is also important. Until we can work through the difficult experiences we cannot know complete healing. Sacramental and ritual actions have a special part to play at this point. The words of a liturgy can be especially helpful at a time when our own words are inadequate to match our feelings. Groups have great value, but there are times when people need to be alone. It can be worth creating a suitable space within the church building, a small room or side chapel, or just a corner where people can retreat and be quiet, or ask for prayer. Some physical thing to give expression to unspoken – and unspeakable – emotions can be helpful, such as the possibility of lighting a candle or drawing something on a sheet of paper or in a book. Sharing the Eucharist with other Christians also opens us up to being able to receive and to express feeling again. Those in the Reformed tradition may need to ponder how they can incorporate things like anointing and confession/absolution in their pastoral ministry with people who are abused and distressed. This can be particularly helpful in situations where whole families are trying to restructure their lives following some disruptive episode. People scar one another to such an extent that it can take some time before it is possible for them to live together again. But we never move on by burying the past, and the one thing the gospel does give us is a way to repent and experience forgiveness and also discover a capacity to forgive other people.

10 Growing old

Most people have negative images of old age: people retire from work, their children leave home, their peers die, their contacts with other people tend to become fewer in number, until they end up, as Shakespeare said, 'sans teeth, sans eyes, sans everything'.[1] The news media reinforce that, by highlighting the plight of old people who are eking out the remnants of their lives unloved and uncared for in run-down care facilities, and probably suffering the destructive effects of dementia into the bargain. These problems are real, but an over-emphasis on them tends to distort the reality, which is rather different. While the incidence of dementia does increase with age, only one in five even of the over-eighties suffers from dementia, which means that 80 per cent of them do not, and they go on to live out their entire lives without any fear of significant mental impairment.[2] In western countries, people now live longer and enjoy better health than ever before, partly as a result of improved diets and healthcare provision, but also (for men especially) due to the relative absence of large-scale warfare over the past fifty years. When Erik Erikson divided the human life span into eight ages, there were just two of them after the age of thirty: 'generativity' (age 30–60), followed by 'facing death'.[3] Nowadays, that understanding of life after sixty seems extraordinarily simplistic: for most people this 'final' stage is likely to last for twenty years or more, and it might easily last longer than the 'generativity' stage. Clearly, 'facing death' is no longer an appropriate way of describing this stage of life.

Several factors are requiring us to redefine 'old age'. Traditionally old age would have been defined by reference to reproduction, but fertility treatments now make it possible for women as old as sixty or more to conceive, and overall there is an expectation that sexual relationships in some form will be possible for most people well into their eighties and beyond.

Greater fluidity of relationships means that men form partner-ships with younger women, and become fathers at an age when previous generations would have expected them to be dead. At the same time, relational breakdown among younger generations means that many older couples find they have neither time nor opportunity just to be old. Instead, they become surrogate parents to their grandchildren in a western re-invention of the extended family. Economic realities are also demanding a redefinition of old age. When pension plans were established as part of the post-war welfare state in Britain, it was assumed that many would die very soon after retirement at age sixty-five, and virtually everyone would be dead before they reached eighty. Greater longevity, coupled with the volatility of the stock market and declining numbers of younger people in the workforce, is changing all that, and increasing numbers of older people are faced with either continuing in work or facing retirement in economic hardship.

Increased life expectancy raises new questions about old people's relationships. In the past a long marriage might have lasted for as little as twenty years: women frequently died young in childbirth, and men died in war. That is why a twenty-five-year marriage was significant, while a fifty- or sixty-year mar-riage was out of the ordinary. Today, the nature of marriage itself is quite different, and older people wrestle with the same challenges as younger ones. It can no longer be assumed that long-term relationships will necessarily last for life. In the UK, there is a peak in the divorce statistics at about the thirty-year mark, a point that often coincides with the departure of the final child from the parental home. Couples discover they no longer know one another, and leave for other partners with whom they hope to discover new aspects of their own identity. Women who have spent all their lives giving out to others now want someone to give to them, and when their long-term spouse is incapable of doing that it can be the occasion for a new liaison with someone who will lavish them with gifts and attention – quite often younger men, who may themselves be looking for a mother figure to nurture them.

There is not even a consensus on what ageing actually is. Common sense suggests that it is a physical process, and most researchers believe there must be a genetic basis to ageing: perhaps we are programmed to decay after our reproductive phase is completed. But there is more to it than that. The *Handbook of the Psychology of Aging* lists four ways of defining old age: chronological or biological age (determined by the condition of an individual's physical systems), psychological age (attitude, motivation, willingness to adapt and change), functional age (determined by what a person is able to do to cope with life and its changes), and social age (reflecting the way in which a person manages to integrate within the wider community).[4] This taxonomy reflects what most people pick up intuitively: that a thirty-year-old can live in an 'old' way, while people in their eighties and nineties can be as 'young' as when they were twenty. Whatever technical definitions may be offered for 'old age', it is clear that we are getting old younger and living old for longer: the 'oldest old' (people over eighty) are now joined by the 'youngest old' (people over fifty).

The youngest old

Some people in this age group will be actively parenting teenagers, while others will be seeing their children leave home. Many will be doing both. The departure of grown children from the family home used to be easy to describe: they left to get married. Today, there can be multiple departures: going to university, taking time out to travel, working in a distant city, and so on. Today's fifty-somethings can never know for certain if their children will leave at all, and there is a growing trend for adult children to remain in the parental home well into their thirties, not to mention the likelihood that they will return after a relationship break-up, sometimes accompanied by their own children.

Parents at all stages of family life constantly wonder how they are doing, but at this stage they really can know the answer to that question. Whatever it is, they will need to reinvent themselves by facing up to some fundamental identity questions: who will we be now that we no longer have the immediate responsibility for children? Some avoid it by having another baby, either their own or by becoming surrogates to other parents who are busy with work. Some dream of having more children, imagining that if they were to start over again they would do a better job. This can be a particularly challenging time for parents (typically mothers) who have been full-time homemakers. Other people of their own age may be thinking of retirement, so when they want to return to work, or even start a new career, they can be treated like a freak and may find themselves the victim of ageist attitudes. Lone parents can encounter particular pressures of loneliness, raising new questions about whether they want to find companionship in some other way.

The way parents relate to their adult children often replicates their experiences with their own parents. Some leave their kids to get on with it, and are apparently satisfied to see them only on rare occasions. Others need to keep in regular contact, perhaps because their own parents never did. Charting a course somewhere between these two extremes is not easy, and many older adults simply do not know how to be caring and supportive without also being controlling. When that happens, it invariably results in major tensions when they get together with their adult children, and leads to a diminution of the relationship. There will be a difference here between those whose vision for their children was centred on their own ambitions as parents, and those who from the outset valued their children as individuals and encouraged them to develop their own separate personality and abilities.

In recent years, churches in the UK have increasingly come to be the preserve of older people, and statistics show a significant increase in the 45–64 age group in all types of church.[5] This does not necessarily indicate that churches are gaining more people over the age of forty-five: the percentage increase in this age cohort could be a statistical illusion, created by the fact that increasing numbers of young people are leaving the churches. But either way, it might be imagined that churches would be well placed to relate effectively to the needs of older people. This does indeed seem to be the case in relation to the 'oldest old', especially those with care needs which Christians feel they can meet. But the church's track record with the youngest old is less encouraging. In the course of writing this chapter, we randomly sought the opinions of a number of people working in the community, among whom was the marketing manager of one of Scotland's tourist agencies. Identifying the over-fifties as one of her key target groups, she described them as follows: 'Over-fifties are different from what you would traditionally think of as "oldies". Their role models are not Victor Meldrew [star of the TV sitcom *One Foot in the Grave*], but Mick Jagger [Rolling Stones, and now in his sixties]. They are the biggest growth group in the population, with money, lots of ideas and an enthusiasm to still really live and contribute to society.' She continued to give further definition to this: 'When promoting to them, we use photos of people in their forties, which is how they perceive themselves. Family is important to them. In the future they will play a key role in their grandchildren's lives as work patterns change for their own children. War and recession are key to this group. They are worried about pensions and the implications of war on their families. They are asking about the meaning of life. They want value for money.'

You might think this offers the church a significant opportunity: the youngest old have time, money, and enthusiasm to see things change – and there are more of them than ever before, a trend that will continue for the foreseeable future. Yet most British churches (their North American counterparts are significantly different in this) pour most of their resources, both money and people, into work among the young. At the time of writing, the current issue of a British Christian periodical advertises sixty-seven positions for full-time church workers, forty-nine of which are for youth ministers, and only one connected with ministry among older people (chaplain to a care home), with one further appointment available for a 'family minister' which, depending on how it is interpreted, could include older people in its remit. It is not hard to identify reasons that might explain this imbalance, most notably the church's failure to keep even its own young people, let alone connect with those who are unchurched. But part of the explanation is also to be found in society's preoccupation with remaining, in the words of Bob Dylan's song, 'Forever Young'. When he composed that for his son he was thirty-two, and the greatest blessing he could wish for him was to be spared the humiliation of growing old. Today, Dylan himself is old and sings about how he sees the world now: paradoxically, his current music puts him in conflict with the very youth culture he helped to nurture.[6] He has learned what some churches forget, that 'staying young' lacks an appropriate eschatological perspective which is necessary for human transformation. As Eugene Bianchi puts it, 'Too often in the aging process we settle for reminiscing rather than creating new memories. To recollect is to gather together past experiences of success or failure as stepping stones for new ventures.'[7]

The inconsistency of churches that are over-concerned with younger people should not be lost on a generation that has done more theological reflection on the nature of faith than any of our Christian forebears. The notion that 'stages of faith' run in parallel with stages of life is so widely accepted as a basis for Christian education theory that when we used it in a previous chapter we felt it needed no particular justification. Yet even within that frame of reference, a majority of those who adopt such understandings tend to concentrate all their efforts on faith development in childhood, with only a token recognition that it is a lifelong quest – and sometimes there is not even that minimal acknowledgement.[8] Actually, it may be a mistake to separate the concerns of younger people from the spiritual aspirations of today's over-fifties. For though many churches have become the preserve of older people, the majority of the youngest old in the wider population are in fact unchurched. This challenges the widely held notion that older people will be knowledgeable about the church, and will also tend to prefer traditional ways of being church. The reverse is more likely to be true, for those who come to faith for the first time in their fifties or later are unlikely to have any prior knowledge at all, and will be more deeply rooted in popular culture than their peers who have been in church all along. Their musical experience alone will enable them to make little sense of an average worship service, and both traditional hymns and so-called worship songs will be as alien to them as they would be to their own teenage children, while the kind of leisure activities that they value might be radically different from those typically found among church people. There is no guarantee that someone in their fifties who has been a lifelong church member will have the same expectations of faith as a person of the same age who has only recently become a Christian. Is this why the church makes so little effort to connect with people in this youngest old age group, because their presence might be too threatening? Young people and their demands for change are easily put down, but the same demands from older people who are more insistent and more articulate can be far more challenging. Is there a major mission opportunity that is being ignored?

Key issues for people in this age bracket will include the following:

Changing job patterns

Generally speaking, people over fifty find themselves discriminated against in the workplace as being past their best. Yet there is no real evidence that older people are any less efficient than younger ones, except for some physically demanding occupations, and the wealth of experience they bring in terms of interpersonal skills will often outweigh any restrictions they may have. The lack of an adequate workforce of younger people able to sustain the economy may be the very thing that will change this in the future. The situation in North America in this respect is quite different from that in the UK, with many more job opportunities open to older people, and less pressure on them to retire at fixed ages. The reasons for this are not always positive, of course, and many need to work till they drop because they would otherwise not have adequate income.

Economics

This is a growing concern all over the western world as even those who thought their pensions were secure are discovering otherwise. This causes real anxiety for younger people as well, who are being warned to invest early for themselves at the same time as they may be worrying about having to provide care for their older relatives. There is also a gender issue here, for retired women are more likely to live in poverty than men. A UK study by Age Concern and the Fawcett Society found that almost 25 per cent of single female pensioners live below the poverty line, and that married women typically receive a third of the pension

income of their husbands. Because of their greater average life
span, they also get lower rates of return when they convert a
pension fund into an annuity.

Relationships

The changes in the family described in previous chapters affect
older people just as much as younger ones. Changing attitudes
to divorce, marriage, and sexual relationships may have offered
greater freedom, but with much less certainty – especially to the
youngest old, who are the first generation ever to live with this,
and therefore have no previous role models to guide them. There
is a growing tendency of men in their sixties starting second and
third families with younger women in their thirties or forties.
The statistics for the USA are virtually identical to the UK, and
display all the same trends. Alongside this reality, though, is the
fact that relationships of all sorts can be more difficult to forge
as people grow older. The opportunities for meeting new people
are less, and often require a great deal of effort. Finding people
who share similar values can be more difficult than it seems, and
those in relationships can find it difficult to relate to others who
are single. All these factors can create instability in the lives of
older people, leading to emotional roller-coasting if not more
serious mental health problems.[9]

Community

This has been a recurring theme throughout this book. It is the
one thing that everyone is searching for and no one seems to
discover. The challenges for older people are fundamentally the
same as for those in younger age groups: friendship, community,
opportunity for fulfilment, meaningful identity, and purpose in
life. The difference is that the youngest old are at a stage in life
where they could help to build the new community which
younger people would like but simply don't have the time to
create, or indeed the experience to do so. Eugene Bianchi highlights this as one of the key features of a spiritual understanding
of ageing, as 'elders who are able to return to the centers of life
with new wisdom become role models for younger persons . . .'[10]

For some, grandparenting will be a way of doing this. One of the reasons for so much discontinuity and fragmentation in our culture can be traced to the way we are disconnected from our roots and our stories. In a time when grandchildren frequently live at a distance from their grandparents, it requires effort to keep these relationships alive. The Hebrew people (in common with most first nations) passed on their faith stories within families long before they were written down, and enabling people to write their own stories as a gift for their grandchildren or to tell them on tape will be a priceless gift for the next generation. Not only will it be the rediscovery of a lost art, but it also enables people to deal with their own history and do the necessary work of integration within their own lives.[11]

These are all fairly obvious things, and it was only after compiling the list that we realized how closely it parallels what Raymond Fung identifies as 'the Isaiah Vision', in which 'Babies will no longer die in infancy, and all people will live out their life span. Those who live to be a hundred will be considered young . . . People will build houses and live in them themselves . . . they will plant vineyards and drink the wine . . . They will fully enjoy the things they have worked for. The work they do will be successful . . .' (Isaiah 65:20–3).[12] With a little imagination the list could easily be expanded, but these concerns offer a starting point where churches might not only make their own distinctive contribution, but could also collaborate with other agencies that are not overtly Christian. An added bonus is the fact that this is surely a vision which even traditionalists in the church should be happy to endorse – indeed, they could be the people most suited to facilitate it.

From one stage of age to the next

The term 'oldest old' is usually reserved for those who are over eighty. But the pattern for the final stages of life has traditionally been determined earlier than that, by reference to what happens when people retire from full-time paid employment. Some regard retirement as a time to do more of the same. Certain lifestyles and occupations lend themselves very well to this. Most retired clergy see things this way: they leave the responsibilities of full-time church work but still expect to be engaged in the activities of ministry. Authors and journalists often find themselves in a similar position – able to retire in the sense of taking a pension, but never really giving up. This is not the only way of doing 'more of the same'. Hobbies or sports that were previously leisure activities can become the equivalent of full-time occupations, though with none of the obligations that would have involved earlier in life. Others would be bored silly by this, and look for new opportunities not previously available to them. Significant numbers of retired people move to a new place, even when they have lived in the same location for many years. Some find this literally gives them a new lease of life, with new situations and possibilities opening up before them, and inspiring them with an enthusiasm and commitment they never thought possible. Some even take up a new occupation, and full-time church work can be especially attractive at this time. Others 'get away from it all' by going to live in the sun, either permanently or for several months each year. Significant numbers of older British people take up winter residence in places like Spain, while their North American counterparts go to Florida. Living among other people who have made the same choices offers scope for new friendships and new experiences – including spirituality. Church can easily become a point of contact with newcomers to an area, at any stage of life. Such radical change also carries risks, of course: loneliness, and not being able to settle or cope in the new situation. Some move to be closer to their adult children, only to find that either they are not welcome or their children move somewhere else. Moving is not the only way to inaugurate change, and others compensate for lost opportunities earlier in life by returning to education or tackling some project that will make a significant difference to themselves and their family or the wider community. Most people who embark on major change never look back, but seem to be energized and empowered by it.

Others, of course, just want to do 'nothing' – by which they usually mean filling their time with trivialities such as walking the dog, going to the shops, or watching TV. For people whose work has been their life, such things can replace the structure they previously found in the workplace. The daily routine of work can leave people feeling dependent and even institutionalized, and the best way to cope with its loss is by keeping busy doing nothing. This often hides a deep-seated uncertainty about meaning, purpose, and identity in people who think they have under-achieved and are unable to face up to who they are. Routines become a distraction, reducing life to a series of purely practical considerations in order to avoid dealing with personal pain. Such people can be negative and cynical about others of all ages, and easily become caricatures of themselves – lonely and introverted and waiting to die (which they often do at a relatively young age). There are very many people like this: disengaged from society and struggling with a pointless existence.

As people move into the final stages of life, their concerns will largely be determined by the kind of choices they made when they retired from full-time work. But there are some questions that inevitably come into clearer focus as we reflect on the prospect of our own death. Meaning and purpose are key themes throughout life, but they become more urgent now as we wonder what it will be like to die, and whether there is anything else after that. The oldest old can find these questions either very comforting or extremely frightening, depending on their inherited worldview. Some know that they are made in God's image, and their previous experience of God's care in their lives gives them the certainty that, whatever happens, God will be there. For others, God is the last thing they want to encounter, because they regard God as angry and punishing, and fear that even by thinking about these questions they might somehow be offending God and making things worse for themselves. Even non-religious people find themselves reflecting on these questions of ultimate meaning.

Loneliness is a more immediate concern for many. This is by no means only an old person's issue, but horror stories of people dying alone and being undiscovered for months can be alarming. Personal worth and dignity is undermined by the possibility of dying in such circumstances. The same is true of past memories, living with one's unresolved shortcomings and failures, whether individual or relational. The need to put things right, especially with close family members, is more urgent than ever before, because the time is short and uncertain. We need to be forgiven by others, and also to be enabled to forgive ourselves. People with strong religious views can find this difficult, especially if they are suffering from ill health which they might be inclined to understand as God's punishment for past failures.

Future hope is vital at this time of life. It is not of course an exclusively Christian virtue, but Christian hope is rooted in a holistic worldview that points forward beyond itself to the kingdom of God and the Church triumphant, and – in personal terms – assures individuals that their life is of significance in the cosmic scheme of things. This in turn is a reaffirmation of the centrality of the two doctrines of creation and incarnation for a truly Christian understanding of what it means to be human: made in the image of God, loved and valued to the very end of all things.

Spiritual care for older people

Traditional cultures throughout the world not only integrate old people in the wider community, but also respect them for their wisdom and maturity. Christians have historically respected and valued the contribution of older people – even of the 'oldest old' – as evidenced in the Bible itself, where Moses was eighty years old before commencing his major life's work! In the west today, however, old people are increasingly regarded as a burden, an attitude that will probably increase as they continue to live longer and cost more to the taxpayer. A consumer society values everyone by reference to their productivity – the things we can do, rather than the persons we are. This has been true for at least the last two hundred years, but it is a bigger challenge for today's ageing population than might have been the case in our grandparents' generation. In our throwaway society, people can be as disposable as packaging. Karen Kaigler-Walker highlights how physical appearance can be a particular issue in the case of older women, but this kind of rejection is by no means restricted by gender.[13]

Older people who find themselves treated with disdain are dehumanized, while younger generations are deprived of those resources of wisdom that could help them create a new future in these times of cultural turbulence. No life is so insignificant that it does not count. In the classic movie *It's a Wonderful Life*, the leading character George Bailey movingly demonstrates the enormous value to a community of even an 'ordinary' life, as in a multitude of small instances he does what he thinks is right, and in the process enriches the lives of all those whom he encounters.[14] It is said that when a butterfly flaps its wings, it sends a wave that is felt around the world and throughout the universe. What is true in chaos theory also applies to human relationships: how we treat one another ripples through others' lives like the butterfly's wings flapping. In theological terms, could this be the 'sin that is visited from one generation to the next' referred to in Ezekiel 18:2? It is unquestionably a point at which many older people find themselves sinned against, as the exploitation of one generation by another not only creates a climate of fear but also results in an enforced stunting of personal development in those who are victimized.

Negative attitudes toward older people are clearly challenged by a proper understanding of the doctrine of creation, which takes seriously the claim that we are all 'made in God's image' – not to mention many biblical references to the importance of community for human wholeness. Many people are likely to find that the later stages of life offer an opportunity to pay more attention to nurture and growth of the spirit, since the demands of family and work are less extensive than they once were. In a world where value is judged on 'results', keeping busy is paramount, and time for meditation or reflection is a marginal activity: those who create it for themselves can be admired and despised at the same time. Yet without these tools we are ill equipped to face the biggest life change of all, the transition to the next stage of being. There is a challenge here, especially to the traditional theological paradigm of Protestantism, with its insistence that spirituality is primarily a matter of cognitive rationality. This can lead to an attitude that writes off the possibilities of further spiritual development in old age, especially for those with degenerative conditions such as dementia or who suffer from impaired understanding or learning difficulties. There is a need for a more fluid approach both in relation to what it means to be 'old' and also to what constitutes 'spirituality'. The values of the gospel are clearly counter-cultural at this point, and as well as challenging the church to think more deeply about ageing it also puts a question mark against the assumptions of much gerontological literature, which tends to interpret old age as reduced involvement in society, based on an understanding of work as the measure of a person's worth. Jesus' encounter with Nicodemus is instructive in this connection, for when he describes himself as too old (John 3:4) Jesus assures him that no one is too advanced in age for spiritual renewal: 'new birth' can lead to untold possibilities of growth and development at any stage of life.

The nurture of spirituality is not the sole responsibility of church leaders: individuals also have a responsibility to respond to the spiritual teaching and support they are receiving, just as they should take responsibility for their physical wellbeing by adopting healthy diets. Older people will not merely be con- sumers of spiritual goodies, but can also make significant contributions to the work of creating relational communities that will reflect gospel values in their own locality. Some churches will find this requires some restructuring of their operations, because they are just not set up to welcome such participation, whether by older people or others. Different ideas will work in different circumstances, but in essence it requires an approach that looks to the needs of people and prayerfully responds by getting along- side others, considering their gifting and life experiences, and then imaginatively working out how these skills might be used to respond to the needs of the wider community. A simple example might involve matching the resources of one individual or group to the needs of another – for instance, someone with experience in financial management offering advice to others who are struggling with debts; or someone with teaching skills helping immigrants to learn a new language; a full-time home- maker who knows how to manage on a limited budget teaching a retired executive how to cook. Others might facilitate work- shops and community events based around interests or need. All such relational groups can naturally become the entry point to faith for friends and neighbours.

This is hardly rocket science: in fact, the possibilities for using the knowledge of older people are so obvious that it is difficult to imagine why every local church is not already doing this sort of thing. Some will be, though the existence of national initiatives to match older people and their skills with local needs suggests that most congregations are unable to do it by themselves. For those who would like to do so, it would require an intentional approach. It is easy to assume that we know what people either want or need, and set up programmes which then never really take off. To be effective, churches need to be methodical in surveying both those who already are part of the church and those with whom they may work in partnership.

There is a lesson to be learned here from mistakes made in the 1960s, when those now in their fifties were children. The church singularly failed to connect with the cultural change that was happening then, and by the time it caught up the response was 'too little, too late' – a failure that explains why so many of those now in mid-life grew up with no living relationship to Christian faith.[15] A cultural shift of similar proportions is now taking place with the emergence of older people as a key group in the community, and it will be both short-sighted and tragic if the church still fails to respond in relevant ways. This is one point at which British churches could learn from churches in other parts of the world, notably in North America and Australia, where there has always been a more intentional approach to ministry among older people, including the youngest old.

In summary, then, even old age is not immune to the redefinition of the family. Today's youngest old in particular offer unique challenges and opportunities to the church. They are the first generation to have been 'teenagers', to have lived most of their adult life with no personal experience of war, to have financial independence, greater education, and increased opportunities for their children. They now face being the first generation to have an extended retirement span. Their desire to do something worthwhile with their accumulated experience and wisdom is shared increasingly with the oldest old, and that trend is bound to grow as today's fifty-somethings become tomorrow's eighties and nineties. At the same time, many do not live close to their own family, indeed an increasing number have complex family relationships – all of which means that (like everyone else, it seems) they are looking for a sense of community and meaningful relationships with others. Most of these people are not Christians, and have never had any living connection with the church. They invite the church to reaffirm its foundational vision of people as made in the image of God, and to appreciate afresh that the gospel is relational, not individualistic. Effective ministry with this expanding people group could provide a source of new energy and enthusiasm that might yet transform the mission of the church, and turn declining congregations into significant outposts of God's kingdom. But to achieve this will require lateral thinking, creative Christian spirituality, and an openness to new ways that may in the event turn out to be just too challenging for the average local church.

Notes

Chapter 1: Family history

1. *The Waltons* is similarly well served, with its own website 'dedicated to the global community that strives to maintain family values as exemplified by the TV series, *The Waltons*.' http//:www.thewaltons.com

2. *The Simpsons* are actually not so very different. Though Homer and Marge Simpson display their affection in very different ways from Charles and Caroline Ingalls, they still exemplify traditional values like loyalty, mutual support, and truthfulness. See William Irwin, Mark T. Conard and Aeon J. Skoble (eds.), *The Simpsons and Philosophy* (Chicago: Open Court, 2001); and, for a religious perspective, Mark I. Pinsky, *The Gospel According to the Simpsons* (Louisville: Westminster John Knox Press, 2001). On portrayals of the family in literature through the ages, see Nicholas Tavuchis and William J. Goode, *The Family Through Literature* (New York: McGraw Hill, 1975).

3. See, for example, Bert N. Adams, *The Family: a Sociological Interpretation* (Chicago: Rand McNally, 1975); Graham Allan, *Family Life* (Oxford: Blackwell, 1985); Mary Farmer, *The Family* (London: Longmans, 1970); Diana Gittins, *The Family in Question*, 2nd edn (London: Macmillan, 1993); B. Gottlieb, *The Family in the Western World* (New York: OUP, 1993); C.C. Harris, *The Family: an Introduction* (London: Allen & Unwin, 1969); Barrie Thorne and Marilyn Yaloms (eds.), *Rethinking the Family* (London: Longman, 1982); Adrian Wilson, *Family* (London: Tavistock, 1985); Robert F. Winch, *The Modern Family* (New York: Rinehart & Winston, 1971). On the family in different cultures, see Ruth Nanda Anshen, *The Family: its Function and Destiny* (New York: Harper & Row, 1959). And from a Christian perspective, Herbert A. Anderson, Don S. Browning, Ian S. Evison and Mary Stewart Van Leeuwen (eds.), *The Family Handbook* (Louisville: Westminster John Knox Press, 1998); Jack O. Balswick and Judith K. Balswick, *The Family* (Grand Rapids: Baker, 1991). Stephen C. Barton (ed.), *The Family in Theological Perspective* (Edinburgh: T & T Clark, 1996); Rodney Clapp, *Families at the Crossroads* (Downers Grove: InterVarsity, 1993); Rosemary Radford Ruether, *Christianity and the Making of the Modern Family* (London: SCM Press, 2001).

4. *The Family in Question*, 60–72.

5. On the history of the family in different cultures, the most comprehensive work is still Willystine Goodsell, *A History of Marriage and the Family* (New York: Macmillan, 1934); see also James Casey, *The History of the Family* (Oxford: Blackwell, 1989). James Wallace Milden, *The Family in*

Past Time (New York: Garland, 1977), provides invaluable bibliographical guidance covering many historical periods.

6. This claim is generally made on the basis of mythology and implied oral traditions, e.g. by Robert Graves, *The White Goddess* (London: Peter Smith, 1983). But this is discounted by serious scholars: cf. Joan Bamberger, 'The Myth of Matriarchy: Why men rule in primitive society', in Michelle Zimbalist Rosaldo and Louise Lamphere (eds.), *Woman, Culture, and Society* (Palo Alto: Stanford University Press, 1974), 263–80; Robert Brown, *Human Universals* (Philadelphia: Temple University Press, 1991).

7. Fred J. Schonell, *The Happy Venture Readers* (Edinburgh: Oliver & Boyd, various dates from 1950 on).

8. John Drane and Olive M. Fleming Drane, 'Breaking into dynamic ways of being Church' in *Breaking New Ground* (Dunblane: Action of Churches Together in Scotland, 2001), 139–54; cf. John Drane, *The McDonaldization of the Church* (London: Darton, Longman & Todd, 2000), 133–8.

9. Edward Goldsmith, *The Way: An Ecological World-View* (London: Rider, 1992), 171. Our emphasis.

10. Awareness of the human rights issues surrounding the patriarchal exploitation of women goes back further than that, at least to the eighteenth century. Mary Wollstonecraft wrote her *Vindication of the Rights of Women* as early as 1792, while William Thompson's *Appeal of One Half of the Human Race against the Pretensions of the Other Half* (1825) and John Stuart Mill's *On the Subjection of Women* (1869) were also influential. The UK government's Married Women's Property Act (1882) began the process of legislative change, though there was still a long way to go after that.

11. For accessible accounts of this, see Charles Handy, *The Age of Unreason* (London: Business Books, 1989), especially 137–402; and *The Empty Raincoat* (London: Hutchinson, 1994).

12. Ulrich Beck, *Risk Society: toward a new modernity* (London: Sage Publications, 1992), 116.

13. Douglas Coupland, *Life After God* (London: Simon & Schuster, 1994). For one of the most sophisticated – and entertaining – presentations of the kind of challenges facing post-modern families, see also his novel *All Families are Psychotic* (London: Flamingo, 2001).

Chapter 2: Who are today's families?

1. The 2001 UK census reported that 22.0% of British children now live in one-parent families, while in the US 27% of all family households with children are headed by lone parents. There is an upward trend in most countries where the nuclear family – as distinct from the 'extended' family – has previously been the norm. Unless otherwise indicated, the statistics quoted in this chapter are taken from the 2001 UK census and the 2000 US census.

2. For some of these, see R.N. Rapoport, M.P. Fogarty and R. Rapoport (eds.), *Families in Britain* (London: Routledge & Kegan Paul, 1982), 121–354; Gwen B. Carr, *Marriage and Family in a Decade of Change* (Reading MA: Addison Wesley, 1977). For a global survey, from a Christian perspective, cf. Don S. Browning, 'World Family Trends' in *The Cambridge Companion to Christian Ethics* (Cambridge: Cambridge University Press, 2001), 243–60.

3. The nature of marriage itself is a major question in contemporary debates about the family, which cannot be tackled here. For a survey of historic Christian understandings, see John Witte Jr, *From Sacrament to Contract* (Louisville: Westminster John Knox Press, 1997); and for a proposal for reconstructing the institution of marriage on a Christian foundation, Don S. Browning, *Marriage and Modernization: how globalization threatens marriage and what to do about it* (Grand Rapids: Eerdmans, 2003). Cf. also Adrian Thatcher (ed.), *Celebrating Christian Marriage* (Edinburgh: T & T Clark, 2002).

4. *http://www.newyorklife.com/NYL2/Article/0,1234,11783,00.html*

5. On life in one-parent families, see S. Lanahan and G. Sandefur, *Growing up with a Single Parent* (Cambridge MA: Harvard University Press, 1994).

6. For first-hand accounts of some of the difficulties facing those who are trying to blend families together, see Frank F. Furstenberg and Graham B. Spanier, *Recycling the Family: Remarriage after Divorce* (Beverly Hills CA: Sage, 1984); Brenda Maddox, *The Half-Parent: Living with Other People's Children* (London: Andre Deutsch, 1975). For a Christian perspective, see Laura Sherman Walters, *There's a New Family in My House* (Wheaton IL: Harold Shaw Publishers, 1993); Merrilyn Williams, *Stepfamilies* (Oxford: Lion, 1998).

7. Ten- to fourteen-year-olds can be especially problematic in this respect: cf. the survey of research in M. Ambert and M. Baker, 'Marriage Dissolution', in B. Fox, *Family Bonds and Gender Division* (Toronto: Canadian Scholars Press, 1988), 453–75.

8. As with marriage, it is not possible to give this topic the attention it deserves in a book of this size. For Christian opinions on it, see Adrian Thatcher, *Living Together and Christian Ethics* (Cambridge: Cambridge University Press, 2002); Duncan Dormor, *Just Cohabiting?: The Church, Sex and Getting Married* (London: Darton, Longman & Todd, 2004).

9. For a suggestion as to how the church might recognize this, see Rosemary Radford Ruether, *Christianity and the making of the Modern Family* (London: SCM, 2001), 206–30.

10. The categories used by the census differentiated between different forms of the single lifestyle, listing 30.2% as 'single' (a definition that, however, includes cohabiting couples), 8.4% 'widowed', 8% 'divorced', and 2.5% 'separated'. When all these single people are added together, they clearly

outnumber 'married' (43.8%) or 'remarried' people (7.1%). The figures
from the USA are gathered slightly differently, but show the same trend
with more than 40% of the adult population being classified as single.

11. There is an absence of well-informed writing on this topic from a
Christian perspective, but see Albert Y. Hsu, *Singles at the Crossroads*
(Downers Grove: InterVarsity, 1997); Kristin Aune, *Single Women:
Challenge to the Church* (Carlisle: Paternoster Press, 2002).

12. For accounts of gay parenting, see A.E. Gottfried and A.W. Gottfried,
Redefining Families (New York: Plenum, 1994), 131–70; Jill S. Pollack,
Lesbian and Gay Families: Redefining Parenting in America (Chicago:
Franklin Watts, 1995); Peggy Gillespie (ed.), *Love makes a Family: portraits
of lesbian, gay, bisexual and transgendered parents and their families* (Amherst:
University of Massachusetts Press, 1999).

13. For a Christian resource, see David K. Switzer, *Pastoral Care of Gays,
Lesbians, and their Families* (Minneapolis: Fortress Press, 1999).

14. On custodial grandparenting, see Gottfried and Gottfried, *Redefining
Families*, 171–220.

Chapter 3:   Being a child in today's family

1. For a recent exposition of these ideas, see Dorothy Law Nolte, Jack
Canfield and Rachel Harris, *Children Learn What They Live: parenting to
inspire values* (New York: Workman Publishing, 1998).

2. Philippe Aries, *Centuries of Childhood* (New York: Vintage Press, 1962).

3. Cf. S. McLanahan and L. Bumpass, 'Intergenerational consequences of
family disruption', in *American Journal of Sociology* 94/1 (1988), 130–52.

4. For children's own stories of the way divorce impacted their lives, see
Jill Krementz, *How it Feels when Parents Divorce* (London: Victor Gollancz,
1985); also Yvette Walczak, *Divorce: the Child's Point of View* (London:
Harper & Row, 1984).

5. For discussions of child sexual abuse from a Christian perspective, cf.
Florence Rush, *The Best Kept Secret: Sexual Abuse of Children* (New York:
McGraw-Hill, 1980); Mary D. Pellauer, Barbara Chester and Jane A.
Boyaiian (eds.), *Sexual Assault and Abuse: A Handbook for Clergy and
Religious Professionals* (San Francisco: Harper & Row, 1987), 5–9, 172–97;
Hilary Cashman, *Christianity and Child Sexual Abuse* (London: SPCK,
1993); Ann Loades, 'Dympna revisited: thinking about the sexual abuse
of children', in Stephen C. Barton (ed.), *The Family in Theological Perspective* (Edinburgh: T & T Clark, 1996), 253–72.

6. Cf. Olive M. Fleming Drane, *Clowns, Storytellers, Disciples* (Oxford: BRF,
2002), 12–16.

7. For more on 'religious abuse', see Wesley R. Monfalcone, *Coping with
Abuse in the Family* (Philadelphia: Westminster Press, 1980), 45–57.

8. Cf. Diana Gittins, *The Family in Question*, 2nd edn (London: Macmillan,
1993), 169–82.

9. In many respects nothing much has changed with regard to some of the root causes of sexual abuse in particular. Cf. the work by Anthony S. Wohl on incest in Victorian families, which identifies bad housing, cramped conditions, and social inequalities as major contributing factors (ch. 10 in Anthony S. Wohl (ed.), *The Victorian Family,* London: Croom Helm, 1978).

10. Michel de Certeau, *The Practice of Everyday Life* (Berkeley: University of California Press, 1984).

11. For a comprehensive treatment of the whole question of ministering to children in today's families, see Andrew D. Lester (ed.), *When Children Suffer: A Sourcebook for Ministry with Children in Crisis* (Philadelphia: Westminster Press, 1987), which despite its age is still of considerable value.

12. Herbert Anderson and Susan B.W. Johnson, *Regarding Children: a new respect for childhood and families* (Louisville: Westminster John Knox Press, 1994), 26.

Chapter 4: **Adults in today's family**

1. Charles Handy, *The Empty Raincoat* (London: Hutchinson, 1994), 178ff.

2. *ibid.,* 232.

3. According to Erik Erikson, this is related to the different ways in which men and women conceptualize space: cf. his essay, 'Inner and Outer Space: Reflections on Womanhood', in N.W. Bell and E.F. Vogel, *A Modern Introduction to the Family* (New York: Free Press, 1968), 442–63.

4. Cf. C. Safilios-Rothschild, 'The study of family power structure: a review', in *Journal of Marriage and the Family* 32 (1970), 539–52; G. McDonald, 'Family Power: the assessment of a decade of theory and research, 1970–1979', in *Journal of Marriage and the Family* 42 (1980), 841–54; M. Szinovacz, 'Family Power', in M. Sussman and S. Steinmetz (eds.), *Handbook of Marriage and the Family* (New York: Plenum, 1987), 651–93.

5. Jessie Bernard, *The Future of Marriage,* 2nd edn (New Haven: Yale University Press, 1982).

6. For more on this research, see the website of the journal *Family Matters* *http://www.aifs.org.au/institute/media/media020918d.html*

7. John Gray, *Men Are from Mars, Women Are from Venus* (New York: Thorsons, 1993).

8. For a comprehensive account of all this, together with pastoral insights into the male psyche, see Christie Cozad Neuger and James N. Poling (eds.), *The Care of Men* (Nashville: Abingdon Press, 1997).

9. Things like sweat lodges and wilderness retreats have much to offer, along with the kind of spirituality reflected in Robert Bly's best-selling book *Iron John: a Book about Men* (Shaftesbury: Element Books, 1991), but are not exactly accessible to most males. For an outstanding account of

the predicament of men in different cultures today, cf. Errol Miller, *Men at Risk* (Kingston: Jamaica Publishing House, 1991). Most Christian books on the subject fail to get to grips with the new social reality at all, but see James Nelson, *The Intimate Connection: Male Sexuality, Masculine Spirituality* (Philadelphia: Westminster Press, 1988); Jack O. Balswick, *Men at the Crossroads* (Downers Grove: InterVarsity, 1992); Mary Stewart Van Leeuwen, *My Brother's Keeper* (Downers Grove: InterVarsity, 2002) = *Fathers and Sons: the search for a new masculinity* (Leicester: IVP, 2003).

10. For a helpful survey of all the issues dealt with in this chapter, from a Christian perspective, see Ann Carr and Mary Stewart Van Leeuwen (eds.), *Religion, Feminism, and the Family* (Louisville: Westminster John Knox Press, 1996).

Chapter 5: **Parenting**

1. On Family Therapy, see A.C. Robin Skynner, *One Flesh: Separate Persons* (London: Constable, 1976) [= *Systems of Family & Marital Psychotherapy* (New York: Brunner-Routledge, 1976)]; Edwin Friedman, *Generation to Generation* (New York: Guilford, 1985); A. Napier and Carl Whitaker, *The Family Crucible* (New York: Bantam, 1978). From a Christian perspective, see Judith K. Balswick *et al.*, *Relationship-Empowerment Parenting: Building Formative and Fulfilling Relationships With Your Children* (Grand Rapids: Baker, 2003); Froma Walsh (ed.), *Spiritual Resources in Family Therapy* (New York: The Guilford Press, 1999).

2. E. Duvall and B. Miller, *Marriage and Family Development*, 6th edn (New York: Harper & Row, 1985).

3. For a comprehensive discussion of family stage theory, from a Christian perspective, cf. Diana R. Garland, *Family Ministry* (Downers Grove: InterVarsity, 1999), 113–71.

4. On this, see C. Broderick and J. Smith, 'The general systems approach to the family', in W. Burr (ed.), *Contemporary Theories about the Family* (New York: Free Press, 1979), 2:112–29; Kathleen M. Galvin and Bernard J. Brommel, *Family Communication: cohesion and change* (New York: HarperCollins, 1991).

5. Ellen Galinsky, *The Six Stages of Parenting* (Reading MA: Addison-Wesley, 1987).

6. John Finney, *Finding Faith Today* (Swindon: Bible Society, 1992), 40–1. For perspectives on practical ministry at this point in a woman's life, see Margaret L. Hammer, *Giving Birth: reclaiming Biblical metaphor for pastoral practice* (Louisville: Westminster John Knox Press, 1994).

7. Herbert Anderson and Susan B.W. Johnson, *Regarding children: a new respect for childhood and families* (Louisville: Westminster John Knox Press, 1994), 91.

8. Erik H. Erikson, *Identity, Youth and Crisis* (New York: Norton, 1968), 96.

9. Erik H. Erikson, *Childhood and Society*, 2nd edn (New York: Norton, 1950), 255.

10. *ibid.*, 259.

11. For a Christian resource, see Peter Brierley, *Reaching and Keeping Tweenagers* (London: Christian Research, 2003).

Chapter 6: **Bible families**

1. Anyone who doubts that should consult the Center for the Prevention of Sexual and Domestic Violence at *http//:www.cpsd.org*

2. See Susan Brooks Thistlethwaite, 'Every Two Minutes: Battered Women and Feminist Interpretation', in L.M. Russell (ed.), *Feminist Interpretation of the Bible* (Philadelphia: Westminster Press, 1985), 96–107. Also the extensive documentation of the social consequences of this teaching in Joy M.K. Bussert, *Battered Women* (Minneapolis: Division for Mission of the Lutheran Church in America, 1986). Typing the phrase 'wives obey your husbands' in an Internet search engine produces a list of more than 40,000 websites, the majority of them offering this kind of advice.

3. See Stanley Ayling, *John Wesley* (London: Collins, 1979), 215–31; Henry D. Rack, *Reasonable Enthusiast* (London: Epworth, 1989), 251–69. On Livingstone, see Tim Jeal, *Livingstone* (London: Heinemann, 1973), 60–2, 110–12, 251.

4. F.F. Bruce, *Paul Apostle of the Free Spirit* (Exeter: Paternoster Press, 1977), 269–70.

5. 'Christians are more likely to experience divorce than non-Christians', in *The Barna Report* (Glendale: Barna Research, 1999). The study was based on almost 4000 adults, with a margin for error of +/- 2%.

6. Marcus Borg, *Reading the Bible again for the first time* (San Francisco: HarperCollins, 2002); see also his book *Meeting Jesus again for the first time* (San Francisco: HarperCollins, 1995).

7. For a survey of all Bible families, see Herbert Anderson *et al.* (eds.), *The Family Handbook* (Louisville: Westminster John Knox Press, 1998), 195–257.

8. For a survey and summary of some of the theological issues arising out of the way we use the Bible, see Rita-Lou Clarke, *Pastoral Care of Battered Women* (Philadelphia: Westminster Press, 1986), 61–85.

9. There are some stories in the Old Testament which show women as having a certain amount of independence (people like Deborah, Esther, and some prophetesses). But in spite of this, they did not as a whole hold positions in government, or become priests. The family was always patriarchal in structure, and after the exile this became even more rigid as its assumptions were hardened into a very strict system of segregation between women and men.

10. For a thorough exposition of all the biblical material on this topic, see

David Instone-Brewer, *Divorce and Remarriage in the Bible* (Grand Rapids: Eerdmans, 2002).

11. For the rabbis' views on women's place, see the survey in O.L. Yarbrough, *Not Like the Gentiles* (Atlanta: Scholars Press, 1985), esp. 21–3.

12. There is of course a specific background to Jesus' teaching, which is well documented in all the standard New Testament commentaries. For a survey of different exegetical opinions, and their impact on the pastoral task, see Cyril J. Barber, 'Marriage, Divorce and Remarriage', in *Journal of Psychology and Theology* 12 (1984), 170–77.

13. Thistlethwaite, 'Every Two Minutes: Battered Women and Feminist Interpretation', in Russell (ed.), *Feminist Interpretation of the Bible*, 102. Another example would be John 4, which shows Jesus unhesitatingly accepting a woman who was caught up in situations of domestic tension, and affirming her worth, while at the same time inviting her to discipleship.

14. For a succinct and accessible account of the cultural context in Roman society, see David Instone-Brewer, *Divorce and Remarriage in the Church* (Carlisle: Paternoster, 2003), 120–23.

15. For more discussion of this matter in relation to contemporary family values, see Elisabeth Schussler Fiorenza, *In Memory of Her* (New York: Crossroad, 1983), 266–70, where it is argued that Paul took the common code of social behaviour and turned it on its head so as to challenge patriarchal domination, by reading it in the light of Jesus' teaching about loving one's neighbour as oneself (Mark 12:31). For a similar understanding, see also James D.G. Dunn, 'The Household Rules in the New Testament', in Stephen C. Barton (ed.), *The Family in Theological Perspective* (Edinburgh: T & T Clark, 1996), 43–63. A different interpretation of the passage is offered by Rosemary Radford Ruether, *Sexism and God-Talk* (Boston: Beacon, 1983), 141–2.

16. R.W.L. Moberly, *The Bible, Theology and Faith* (Cambridge: Cambridge University Press, 2000), 129.

17. *ibid.*

18. Karl Barth, *Church Dogmatics*, Vol. 3, section 4 (Edinburgh: T & T Clark, 1975), 116–240. See Paul S. Fiddes, 'The status of women in the thought of Karl Barth', in Janet Martin Soskice (ed.), *After Eve: Women, Theology, and the Christian Tradition* (London: Marshall Pickering, 1990), 138–55.

Chapter 7: Nurturing the spirituality of the family

1. John H. Westerhoff III, *Will our Children have Faith?* (Harrisburg PA: Morehouse, 2000), revised edition of a book first published in 1976. For a popular presentation of this thinking from a British perspective, see the report of the Church of England General Synod Board of Education, *How Faith Grows* (London: Church House Publishing, 1991).

2. Walter Brueggemann, 'Will our Faith have Children?' in *Word and World* 3/3 (1983), 272–83.
3. The classic work is James W. Fowler, *Stages of Faith* (San Francisco: Harper & Row, 1981). Cf. also James Fowler, *Becoming Adult, Becoming Christian* (San Francisco: HarperCollins, 1984), James Fowler, *Faith Development & Pastoral Care* (Philadelphia: Fortress, 1987), Jeff Astley and Leslie Francis, *Christian Perspectives on Faith Development* (Grand Rapids: Eerdmans, 1992), Lindell Sawyers (ed.), *Faith and Families* (Philadelphia: Geneva Press, 1986).
4. Cf. Thomas A. Droege, *Faith Passages and Patterns* (Philadelphia: Fortress, 1983), V. Bailey Gillespie, *The Experience of Faith* (Birmingham: Religious Education Press, 1988).
5. Cf. William A. Strange, *Children in the Early Church* (Carlisle: Paternoster Press, 1996).
6. David Hay and Rebecca Nye, *The Spirit of the Child* (London: Fount, 1998); cf. also Robert Coles, *The Spiritual Life of Children* (Boston: Houghton Mifflin, 1990), Doris A. Blazer (ed.), *Faith Development in Early Childhood* (Kansas MO: Sheed & Ward, 1989).
7. Albert Mehrabian, *Silent Messages* (New York: Penguin, 1971).
8. For more on this, see Perry G. Downs, *Teaching for Spiritual Growth* (Grand Rapids: Zondervan, 1994), Jerome Berryman, *Godly Play* (Minneapolis: Augsburg Fortress, 1995).
9. For an interesting presentation of Jesus' relational style, see Laurie Beth Jones, *Jesus CEO* (New York: Hyperion, 1995).
10. For extensive resources on family ministries, see especially Diana R. Garland, *Family Ministry*; K. Brynoll Lyon and Archie Smith Jr, *Tending the Flock* (Louisville: Westminster John Knox, 1998).
11. John Finney, *Finding Faith Today* (Swindon: Bible Society, 1992), 41.
12. Cf. John Drane, *Faith in a Changing Culture* (London: HarperCollins, 1997), Raymond Fung, *The Isaiah Vision* (Geneva: World Council of Churches, 1992).
13. For an example of one such particularly adventurous programme, see Olive M. Fleming Drane, *Clowns, Storytellers, Disciples* (Oxford: BRF, 2002), 211–18.
14. On storytelling, see Janet Litherland, *Storytelling from the Bible* (Colorado Springs: Meriwether, 1991); Thomas E. Boomershine, *Story Journey* (Nashville: Abingdon Press, 1988), William J. Bausch, *Storytelling, Imagination and Faith* (Mystic CT: Twenty-Third Publications, 1984).
15. For fuller treatment of all these ideas, see Fleming Drane, *Clowns, Storytellers, Disciples*.
16. Kathryn Goering Reid with Marie M. Fortune, *Preventing Child Sexual Abuse: A Curriculum for Children Ages 9 through 12* (New York: United Church Press, 1989).

Chapter 8: **The family and the church**

1. On the question of all-age or intergenerational worship, see David Ng and Virginia Thomas, *Children in the Worshiping Community* (Atlanta: John Knox Press, 1981); Megan Coote, *Growing Together* (Melbourne: JBCE, 1988); Peter Graystone and Eileen Turner, *A Church for All Ages* (London: Scripture Union, 1993). For a helpful series of case studies, see David Merritt and Muriel Porter, *What will we do with the Children?* (Melbourne: JBCE, 1990).

2. John Drane, *Faith in a Changing Culture* (London: HarperCollins, 1997), 218–23; cf. Richard V. Peace, *Conversion in the New Testament* (Grand Rapids: Eerdmans, 1999). St Paul's life follows the same pattern of the primacy of discipleship and community, with belief systems emerging out of reflection on that experience: cf. Seyoon Kim, *The Origin of Paul's Gospel* (Grand Rapids: Eerdmans, 1984).

3. Cf. Drane, *Faith in a Changing Culture*, 108–14; Olive M. Fleming Drane, *Clowns, Storytellers, Disciples* (Oxford: BRF, 2002), 148–71.

4. Raymond Fung, 'Mission in Christ's Way', in *International Review of Mission* LXXIX (1990), 82–103.

5. For more on this, see John Drane, *The Bible Phenomenon* (Oxford: Lion, 1999), 167–70; Olive M. Fleming Drane, *Clowns, Storytellers, Disciples* (Oxford: BRF, 2002), 136–8.

6. For some examples, see Mike Riddell, *Threshold of the Future* (London: SPCK, 1998), 157–71.

7. For an understanding of the New Testament churches along these lines, see Robert Banks, *Going to Church in the First Century* (Parramatta NSW: Hexagon, 1985); and for a contemporary application, Robert and Julia Banks, *The Church Comes Home* (Peabody: Hendrickson, 1998).

8. D. Bonhoeffer, *Letters and Papers from Prison* (New York: Macmillan, 1967).

9. John Westerhoff, *Living the Faith Community* (San Francisco: Harper & Row, 1985), 9–10.

Chapter 9: *Families in times of crisis*

1. Erin Pizzey, *Scream Quietly or the Neighbours Will Hear* (London: Penguin, 1974).

2. Erin Pizzey and Jeff Shapiro, *Prone to Violence* (London: Hamlyn, 1982).

3. *Domestic Violence: Home Office Research Study 191* (London: HMSO, 1999).

4. P.G. Tjaden and N. Thoennes, *Full Report of Prevalence, Incidence and Consequences of Violence Against Women: Findings from the National Violence Against Women Survey* (Washington, DC: U.S. Department of Justice, National Institute of Justice & Centers for Disease Control and Prevention Research Report, 2000); *Family Violence in Canada: A Statistical Profile* (Ottawa: Statistics Canada, 2000).

5. For all this, see Helen L. Conway, *Domestic Violence and the Church*

(Carlisle: Paternoster, 1998); Stephen Parsons, *Ungodly Fear* (Oxford: Lion, 2000).

6. For more extensive discussion of the historical and philosophical background to all this within Christianity, see Joy M.K. Bussert, *Battered Women* (Minneapolis: Division for Mission of the Lutheran Church in America, 1986), 5–15, 55–66; Rita-Lou Clarke, *Pastoral Care of Battered Women* (Philadelphia: Westminster Press, 1986), 321–35.

7. Marie M. Fortune, *Keeping the Faith* (San Francisco: Harper, 1987).

8. Cf. Gary P. Liaboe, 'The Place of Wife Battering in Considering Divorce', in *Journal of Psychology and Theology* 13 (1985), 129–38. For a balanced discussion of many of the issues in this chapter, from a biblical perspective, see David Instone-Brewer, *Divorce and Remarriage in the Church* (Grand Rapids: Eerdmans, 2002), 82–95.

9. The expression of Richard Gelles, *The Violent Home* (Beverly Hills CA: Sage, 1972), 74. For a general account of the psychological dimensions of what may be going on in violent relationships, albeit exclusively from a female perspective, see Clarke, *Pastoral Care of Battered Women*, 36–60.

10. For this reason, helping men who are also religious to overcome their violent tendencies can be a particularly tough assignment: see A.L. Horton and J.A. Williamson (eds.), *Abuse and Religion: When Praying Isn't Enough* (Lexington MA: Lexington University Press, 1988).

11. A survey conducted in 12,000 evangelical Christian homes came to the conclusion that 'although many Christian families are not marked by physical violence, many do experience emotional abuse.' Cf. Clyde Narramore, 'Abusing Children Emotionally', in *Fundamentalist Journal* 5/5 (1986), 32–4.

12. For more on handling abuse stemming from religious faith, see Wesley R. Monfalcone, *Coping With Abuse in the Family* (Philadelphia: Westminster Press, 1980), 45–57.

13. One of the most comprehensive and well informed is Marie M. Fortune, *Violence in the Family. A Workshop Curriculum for Clergy and Other Helpers* (Cleveland OH: Pilgrim Press, 1991).

14. *http://www.victoria-climbie-inquiry.org.uk/Evidence/Archive/Oct01/081001latestp2.htm*

15. Randy Frame, 'Child Abuse: The Church's Best Kept Secret?', in *Christianity Today* 29/3 (15 Feb. 1985), 34. For helpful insights on the theological significance of abuse, see James N. Poling, 'Child Sexual Abuse: A Rich Context for Thinking about God, Community, and Ministry', in *Journal of Pastoral Care* XLII/1 (1988), 58–61. On the broader religious ramifications, Joanne Carlson Brown and Carole R. Bohn (eds.), *Christianity, Patriarchy and Abuse* (Cleveland OH: Pilgrim Press, 1989).

16. Jennifer Craven, 'Sexual Abuse in Children: Factors, Effects, Treatment, and Ministry Implications', in *Christian Education Journal* 7/1 (1986), 73.

17. See Marie M. Fortune, *Sexual Violence: the Unmentionable Sin* (New York:

Pilgrim Press, 1983), 176–89. For more on work with perpetrators, cf. Graham C. Willis, *Unspeakable Crimes* (London: Children's Society, 1993), which is especially useful as it documents and compares the British and North American experience.

18. But this is not the only cause: cf. Alfred Kadushin and Judith A. Martin, *Child Abuse: An Interactional Event* (New York: Columbia University Press, 1981), who identify the key components of abuse as being within the abusive event itself.

Chapter 10: Growing old

1. *As You Like It*, II.vii.166.
2. Of approximately 750,000 people in the UK with dementia, only 18,500 are aged under sixty-five, and one in twenty people aged over sixty-five can expect to have the condition, rising to one in five of the over-eighties. See *Older people in the United Kingdom: some basic facts 2002* (London: Age Concern); 'Dementia in people aged 65 years and older: a growing problem?', *Population Trends* 92, Summer 1998 (London: HMSO, 1998).
3. Erik Erikson, *Childhood and Society* (London: Penguin, 1954).
4. J.E. Birren, K.W. Schaie and V.J. Renner, *Handbook of the Psychology of Aging* (San Diego: Academic Press, 2001).
5. *UK Christian Handbook Religious Trends No 4, 2003/4* (London: Christian Research, 2003).
6. Michael Apichella, *The Church's hidden asset: empowering the older generation* (Stowmarket: Kevin Mayhew, 2001), 14–15.
7. Eugene C. Bianchi, *Aging as a Spiritual Journey* (New York: Crossroad, 1997), 15.
8. For a corrective, see Melvin A. Kimble *et al.*, *Aging, Spirituality, and Religion* (Minneapolis: Fortress Press, 1995); also L. Eugene Thomas and Susan A. Eisenhandler (eds.), *Religion, Belief, and Spirituality in Later Life* (New York: Springer, 1999).
9. See Harold G. Koenig and Andrew J. Weaver, *Counseling Troubled Older Adults* (Nashville: Abingdon Press, 1997).
10. Bianchi, *Aging as a Spiritual Journey*, 8.
11. For an excellent 'how-to' on this, see Mike Paterson, *With Love: gifting stories to grandchildren*, 2nd edn (North Shore City, New Zealand: Tandem Press, 2001).
12. Raymond Fung, *The Isaiah Vision* (Geneva: WCC, 1992).
13. Karen Kaigler-Walker, *Positive Aging* (Berkeley: Conari Press, 1997).
14. *It's a Wonderful Life*, directed by Frank Capra (Republic Pictures, 1947).
15. See the analysis of the 1960s in Callum Brown, *The Death of Christian Britain* (London: Routledge, 2001).

Booklist

Adams, Bert N., *The Family: a Sociological Interpretation* (Chicago: Rand McNally, 1975)

Allan, Graham, *Family Life* (Oxford: Blackwell, 1985)

Anderson, Herbert A., Don S. Browning, Ian S. Evison and Mary Stewart Van Leeuwen (eds.), *The Family Handbook* (Louisville: Westminster John Knox Press, 1998)

Anderson, Herbert, and Susan B.W. Johnson, *Regarding Children: a new respect for childhood and families* (Louisville: Westminster John Knox Press, 1994)

Anshen, Ruth Nanda, *The Family: its Function and Destiny* (New York: Harper & Row, 1959)

Apichella, Michael, *The Church's hidden asset: empowering the older generation* (Stowmarket: Kevin Mayhew, 2001)

Aries, Philippe, *Centuries of Childhood* (New York: Vintage Press, 1962)

Astley, Jeff, and Leslie Francis, *Christian Perspectives on Faith Development* (Grand Rapids: Eerdmans, 1992)

Aune, Kristin, *Single Women: Challenge to the Church* (Carlisle: Paternoster Press, 2002)

Balswick, Jack O., and Judith K. Balswick, *The Family* (Grand Rapids: Baker, 1991)

Balswick, Jack O., *Men at the Crossroads* (Downers Grove: InterVarsity, 1992)

Balswick, Judith K. et al., *Relationship-Empowerment Parenting: Building Formative and Fulfilling Relationships With Your Children* (Grand Rapids: Baker, 2003)

Banks, Robert, and Julia, *The Church Comes Home* (Peabody: Hendrickson, 1998)

Barton, Stephen C. (ed.), *The Family in Theological Perspective* (Edinburgh: T & T Clark, 1996)

Beck, Ulrich, *Risk Society: toward a new modernity* (London: Sage Publications, 1992)

Bell, N.W., and E.F. Vogel, *A Modern Introduction to the Family* (New York: Free Press, 1968)

Bianchi, Eugene C., *Aging as a Spiritual Journey* (New York: Crossroad, 1997)

Birren, J.E., K.W. Schaie and V.J. Renner, *Handbook of the Psychology of Aging* (San Diego: Academic Press, 2001)

Blazer, Doris A. (ed.), *Faith Development in Early Childhood* (Kansas MO: Sheed & Ward, 1989)

Brierley, Peter, *Reaching and Keeping Tweenagers* (London: Christian Research, 2003)

Browning, Don S., *Marriage and Modernization: how globalization threatens marriage and what to do about it* (Grand Rapids: Eerdmans, 2003)

Brynoll, Lyon K., and Archie Smith Jr, *Tending the Flock* (Louisville: Westminster John Knox Press, 1998)

Burr, W. (ed.), *Contemporary Theories about the Family* (New York: Free Press, 1979)

Bussert, Joy M.K., *Battered Women* (Minneapolis: Division for Mission of the Lutheran Church in America, 1986)

Brown, Joanne Carlson, and Carole R. Bohn (eds.), *Christianity, Patriarchy and Abuse* (Cleveland OH: Pilgrim Press, 1989)

Carr, Ann, and Mary Stewart Van Leeuwen (eds.), *Religion, Feminism, and the Family* (Louisville: Westminster John Knox Press, 1996)

Carr, Gwen B., *Marriage and Family in a Decade of Change* (Reading MA: Addison Wesley, 1977)

Casey, James, *The History of the Family* (Oxford: Blackwell, 1989)

Cashman, Hilary, *Christianity and Child Sexual Abuse* (London: SPCK, 1993)

Certeau, Michel de, *The Practice of Everyday Life* (Berkeley: University of California Press, 1984)

Clapp, Rodney, *Families at the Crossroads* (Downers Grove: InterVarsity, 1993)

Clarke, Rita-Lou, *Pastoral Care of Battered Women* (Philadelphia: Westminster Press, 1986)

Coles, Robert, *The Spiritual Life of Children* (Boston: Houghton Mifflin, 1990)

Conway, Helen L., *Domestic Violence and the Church* (Carlisle: Paternoster, 1998)

Coupland, Douglas, *All Families are Psychotic* (London: Flamingo, 2001)

Drane, John, *Faith in a Changing Culture* (London: HarperCollins, 1997)
  The McDonaldization of the Church (London: Darton, Longman & Todd, 2000)

Droege, Thomas A., *Faith Passages and Patterns* (Philadelphia: Fortress, 1983)

Erikson, Erik H., *Childhood and Society*, 2nd edn (New York: Norton, 1950)
  Identity, Youth and Crisis (New York: Norton, 1968)

Farmer, Mary, *The Family* (London: Longmans, 1970)

Fleming Drane, Olive M., *Clowns, Storytellers, Disciples* (Oxford: BRF, 2002)

Fortune, Marie M., *Sexual Violence: the Unmentionable Sin* (New York: Pilgrim Press, 1983)
  Keeping the Faith (San Francisco: Harper, 1987)
  Violence in the Family. A Workshop Curriculum for Clergy and Other Helpers (Cleveland OH: Pilgrim Press, 1991)

Fowler, James W., *Stages of Faith* (San Francisco: Harper & Row, 1981)
  Becoming Adult, Becoming Christian (San Francisco: HarperCollins, 1984)
  Faith Development & Pastoral Care (Philadelphia: Fortress, 1987)

Furstenberg, Frank F., and Graham B. Spanier, *Recycling the Family: Remarriage after Divorce* (Beverly Hills CA: Sage, 1984)

Galinsky, Ellen, *The Six Stages of Parenting* (Reading MA: Addison-Wesley, 1987)

Garland, Diana R., *Family Ministry* (Downers Grove: InterVarsity, 1999)

Gelles, Richard, *The Violent Home* (Beverly Hills CA: Sage, 1972)

Gillespie, V. Bailey, *The Experience of Faith* (Birmingham: Religious Education Press, 1988)

Gittins, Diana, *The Family in Question*, 2nd edn (London: Macmillan, 1993)

Goering Reid, Kathryn, with Marie M. Fortune, *Preventing Child Sexual Abuse: A Curriculum for Children Ages 9 through 12* (New York: United Church Press, 1989)

Goodsell, Willystine, *A History of Marriage and the Family* (New York: Macmillan, 1934)

Gottfried, A.E., and A.W. Gottfried, *Redefining Families* (New York: Plenum, 1994)

Gottlieb, B., *The Family in the Western World* (New York: OUP, 1993)

Graystone, Peter, and Eileen Turner, *A Church for All Ages* (London: Scripture Union, 1993)

Hammer, Margaret L., *Giving Birth: reclaiming Biblical metaphor for pastoral practice* (Louisville: Westminster John Knox Press, 1994)

Harris, C.C., *The Family: an Introduction* (London: Allen & Unwin, 1969)

Hay, David, and Rebecca Nye, *The Spirit of the Child* (London: Fount, 1998)

Horton, A.L., and J.A. Williamson (eds.), *Abuse and Religion: When Praying Isn't Enough* (Lexington MA: Lexington University Press, 1988)

Hsu, Albert Y., *Singles at the Crossroads* (Downers Grove: InterVarsity, 1997)

Instone-Brewer, David, *Divorce and Remarriage in the Bible* (Grand Rapids: Eerdmans, 2002)

Divorce and Remarriage in the Church (Carlisle: Paternoster, 2003)

Kaigler-Walker, Karen, *Positive Aging* (Berkeley: Conari Press, 1997)

Kimble, Melvin A. et al., *Aging, Spirituality, and Religion* (Minneapolis: Fortress Press, 1995)

Krementz, Jill, *How it Feels when Parents Divorce* (London: Victor Gollancz, 1985)

Lanahan, S., and G. Sandefur, *Growing up with a Single Parent* (Cambridge MA: Harvard University Press, 1994)

Lester, Andrew D. (ed.), *When Children Suffer: A Sourcebook for Ministry with Children in Crisis* (Philadelphia: Westminster Press, 1987)

Maddox, Brenda, *The Half-Parent: Living with Other People's Children* (London: Andre Deutsch, 1975)

Milden, James Wallace, *The Family in Past Time* (New York: Garland, 1977)

Monfalcone, Wesley R., *Coping with Abuse in the Family* (Philadelphia: Westminster Press, 1980)

Napier, A., and Carl Whitaker, *The Family Crucible* (New York: Bantam, 1978)

Nelson, James, *The Intimate Connection: Male Sexuality, Masculine Spirituality* (Philadelphia: Westminster Press, 1988)

Neuger, Christie Cozad, and James N. Poling (eds.), *The Care of Men* (Nashville: Abingdon Press, 1997)

Ng, David, and Virginia Thomas, *Children in the Worshiping Community* (Atlanta: John Knox Press, 1981)

Parsons, Stephen, *Ungodly Fear* (Oxford: Lion, 2000)

Pellauer, Mary D., Barbara Chester and Jane A. Boyaiian (eds.), *Sexual Assault and Abuse: A Handbook for Clergy and Religious Professionals* (San Francisco: Harper & Row, 1987)

Rapoport, R.N., M.P. Fogarty and R. Rapoport (eds.), *Families in Britain* (London: Routledge & Kegan Paul, 1982)

Ruether, Rosemary Radford, *Christianity and the Making of the Modern Family* (London: SCM Press, 2001)

Rush, Florence, *The Best Kept Secret: Sexual Abuse of Children* (New York: McGraw-Hill, 1980)

Russell, L.M. (ed.), *Feminist Interpretation of the Bible* (Philadelphia: Westminster Press, 1985)

Sawyers, Lindell (ed.), *Faith and Families* (Philadelphia: Geneva Press, 1986)

Skynner, A.C. Robin, *One Flesh: Separate Persons* (London: Constable, 1976) = *Systems of Family & Marital Psychotherapy* (New York: Brunner-Routledge, 1976)

Strange, William A., *Children in the Early Church* (Carlisle: Paternoster Press, 1996)

Sussman, M., and S. Steinmetz (eds.), *Handbook of Marriage and the Family* (New York: Plenum, 1987)

Tavuchis, Nicholas, and William J. Goode, *The Family Through Literature* (New York: McGraw Hill, 1975)

Thomas, L. Eugene, and Susan A. Eisenhandler (eds.), *Religion, Belief, and Spirituality in Later Life* (New York: Springer, 1999)

Thorne, Barrie, and Marilyn Yaloms (eds.), *Rethinking the Family* (London: Longman, 1982)

Van Leeuwen, Mary Stewart, *My Brother's Keeper* (Downers Grove: Inter-Varsity, 2002) = *Fathers and Sons: the search for a new masculinity* (Leicester: IVP, 2003)

Walczak, Yvette, *Divorce: the Child's Point of View* (London: Harper & Row, 1984)

Walsh, Froma (ed.), *Spiritual Resources in Family Therapy* (New York: The Guilford Press, 1999)

Walters, Laura Sherman, *There's a New Family in My House* (Wheaton IL: Harold Shaw Publishers, 1993)

Westerhoff III, John H., *Will our Children have Faith?* 2nd edn (Harrisburg PA: Morehouse, 2000)

Williams, Merrilyn, *Stepfamilies* (Oxford: Lion, 1998)

Wilson, Adrian, *Family* (London: Tavistock, 1985)

Winch, Robert F., *The Modern Family* (New York: Rinehart & Winston, 1971)

Witte Jr, John, *From Sacrament to Contract* (Louisville: Westminster John Knox Press, 1997)

Index

People and Subjects

abuse 20, 27, 31, 47, 51–4, 60, 68, 69–71, 76–7, 96, 102, 105, 108–9, 115–16, 138, 140–1, 158–78
adolescent, adolescence 50, 60, 80, 94–8, 150, 152–7, 181

Barth, Karl 116
Beck, Ulrich 19
Bible, teaching on families 4, 8, 15, 44, 55–6, 99–117
Bonhoeffer, Dietrich 153
Borg, Marcus 106
Bruce, F. F. 104
Brueggemann, Walter 118
Burns, Robert 1, 11

child, children, childhood: in family 11–13, 20, 42–57, 82; discipline of 33, 45–6, 85, 89–91; and divorce 49–51; and values 92–3; spirituality of 122–5, 173; toddlers 91, 129–32; *see also* faith, sharing and nurture of
childlessness 35–7, 112, 146
church 32–3, 43–4, 51, 55–7, 93–4, 125; attitudes to children 91–2, 118–19, 128–9, 152–3; support for parents 53, 64–5, 87, 89, 98, 125–57; and older people 183–5, 188
cohabitation 34–5, 81, 82, 100
community, search for 19–20, 23–4, 38, 4–44, 56, 79, 146–7, 151–4, 157, 186–7, 191–2; *see also* meals

consumers, consumerism 10–13, 43, 56–7, 94, 96, 190
Coupland, Douglas 19
de Certeau, Michel 55

Dickens, Charles 2
divorce 28–9, 32, 37, 48, 49–51, 63, 68, 76–7, 82, 89, 93, 104, 111–13, 140, 180; *see also* marriage

Enlightenment 9–14, 16, 18–19, 22; *see also* family: industrial nuclear
Erikson, Erik 80, 82, 88, 93, 179

faith, sharing and nurture of 4, 11–12, 88, 118–41, 173; *see also* children: spirituality of
family, definition of 5–7, 15, 22–41; traditional 1–3, 7–9, 67, 73–4; industrial nuclear 10–13, 32, 40, 45, 74, 81, 83, 103, 105, 107, 146, 166; post-modern 14–20, 59–62, 95–6; blended 31–3, 63, 81, 83, 90, 93; & Christian values 3–5, 56–9, 103–7, 110–11; *see also* Bible, teaching on families
Finney, John 85, 128
food: *see* meals

Gittins, Diana 6
Goldsmith, Edward 15–16
grandparents 33, 34–5, 39, 60, 81, 83, 87, 88, 180, 187
Gray, John 72

Handy, Charles 65–6

homosexuality 38–9; *see also* sex, sexuality

identity, personal 19–20, 42–3, 61–2, 75–7, 90–1, 181–7, 189; *see also* community, search for

Jesus 22–3, 47, 55–6, 58, 109–13, 126, 130, 148, 159, 167, 192; *see also* Bible, teaching on families

Livingstone, David 104

marriage 2, 99–102; *see also* divorce
meals 1, 31, 38, 46, 70, 95, 134–5, 151–2; *see also* community
Mehrabian, Albert 125
men, place in family 1–3, 8–13, 17, 19–20, 24–7, 48–9, 71–9; as lone parents 30–1, 75, 78–9, 140; and emotions 75–7, 136; *see also* family, industrial nuclear; patriarchy; women
middle age, mid-life 96–8, 181–7
Modernity: *see* Enlightenment
money: *see* consumerism
music 95, 184

old age 47, 83, 179–94

parents, parenting 80–98, 126–41, 181–2; single parents 27–31, 47, 87, 90; step-parents 31–3, child care 23–4, 65, 88, 129–30; support groups 135–40
patriarchy 8–9, 10–11, 25–6, 53, 69–74, 97, 107–9, 111–14, 130, 150, 165–7; *see also* family, industrial nuclear; men; women
Pizzey, Erin 160

Revolution, Industrial 9–13, 17, 22; *see also* Enlightenment
sex, sexuality 7, 17, 36, 61–2, 68, 70, 85, 94–5, 143; *see also* homosexuality
Simpsons, The 3
singles, singleness 20, 37–8, 112, 143, 146, 186; as parents 22, 27–31, 67
suicide 54, 76, 153

teenagers: *see* adolescents

violence: *see* abuse

Wesley, John 104
Westerhoff, John H. 118, 119, 157
Wilder, Laura Ingalls 3
women, role in family 1–3, 7–13, 17, 19–20, 25–7, 62–71; as lone parents 29–30, 48, 67, 68, 134–5; in teaching of Jesus 112–13; in St Paul 113–14; *see also* family, industrial nuclear; men; patriarchy
work 6–7, 9–13, 16–20, 23–7, 35–6, 39–40, 44, 65–7, 73, 76, 78–9, 129–30, 144–5, 165–7, 185

Bible references

Genesis 1:27–8 45, 55, 74, 107
   2:25 107
   3:16 107
   4:1–16 108
   12:10–20 108
   16:1–4 108
   21:9–12 108
   22:1–14 108
   27:1–45 109
   37:1–36 109
Exodus 20:3 107
   20:17 111
   32:1–35 109
Numbers 12:1–16 109

Deuteronomy 24:1–2 111
1 Samuel 2:27–36 109
  3:11–14 109
  2 Kings 8–12 109
Isaiah 11:6 91
  42:9 59
  65:20–3 187
Ezekiel 18:2
Hosea 1:2–3:5 109
Ruth 109
Ben Sirach 30:1–13 45
Matthew 5:38–42 59
  19:1–12 112
  19:30 59
Mark 1:16–20 147
  2:12 59
  3:31–5 110
  9:33–7 56
  9:42 47
  10:1–12 23, 112
  10:14 55
Luke 8:3 112
  8:43–8 167
  10:42 112
  15:11–32 98, 110

John 1:14 55
  3:4 192
  3:5–8 59
  4:4–26 110
  7:53–8:11 110, 112
  12:1–8 110
  13:34–5 146
Acts 17:6 59
Romans 16:7 113
1 Corinthians 1:25 59
  7 114
  11 113
Galatians 3:6–4:31 108, 113
Ephesians 4:15–16 92
  5:21–33 102, 113
  6:5–9 117
Philippians 2:4 114
Colossians 3:18–4:1 113
2 Thessalonians 2:1–4 53
1 Timothy 2:8–15 113
  6:1–2 113
Titus 2:1–10 113
Hebrews 11:18–19
1 Peter 2:18–3:7 113
  3:6 114